Panic!

Panic!

MARKETS,
CRISES, &
CROWDS IN
AMERICAN
FICTION

David A.
Zimmerman

The University of
North Carolina Press
Chapel Hill

Designed by Kimberly Bryant
Set in Quadraat by Keystone Typesetting, Inc.
Manufactured in the United States of America

The paper in this book meets the guidelines for permanence
and durability of the Committee on Production Guidelines
for Book Longevity of the Council on Library Resources.

Library of Congress Cataloging-in-Publication Data
Zimmerman, David A. (David Andrew), 1964–
Panic! : markets, crises, and crowds in American fiction / by
David A. Zimmerman.
p. cm. — (Cultural studies of the United States)
Includes bibliographical references and index.
ISBN-13: 978-0-8078-3023-9 (cloth: alk. paper)
ISBN-10: 0-8078-3023-2 (cloth: alk. paper)
ISBN-13: 978-0-8078-5687-1 (pbk: alk. paper)
ISBN-10: 0-8078-5687-8 (pbk: alk. paper)
1. American fiction—19th century—History and criticism.
2. Financial crises in literature. 3. American fiction—20th
century—History and criticism. 4. Depressions in literature.
5. Popular culture—United States—History. 6. Literature and
society—United States—History. 7. Financial crises—United
States—History. I. Title. II. Series.
PS374.E4Z56   2006
813'.4093553—dc22   2005035089

10 09 08 07 06   5 4 3 2 1

A version of chapter 3 appeared as "Frank Norris, Market Panic,
and the Mesmeric Sublime," American Literature 75 (March 2003):
61–90; used by permission of Duke University Press. A version
of chapter 5 was published as "The Financier and the Ends of
Accounting," Dreiser Studies 35 (Winter 2004): 3–28; used by
permission of Dreiser Studies.

For Susan, who kept me from panicking,
and for the kids, who still think this book
is about the farmers' market

Contents

Illustrations

Acknowledgments

Like the financiers who populate the novels I write about, I have incurred more debts than I can possibly repay. I could not have written this book without the advice and support of friends, colleagues, and specialists across a range of disciplines who, never having met me, were kind enough to answer my sometimes loopy email queries and generous enough to share their expertise and read drafts of my work. For their discerning counsel and criticism, I thank David Anthony, Greg Bell, Stephen Brennan, the late Jenny Franchot, Catherine Gallagher, David Hollinger, Lynn Keller, Randall Knoper, James Livingston, Donald McQuade, James Miller, Benjamin Reiss, Thomas Riggio, Thomas Schaub, Jeffrey Steele, and Cecelia Tichi. I am especially grateful to Russ Castronovo, whose rigorous criticism, sage guidance, and unstinting encouragement make him a model mentor. I also thank Dorothy Brown, whose keen ear and professional wisdom enabled me to see writing impasses as launching points.

I was fortunate to receive two awards that allowed me to complete this book: a Vilas Associate Award given by the Graduate School at the University of Wisconsin, Madison, and a Junior Faculty Research Leave Award, willed into being by my senior colleagues in the Department of English, especially Susan Friedman, the department chair.

I received invaluable research assistance from Mark Pettus, a graduate student and extraordinary cook who delivered freshly baked desserts along with bags of library books to my home. Adam Kadlec also offered important research help as part of an Honors Summer Sophomore Research Apprenticeship sponsored by the College of Letters and Science Honors Program at the University of Wisconsin, Madison.

As noted on the copyright page, parts of this book have previously been published. A version of chapter 3 appeared in *American Literature*; a version of chapter 5 won the 2004 Dreiser Essay Prize given by the International Theodore Dreiser Society and was published in *Dreiser Studies*. I thank the editors of each of these journals for their painstaking readings and for permission to reprint these articles. I am also grateful to the anonymous readers associated with the University of North Carolina Press for their cogent criticism and helpful suggestions for revising my manuscript. Like everyone who read earlier drafts and recommended changes, they made this a better book.

Above all, I wish to thank my wife, the only person happier than I am that I finished this book. To her I owe everything. This book is a testament to her love and tireless support, the marks of which appear on every page.

Panic!

Introduction

At the turn of the twentieth century, along with natural disasters, military actions, and labor strikes, financial panics were the most sensational mass events experienced and discussed by all classes of Americans. Dramatic, confusing, and calamitous, they brought out seemingly freakish behavior in individuals, financial markets, and the economy at large. Haunting commercial and cultural life, they affected virtually every area of national and private experience. No economic problem appeared more fundamental or far reaching, and none generated as much expert and popular controversy. Precipitating violent conflict and cultural upheaval—indeed, pitching the nation, many thought, toward class Armageddon—financial panics provoked social, political, scientific, and ethical debates that, for many Americans, had apocalyptically high stakes.

Americans literally read their fate in panics. In the 1890s and the first decade of the 1900s, waves of pamphlets, financial primers, magazine and journal articles, and fictional works were rushed into print to meet Americans' desperation to understand these convulsions. Although I draw on all of these kinds of texts, my study focuses on panic novels—that is, novels overtly preoccupied with financial panic and economic crisis. I explore how American novelists and their readers during this period understood and shaped the popular discourse of financial panics and how, in one astonishing case, they actually colluded to produce a panic. *Panic!* has three overarching objectives. First, it studies how panic novelists made historical and ideological sense of panics, both the massive crises that upended the U.S. economy in 1893 and 1907 and the minor crashes that rocked Wall Street and the nation's commodity exchanges several times a year. Second, it analyzes Americans' emergent understandings of collective economic behavior and this behavior's extraordinary historical agency; specifically, it examines how American writers turned to the science of mob psychology, psychic research, new conceptions of sympathy, and new forms of conspiracy discourse to understand how market crowds, giant corporations, and mass readerships—more exactly, mass acts of reading—could cast economic ruin on the nation and inflect its historical development. Third, focusing on writers' deployment of sensation, sentiment, the sublime, melodrama, and naturalism, *Panic!* analyzes how financial panic, as an exemplary instance of and metaphor for baffling excess and unplottable contagion, provided fiction writers with a potent resource for interrogating the limits and capacities of novelistic form and accounting. It details how the market in crisis offered fiction writers an instrument and idiom in which to explore the limits—sociological, psychological, ideological, and ethical—of narratability.[1]

Novelists were drawn to market panics as both subject and setting of their fiction because panics exposed cultural and economic dynamics that were invisible under normal conditions, either cloaked by the apparent naturalness of the economy's functioning or latent as mere possibilities, awaiting the pressure of rupture and ruin to become activated. Writers were equally fascinated with the process of revelation itself, the ways natural and artificial energies, physical and psychical forces, and material and metaphysical laws incorporated themselves in and expressed themselves through the behavior of frenzied market crowds and collapsing prices. Like seismologists converging on the epicenter of a recent earthquake or psychic researchers gathered at a séance, panic novelists were attracted to extraordinary, often spectacular, forms of social and economic behavior, hoping to behold in them laws or lessons that comprehended the larger workings of the economy and explained the mystifying interdependencies both energizing and threatening modern economic life. As moments of crisis and discontinuity, panics promised to expose what other events and phenomena could not: the source and scope of market effects, the forces binding and driving crowds, and the social trauma shadowing corporate and financial modernity. As agents of revelation and reckoning, panics seemed to perform the work of novelists themselves—not only literary naturalists itching to excavate the landscape of the quotidian and study the forces churning dramatically beneath, or critical realists dedicated to unveiling the economic and political laws that structured social life, but also romance novelists and melodramatists committed to spotlighting human causes and costs in an increasingly reified economy that seemed to dull sensation and deaden sentiment.

Panic novels reveal how writers across class, region, and ideological disposition conceptualized the new cultural centrality of modern financial markets and how they imagined individuals' entanglement within—and potential release from—far-flung causal webs brought sensationally to view, if not actually conjured into being, by economic catastrophe. Because they implicated and illuminated so many features of social life, panics provided novelists with an extraordinary thematic and formal resource. Panics allowed novelists to figure out— that is, to present in literary form and also to solve, at least on the page—conceptual and cultural problems traversing a range of disciplines, including sociology, psychology, political economy, and history. These problems include not only how to bring the anarchic economy to order, but also how to quarantine the infectious hysteria of feminist mobs and how to preserve forms of ethical accountability in a financial universe where the link between private intentions and public outcomes is no longer discernible. Exploiting the capacity of novels to forge linkages between diverse arenas of social experience, panic novelists used their narratives to construct figural equations as well as causal ties between financial crisis and other forms of cultural, psychological, and philosophical breakdown. This is perhaps panic's most obvious literary service, and it clarifies an important way in which panic novels differ from other kinds of business and finance novels: market crises offered novelists story lines and symbols for remarkably varied forms of modern excess and confusion. Deploying a range of styles and genres, including sensational historical romances, shrill political melodramas, sentimental potboilers, epic artist fables, and patient naturalist dramas, novelists used panic narratives to clarify the cause and consequence of gender trouble, psychological fracture, class violence, moral confusion, and other forms of unanchoring seemingly collateral with the transformation reshaping American capitalism at the turn of the century. In a similar way, novelists harnessed these forms of rupture, exploiting popular fears and memories to clarify the source and social meaning of economic crisis.

While one of my aims is to recuperate the cultural problems figured out by these novels and to explain their sensational urgency for contemporary audiences, a second aim, one that makes *Panic!* a literary as well as a cultural study, is to detail how these figurings actually worked, how novelists staged, solved, and sidestepped these problems, including those that tested the limits of their own enterprise, through their formal, rhetorical, and stylistic choices. Panics, I show, challenged and enabled novelists to work out a number of literary problems—how, for example, to convey the endlessly and unpredictably ramifying social effects of a financial panic within a narrative form that privileges closure; or how to produce sympathy so affecting that it will compel fiction readers to join together into a stock market army capable of unleashing financial terror. I argue that as historical events, political symptoms, cultural allegories, and aesthetic objects, financial panics invited, and, in some cases, necessitated, remarkable kinds of literary experimentation.

What links the diverse set of cultural and literary figurings I examine is their overt concern with market crowds, not only the congealed and spectacular agglomerations that so fascinated photographers and tourists at the turn of the century (such as hordes of terrified investors packing the streets around the New York Stock Exchange) but also the more dispersed and formalized aggregations seemingly coextensive with "the market" itself (such as the stock market and financial networks). Novelists were fascinated and flustered by the ways market crowds bedeviled, even disabled, causal explanations; how their effects spread ungovernably, sending the future spinning in unplottable ways; how their sociological and psychological dynamics unmoored individuals' psychological and ethical autonomy; and how they excited mass emotions, including rage and tearful sympathy, that spilled dangerously out of the market into the home, the street, and the halls of government. At bottom, market crowds served as field sites for investigating economic and emotional interdependencies conjured into being by the widening scale and complexity of financial life at the turn of the century—interdependencies that roiled, and some said doomed, the nation's cultural and political life.

Since the early days of the republic, American writers, including many preoccupied with financial crisis and ruin, had elaborated the private and public dangers of dependency, the manifold threats posed by economic and sentimental intimacy not only to the nation's commercial stability but also to popular notions of self-determination, gender, virtue, and class.[2] The panic narratives I examine, while they register some of these older threats, are different in that their protagonists overtly confront *collective* entanglements and *mass* emotions and, most dramatically, the runaway effects these produced—the commercial vertigo and civic catastrophe that radiated across the chains of exchanges and obligations latticing the market system, borne along, seemingly inexorably, by uncanny forms of "sympathetic affection" (as Edith Wharton phrased it) and collective fear.[3] Like epidemiologists, panic novelists fixated on the source and spread of this contagion, elaborating a number of questions about causality, affect, and collectivity itself: In the face of the bewildering concatenation of financial and emotional entanglements comprising modern markets, how could one trace the cause of market crises and predict their consequences across the economic and social universe? How and why did seemingly autonomous individuals coalesce into market mobs, especially when by doing so they knew they were abetting disaster for themselves and the nation? Was crowd hysteria an anomalous or fundamental feature of financial markets? Given the central role played by the stock market in the emerging industrial order at the turn of the century, how could the pandemic effects of market crowds be quarantined—or harnessed for civic, even moral, purposes?

The heterogeneity of collectivities convened under the concept of "market crowd" is important, for I argue that novelists focused on crowded spaces, especially the interiors of stock and commodity exchanges (sometimes pairing them with streets churning with rioters or theaters thronged with opera lovers), not only to theatricalize ambient forms of human sociality (such as social suggestibility) but also to displace and, indeed, mask culturally and ideologically threatening forms of political and economic solidarity (such as labor militancy and corporate conspiracy). In mapping the reach of market crowds' effects across economic, social, and psychic spaces, panic novelists made visible how individuals were lodged within economic and affective matrices otherwise too vast and abstract to apprehend and how they bore—suffered as well as passed along—the emotions and designs of myriad other individuals across these matrices, spreading trauma and disruption (or, conceivably, salvation) along the way.

For panic novelists, market crowds were not only social bodies; they were also, crucially, events that unfolded in time. They were social processes, chains of causes and effects that spread across history as well as geography, implicating new individuals as they advanced. Panic novels invariably narrate the fate of market players caught up in these chains—speculators trapped in falling markets, financial titans hypnotized by collapsing prices, investors entangled in the speculative designs of market insiders, capitalists caught in revolutionary riots. Panic fiction details how market players react to their entanglement and records the personal and public effects ensuing from these individuals' subjection. By giving dramatic form to the mechanics and ramifications of this implication, panic novels conventionalized certain ways of representing how individuals come to understand and experience their participation in market processes and economic structures, dynamics that normally functioned outside readers' awareness or comprehension. The characters' financial dependence frequently figures metonymically for more diffuse forms of enlistment and subjection—in the case of political writers, it stands for interpellation or ideological recruitment; in the case of philosophical writers, the social interdependencies that condition all human designs.

One of the things clearly at stake in these dramas of subjection is the fate of individuals' psychological, political, and ethical autonomy. Some novelists, predictably, constructed their narratives to mourn or warn against the dissolution of personal autonomy, depicting how market panics and the collective processes they exemplified set fatal constraints on traditional forms of republican virtue, masculine self-determination, and liberal subjectivity. Other novelists, rather than lamenting individuals' fall into organized and unorganized social networks, dramatized counterforms of enlistment and absorption. They documented how individuals could dismantle the causal webs that trapped them by forging new collectivities within as well as without the marketplace, and they showed how these activist communities, mimicking and even exploiting panic's social dynamics, gave rise to liberating forms of selfhood and sociality. Other novelists saw these dramas of conscious withdrawal and enlistment as weak-minded fictions that masked the inescapable intersubjectivity of modern economic and cultural life. They perceived the attenuation of individuality not as a cultural threat but rather as an impetus for new, more realistic forms of fiction.

The varied depictions of individuals succumbing to or seeking freedom within speculative markets, financial networks, and economic institutions taught readers how to conceptualize market collectivities and conduct themselves toward them. Panic novels performed this pedagogical work through different kinds of formal experiments. Calling attention to the artifactuality of their own design, some narratives invited readers to compare the experience of reading their melodramatic plots with the experience of being caught within conspirators' financial and political designs. The obviously fabricated causal machinery of their over-the-top dramas gave form and feeling to the widespread charge that all aspects of modern financial life were shaped by the plots of a seemingly omnipotent banker regime. Other panic novels constructed narrative forms that obscured the connection between economic and social life. One historical romance, which I discuss in chapter 1, painstakingly extricates its hero, a corporate titan, from the causal chains connecting corporate capitalism and cultural chaos. Its narrative is built around sensational analogies between financial crisis and social cataclysm (such as feminist revolt and mob violence), but these evocative equations, performing obvious thematic work in the novel, function to occlude any cause-and-effect relation between the economic system and social fracture.

Other panic narratives broadened the self-reflexive rhetorical and pedagogical work of the genre by instructing readers in how to manage their emotional investments and how to discern the political, psychological, and ethical risks and rewards of their sentimental affiliations within market crowds. They established the act of reading fiction as a surrogate and preparatory form of real-world economic and political behavior. Panic novels functioned as training tools, imaginative testing grounds in which readers could practice how to *feel* in the market and how to feel about feeling itself. Educating readers in how to feel about market collectivities had monumental social stakes, at least in the minds of novelists and their critics, since panics, whatever their specific precipitants, were effects of dangerously massified and epidemic emotions. ("Sentiment is often as powerful as fact in the regulation of values," observed one economic theorist.)[4] Like seduction tales, the sentiment-saturated melodramas of panic modeled healthy and hazardous kinds of affective entanglements. They encouraged readers to see the market as a sentimental community comprised of individuals linked by grief or guilt, and they harnessed a range of formal devices to compel readers to identify with characters who, themselves victims of market crowds, learned to feel the grief or guilt of others.

These novels were not simply cautionary tales. They were also recruitment manuals, and, indeed, they performed their most striking rhetorical work by exploiting sentimentality and sympathy to forge their readers, sometimes overtly, into economically, politically, and ethically efficacious crowds. Deploying formal novelties such as appendixes filled with readers' personal testimonials or narrative framing devices that immunized readers from the potentially ungovernable emotional appeal of melodrama itself, they compelled readers not only to see the market as a network of hearts "systematically skewered" together (as one writer put it) but also to view themselves and other readers as purposeful agents within a sentimental collective constituted through their common feelings for literary characters (and, in one case, for the author himself).[5] Terror and tears bound the nation, as the devastating financial crises in 1893 and 1907 sensationally confirmed, but panic novelists explored the possibility that these emotional bonds could be harnessed and disciplined in an otherwise anonymous market, that the emotional currents driving the financial universe could be rechanneled, if not reversed, by novel reading, and that literary sentiment and sympathy might empower rather than enslave individuals caught within these flows.

Most panic novelists treated market crises and crowds as urgent cultural problems, which they attempted to relieve or repress by mining the rhetorical and formal resources of their art. However, Frank

Norris and Theodore Dreiser, each offering a distinct brand of naturalism, treated market crises and crowds primarily as literary and philosophical problems, and by structuring their novels around financial panics, they sought to clarify and illuminate problems associated with literary form itself. These writers, as I discuss more fully later in this introduction, investigated how the chaotic and unpredictable character of market crises both invited and defied literary containment. Their narratives elaborate parallels between the speculative campaigns of market titans and novelists' own attempts to give formal shape and aesthetic coherence to the world they work on. Norris and Dreiser detail, more exactly, how the effort to bring the economic, psychic, and social dynamics driving market crowds to financial and narrative order fails. In their novels, the market in crisis (shown by frenzied traders' generating a babble of price quotations or the maddening inexorability of crowd effects) enacts and allegorizes the sublime unaccountability of nature's laws and processes. No plan or plot can comprehend nature or bring its economic and social expressions to account. Indeed, Norris and Dreiser document how the very attempt to speculate on nature—to predict and exploit the behavior of market crowds—sets in motion the textual effects, the narrative automatism and contagion, that loose themselves from the speculator-writer's grip.

Panic Fiction, 1898–1913

Economic and finance fiction was popular throughout the Gilded Age and Progressive Era. By one count, around three hundred novels focusing on economic and financial questions were published between 1870 and 1900.[6] As it had after the panics of 1837 and 1857, economic crisis inspired its own fiction boomlet. At least two dozen economic novels appeared in the months after the panic of 1893, a fraction of the hundred or so economic novels, many of them shrill antibanker polemics, published during the ensuing depression. Although the fiction written during that crisis plays an important role in my study, I concentrate on the wave of panic fiction published between 1898 and 1913. These years correspond to, on one end, the launching of the industrial "trust" boom that transformed the United States economy with awesome and, for many, awful swiftness; and, on the other end, the passage of the Federal Reserve Act, the federal government's controversial attempt to end the ravages of financial crises. The fifteen years under discussion constitute a watershed in American economic and cultural history, a period of acute and far-reaching change motivated in large part by the jarring social and economic effects of the depression in the 1890s and the enduring threat, realized in 1907, of another major financial crisis.

The historical specificity of my investigation is crucial, not least because during these years, novelists, publishers, and mainstream (that is, popular, urban, and middle-class) magazines realized the commercial possibilities of finance fiction for the first time. Writers churned out dozens of novels about Wall Street, commodities markets, and banking, many of them focusing on panics. Some of these writers—including Frank Norris, Upton Sinclair, Harold Frederic, Theodore Dreiser, Emerson Hough, David Graham Phillips, Will Payne, Robert Herrick, and Alfred O. Crozier—had already established themselves as novelists, journalists, or, in the case of Edwin Lefèvre and Thomas Lawson, Wall Street stock operators. Others, including Frederic Isham, Henry Webster, Frederick Upham Adams, William Hudson, James Clews, and A. Newton Ridgely, escaped fame, at least as novelists. Some panic novels, such as Hough's The Mississippi Bubble (1902) and Norris's The Pit (1903), were national bestsellers. Others gained brief but explosive notoriety. Thomas Lawson's sentimental panic novel Friday, the Thirteenth (1907), one of the most anxiously anticipated first novels in U.S. history, played a key role in Lawson's sensational campaign to undermine the nation's financial system. Alfred Crozier's conspiracy melodrama The Magnet, considered by the editor of the Arena to be "the most important politico-economic novel" of 1908, achieved sudden fame when Robert La Follette, then a freshman senator from Wisconsin, read from it during an eighteen-hour speech to Congress following the panic of 1907.[7]

Panic novelists capitalized on and contributed to the surge of popular interest in high finance and the stock exchange between 1898 and 1913. It was during these years that Wall Street emerged as a national thrill park, equal parts casino, sporting arena, and magic show. The defeat of William Jennings Bryan and the silver movement in the elections of 1896 and 1900, the revival of the nation's moribund railroad industry, and other factors at home and abroad combined to lift the nation out its paralyzing depression late in the nineties, and "with almost magical suddenness" the economic mood on Wall Street changed from despair to giddiness.[8] Beginning in 1899, a frenzy of speculation possessed middle-class investors, who stampeded Wall Street en masse for the first time, eager to buy and trade shares in hundreds of new, breathtakingly huge industrial corporations, or "trusts," suddenly arising—or, more precisely, amassing—out of the business rubble of the nineties. American investment in U.S. companies outpaced European investment for the first time, a long-awaited confirmation, for many economic patriots, of America's financial independence and maturity. For the first time since the boom years after the Civil War, finance became gripping popular entertainment. Financial news, formerly restricted to the back page of city papers, was now "blazoned forth" in dramatic headlines.[9] Crowds of tourists and sensation-seekers thronged the streets of the financial district and the viewing galleries of New York's exchanges to see the pyrotechnics. According to one writer, the city had "no more entertaining public exhibition."[10]

Novelists found ample drama not only on Wall Street but also in the Chicago Board of Trade and other organized exchanges around the nation. Stock and commodity markets featured high-stakes competition, harrowing suspense, riveting twists and climaxes, extraordinary personal performances, the unpredictable handiwork of chance, and the anarchic influence of crowds. Here, captivated by the spectacle of price swings, fiction writers gave themselves over to a world of narrative possibilities. Unanchored to concrete things, writers' minds were free to speculate on—to imagine, to wager on—the fate of individual stocks or commodities, the wealth their movement mysteriously created or annihilated, and the extensive effects their sudden rise or decline might have on the nation.

No market events produced more sensational or far-reaching effects than panics. Sweeping away business gains and family incomes, even the smallest panics—the minor shakedowns and collapses that haunted the nation's financial marketplaces as well as the bank runs that routinely terrified depositors in towns across the country—brought sudden ruin to thousands of businessmen, investors, and their families. The largest panics, those that bloomed mysteriously into full-blown economic crises, produced forms of public and personal trauma on a national scale. They upset markets, paralyzed industry, threw millions of laborers out of work, bankrupted thousands of firms and farmers, and, by jarring the price of money, put all values, including cultural values, in flux. In the months after the panic of 1893, 600 banks closed their doors and 16,000 businesses failed. Two to three million people—around a fifth of the nation's labor force—were left without work. In industrial cities such as Chicago, the jobless numbered 100,000. The panic of 1907, coming after ten years of unparalleled prosperity, likewise staggered the nation.[11]

Fiction writers attempted to bring these chaotic, mystifying events to interpretive order by rendering them into analytically and ideologically serviceable narrative shapes. Taking full advantage of their license as fiction writers, they invented tropes, evoked images, and drew on idioms that made abstractions such as "the economy" and "money supply" and "crisis" familiar in vernacular terms; they also offered story lines embedded within recognizable master plots of nation, history, and civilization that invested these abstractions with aesthetic and cultural meaning, allowing audiences to interpret and assess them. Conveying alarms and assurances about the economy's sweeping transformation, panic novelists intertwined their finance plots with politically charged courtship and adventure stories, offered propagandistic retellings of economic and cultural history, unfolded sensational prophecies of future crises, and in other ways threaded panics into (or disarticulated panics from) ideologically encrusted—and bitterly contested—cultural and historical grand narratives. In short, they adapted old narrative grammars and fashioned new ones to focus and frame the dizzying change they witnessed.

Most panic novelists saw themselves as participants in the ideological and intellectual construction of financial modernity. They informed and consolidated public opinion, set the terms and tone of public debate, and pressured financial policymakers, often encouraging reform or revolution that would, they insisted, make economic crises and their devastation a thing of the past. Their efforts remind us that economic developments are inseparable from the narratives used to interpret and evaluate them. What we call "the market" is a social and political—and thus linguistic—construction. It is a discursive realm fought over by more or less self-conscious social factions seeking to normalize their interests and justify their mission or struggle. Crisis and upheaval incite explosive battles over the market's conceptualizations, its forms and functions, and its social meanings.[12]

Consciously and unconsciously participating in these battles, panic novelists were animated by diverse political and ideological agendas. Some writers used their narratives to celebrate the corporate transformation of the economy, dramatizing for middle-class audiences the cultural and ethical wisdom of investing in the new trusts. They identified corporate leaders as enlightened, progressive, and patriotic guardians of cultural tradition and stability, heroes ridding the nation of the scourge of crises and chaos. Other writers crafted sensational warnings against corporate modernity, dramatizing the dire need to reverse the corporate industrial juggernaut (as populists and pro-silver writers desired) or put management of the trusts in the hands of "the people" (as socialists urged). Many of these narratives represented financial crises as weapons of economic mass destruction deployed by vicious Wall Street financiers who conspired to pilfer middle-class wealth and extort favorable legislation from Congress. Others illuminated how panics were endemic features of industrial capitalism's advance, inevitable effects of the unprecedented concentration of economic and political power in the hands of a few financial barons. Some novelists drew richly on historical myths and sources to rewrite American economic history. Others contrived over-the-top fantasies or thought experiments, political economic science fiction that staged alternative futures toward which current economic trends or conflicts seemed to point. Whatever their ideological aims, all of these novelists imagined or suggested ways to remedy financial crises and contain the social trauma they produced.

What made the problem of ending or mitigating these convulsions so vexing—and, indeed, what helped inspire such a vast body of writing about panics in the first place—was that there existed no consensus about how to explain, or even describe, a financial crisis. Clergymen and moralists, as they had been doing throughout the nineteenth century, blamed financial crises on the moral laxness and financial recklessness of the community; manufacturers cited labor legislation, agitation, and overproduction; workers pointed to low wages and mechanization; populists pointed to Wall Street's stranglehold on credit; and bankers pointed to overinvestment and the creakiness of the nation's outdated financial system.[13] A portion of the public discerned only the chastening hand of Providence behind these "fearful visitations."[14] Among professional economists, a group that achieved popular authority around the turn of the century, "irreconcilable differences" existed over how to untangle the knot of variables that shaped investor confidence, the circulation of money and credit, and all the other factors, global and local, structural and seasonal, economic and psychological, seemingly at work behind these uncanny events.[15]

The challenge of comprehending financial upheavals fueled fierce, wide-ranging debates about the identity of the nation, the future of its political and economic traditions, and the demise of its cultural institutions. For economic observers, even the most basic questions carried seemingly monumental implications. Were crises freakish economic abnormalities, or were they inseparable from industrial economic development? Were they symptomatic of economic progress or progress's limits? Were they salutary, a sobering reality check on investors, or catastrophic, proof that industrial capitalism would destroy itself and the nation? Were they the most or least illuminating features of the economy?

The problem, as novelists and other participants in these debates made clear, was that different explanations told very different stories, not just about how panics and crises erupted and ended but also about the moral premises and social meanings of open markets, economic centralization, and, looming over these and other companion narratives, the political and cultural fate of the republic.

The New Order

Financial crisis provoked such urgent commentary because it constituted a primary symptom, and, for many observers, a primary cause, of the massive corporate makeover that reshaped the United States economy and society between 1890 and 1910, a makeover that entrenched large corporations, the stock market, and financial titans at the center of the economy. For this reason, when their narratives pointed to a panic's cause (at least a cause beyond the madness or capriciousness of financial crowds), novelists inevitably implicated themselves in national debates—erupting at times into violent conflict —over the rise of big business and high finance.

The basic outlines of this rise are familiar. Business leaders saw the bitter depression of the 1890s as the consequence of an outmoded economic system in which companies, trying to survive in unregulated markets, engaged in reckless investment and ruinous competition. Such desperate practices, what Walter Lippmann called the "planless scramble of little profiteers," led to unpredictable markets, overproduction, falling price levels, and economic crises.[16] These crises, in turn, led to massive wage cuts and layoffs, which triggered labor "riots and social anarchy."[17] Viewing themselves as "trustees of the national prosperity," captains guiding the nation's economy and culture across unfamiliar and perilous seas, leading industrialists and metropolitan bankers saw the emergence of large corporations as the best means of rationalizing production and preventing financial crises and class war.[18] Supported by a gold standard to stabilize price levels and investment, a banking system supple and centralized enough to douse money panics before they got out of hand, and new markets overseas to absorb industry's surplus capital, industrial organization—or, as many called it, Morganization—would defang the growing menace of labor activism and direct the juggernaut of capital accumulation smoothly, irresistibly forward.

Observers marveled at the swiftness of the trusts' emergence. Between 1898 and 1904, more than three hundred mammoth industrial and manufacturing corporations came into being, most of them products of mergers. At least fifty of them dominated their industry, producing more output than all of their competitors combined. Whereas only a few "industrials" with a capitalization of $10 million existed in 1890, nearly a hundred had sprung up by 1902. One of them, J. P. Morgan's United States Steel Corporation, controlling 70 percent of the steel industry, had a capitalization of over a billion dollars. Railroads, subject to notoriously cutthroat and self-destructive competition, also consolidated. By 1904, over a thousand railroad lines came under the control of six combinations associated with either Morgan or Rockefeller.

Wall Street and high finance assumed their central place in the national and world economy—and popular panic discourse—during these years. To finance the mergers, industrial corporations required immense amounts of capital, far more than regional banks could provide, so they turned to Wall Street's investment houses to orchestrate the sale of their stocks and bonds to American and European investors. Only large investment firms, centered in New York, had the resources and prestige to market securities on such a scale. Between 1898 and 1904, these banks oversaw the issue of $4 billion of new stocks and bonds to the public, setting in motion what one prominent banker called an "industrial debauch"—the sensational middle-class stock binge I described earlier.[19] For their organizing and underwriting efforts, bankers insisted that they or their proxies receive seats on the boards of the new corporations, where they could supervise the corporations' financial policies. In this way, as the business historians Thomas Cochran and William Miller put it, "a small clique acquired a voice in every one of the great 'trusts' that came increasingly to dominate the everyday life of the nation."[20]

These years marked the heyday of banker power. In 1912, a sensational congressional investigation into an alleged "Money Trust" revealed that a coterie of bankers associated with Morgan, perched atop the sluice gates through which rivers of investment dollars flowed, had come to control 342 directorships in 112 corporations, giving a few financiers influence over an amount of capital worth more than all the property in the twenty-two states west of the Mississippi.[21] Even more ominous than the financiers' presence inside corporate boardrooms, at least to those suspicious of banker oligarchy, was the financiers' growing hegemony over the public's savings. Between 1903 and 1913, Wall Street's leading bankers came to control major insurance companies, national banks, and trust companies (a new species of loosely regulated banks, not to be confused with the industrial "trusts"), giving them leverage over roughly three-quarters of the total bank deposits in the country.

With the storehouses of middle-class savings as well as corporations' ballooning deposits at their disposal, and with the money of hundreds of thousands of small investors already under their management, six groups of bankers—fewer than a dozen individuals, according to the congressional counsel Samuel Untermyer[22]—were able to buy up and issue corporate stocks, manipulate the price of those stocks in the stock market, and thereby guarantee a market for the securities of the corporations whose financial policies they directed. According to the Money Trust investigation, Morgan and a handful of proxies were able to "dominate the New York Stock Exchange" and "create, avert, and compose panics" at will. By presiding over the nation's major lending institutions, they could set loan rates around the United States, ration credit to sustain or starve businesses, and exert, according to a congressional subcommittee, "a power over the business, commerce, credits, and finances of the country that is despotic and perilous."[23]

Panic fiction served as a major propaganda outlet for enemies of the banker regime, a forum where they could sketch out their fears and most fevered charges. Upton Sinclair's The Moneychangers (1908), for example, locates the cause of the panic of 1907 in Morgan's financial and sexual rapaciousness. Alfred Crozier's The Magnet (1908) unveils how the arch villain, a Morgan stand-in, plans and unleashes a spectacular panic, "the greatest thunderbolt of destruction and ruin ever hurled by a hand less than that of the Almighty."[24] Such narratives, good examples of the "hysteria and triteness" attributed to much popular Wall Street writing in the first decade of the 1900s, drew on the melodramatic formulas of populist fiction and pro-silver tracts of a generation before.[25] These texts depicted financial panics as the deliberate work of a cabal of malevolent bankers, a "secret society that has more power than the million Masons, the million Odd Fellows, and the half million Knights of Pythias combined," as one Ohio congress-man put it.[26] Panics were portrayed as constituting the most terrifying weapon in bankers' arsenal, a means of plundering the wealth of the producing classes, triggering bankruptcies and foreclosures on which creditors could scavenge, and frightening politicians into passing leg-islation strengthening capitalists' financial hegemony.[27]

Since before the Civil War, financial antimonopolists (as the histo-rian Gretchen Ritter labels these polemicists) argued that northeastern capitalists and Wall Street bankers, aided if not prompted by British financiers and Jewish money lords across Europe, had hijacked the American economy, corrupted the government, and crippled small-producer democracy.[28] In the master narrative that these antimonopol-ists repeatedly spun, capitalists held the money supply of the na-tion hostage, rigging the nation's banking and currency machinery to favor creditors and industrialists and destroying the economic and political sovereignty of farmers, wage earners, and small business-men. Organized capital strangled credit and competition, stifling the entrepreneurial energies and repudiating the proprietary ideals of this broad class of producers.

The antimonopolists made the political and social ramifications of financial panics terrifyingly clear. Banker hegemony, they insisted, was projecting the nation toward class Armageddon. Unless capitalists were stymied and control over the financial system given back to the people through some kind of federal intervention, corrupt and reckless eastern speculators—that is, bankers and corporate directors—would not only continue to produce epidemics of "despair and death" but also, enriched by these crises, enthrone themselves in Washington.[29] The political republic, sustained by economic democracy, would col-lapse. Repeatedly, they warned that millions of citizen paupers would take to the streets in revolt, that the nation was on the brink of class war. Indeed, with the Haymarket bombing and other explosions of labor violence fresh in their memory, populist propagandists saw at hand the final battle between capital and labor, between Wall Street and "the people." Financial panics were portents and precipitants of this apocalypse.

Socialist writers, too, made the connection between financial crisis and the asphyxiation of political and economic democracy explicit, offering their own apocalyptic prophecies. Unlike financial antimonopolists, "scientific" socialists (those who read social and economic change as expressions of strict laws laid out by Karl Marx) viewed the trust movement as the logical culmination of capitalist evolution, an advanced mode of industrial organization that must be harnessed by working people, not dismantled or stalemated as populists urged. They saw economic crises as structurally embedded features of industrial capitalism itself, logical products of the "insatiate greed of the competitive system," which continually squeezed profit rates and necessitated reckless overproduction that glutted markets and paralyzed trade.[30]

To socialists, the trust boom at the turn of the century, intensifying the concentration of wealth and accelerating the progress toward a climactic industrial breakdown, seemed propitious for revolution. The search for new markets in which industrial corporations could dump surplus products would soon come up empty, rates of profit would bottom out, and the whole system would collapse. When that happened, the laboring classes, sufficiently aroused and enlightened, would demand the overthrow of the industrial oligarchy and the competitive order itself, either by ballot or bloodshed. "The whole moneyed structure of society" would topple "over in a huge wreck," as an anarchist puts it in Will Payne's panic novel *Mr. Salt* (1903).[31] The question, socialists writers emphasized, was not if but rather when and in what form the "smash-up" would come. In *The Industrial Republic*, published just before the panic of 1907, Upton Sinclair predicted that depression and revolution would sweep the nation within a decade, most likely following the 1912 presidential election.

The panic of 1907 played a pivotal role in the socialists' prognostications. "The hour predicted by Socialists for over a decade past is TODAY HERE," proclaimed a special panic edition of the socialist weekly *Appeal to Reason*.[32] According to the paper, the collapse of New York's major banks and the ensuing wave of business failures provided dramatic proof of the futility of capitalism and signaled the "birth-pangs of the new social order."[33] Socialist editors saw the crisis as the propaganda moment they had long been waiting for. "The panic has prepared the people for our logic, and we must not allow this golden opportunity to go by," insisted *Appeal to Reason*; the financial disaster had at last brought people "to their senses. They are now ready to reason, to argue, to think and to act. Now is the time to place the right kind of literature in their hands."[34] Socialist writers rushed to the task. Sinclair, for example, immediately wrote *The Moneychangers*, tracing a web of connections—a collusion of vested interests, congealing melodramatically into villainous conspiracy—that linked the financial panic, banker omnipotence, industrial exploitation, and the suffocation of democracy.

Turn-of-the-century metropolitan bankers and business leaders saw things quite differently. Convinced that corporate capitalism was here to stay and needed only federal oversight, not popular expropriation, to fulfill its economic and social promise, they looked upon the propaganda of the silver insurgents and socialists with dismay and launched educational campaigns of their own. Only by convincing the working and urban middle classes that large corporations and the gold standard were socially necessary could corporate leaders expect to bring stability to the economy, manage economic crises, and preempt the social violence they produced. Even after the fight over the gold standard was decided in 1900, corporate reformers—that is, the business leaders and bankers who supported "sound money" as a cure for the economy's anarchism—felt the need to continue to teach the public about crises, their causes, and their remedies. Pro-corporate novelists took part in these instructional campaigns, deploying the same apocalyptic sensationalism as the enemies of the new order. Like the writers bent on derailing corporate modernity—the silverites by turning back time, reversing the corporate juggernaut, and the socialists by radically accelerating it, conjuring forth the revolutionary future latent within the trust boom—corporate advocates viewed financial panics as symptoms and engines of epochal transformation, moments when class warfare, social trauma, and cultural breakdown might spin the nation's destiny from its progressive course. To pro-corporate fiction writers (whose ideological commitments have rendered them all but invisible to literary scholars), industrial massification, guided by capitalist visionaries, would rescue America from such threats. At a time when high finance and big business came under fire for the first time in mainstream monthlies, when labor violence spiked and the Socialist Party amassed unprecedented political strength (garnering a million votes in the 1912 presidential election), pro-corporate novelists made the case for capitalists' public and patriotic service.

Making History

Destiny is the animating preoccupation of many finance novels written during the trust boom. The future of the nation, threatened by economic crisis and bitterly contested in strikes, protests, reform meetings, and elections, seemed up for grabs. Panic novels register the widespread sense of being cast toward an uncertain or ominous future, borne toward irreparable ruin or endless prosperity by the sweep of economic transformation. Overtly and obliquely, panic novels spin out visions of the future, adumbrate the laws and trajectory of its development, define the "acceptable grounds" and agents of social change, and parse this change's moral, political, intellectual, and cultural meaning.[35]

It is hard to overstate the sense of disorientation Americans felt during the corporate restructuring. Contemporary observers, those who mourned the loss of "the old and simple life of America, a life that was doomed by the great organization that had come into the world," as well as those who celebrated the new dispensation, routinely figured the emergence of the new corporate financial regime as an economic typhoon that, within a single generation, had upended the country's cultural and political landscape.[36] Looking back in 1910, Woodrow Wilson concluded: "Our development has run so fast and so far . . . that a new nation seems to have been created which the old formulas do not fit or afford a vital interpretation of."[37] Panic novels, highlighting the relation between economic crisis and the development—or dissolution—of the nation, invoked the economic past and future to help readers make sense of the passage across this altered terrain. Cast in the cultural vortex between economic dispensations, panic novels provided the "formulas" to interpret the emergent nation and explain the forces shaping the new organization of its life.

Some panic writers, predictably, turned to history to reconstruct what capital development and economic crisis had destroyed or changed beyond recognition. Agitating to restore a political economy that by 1907 had "ceased to exist," anticorporate writers, according to Walter Lippmann, made "their histories to fit their illusions."[38] They repeatedly traced the demise of small-producer democracy to pro-banker legislation passed at the end of the Civil War, sometimes, as in James Goode's *The Modern Banker* (1896), linking their economic nostalgia with idealizations of the Old South and plantation paternalism. Even socialists spun out fantasies of a golden republican past, a period of full employment, disciplined consumption, and representative government that would be corrupted by corporate developments after the Civil War.

Less familiar than these forms of memorialization are the attempts by pro-corporate writers around the turn of the century to endow corporate capitalism with a long, progressive history, one that not only viewed business leaders as the "sole and legitimate heirs of the American tradition," as the historian Mike Wallace puts it, but also, more strikingly, established bankers and financiers as America's founding fathers.[39] Viewing capitalism as a bulwark against cultural dissolution and amnesia, pro-corporate panic novelists sought to give the United States a business paternity. They countered populist archaeology and revolutionary demolition with capitalist genealogy.

The key text of my first chapter, Frederic Isham's *Black Friday* (1904), structured around an account of the Paris Commune of 1871 and an account of the famous New York gold panic of 1869, offers one of the most sensational examples of this genealogical imperative. Isham's strategy for erasing capitalist crisis and class conflict from the historical record differs from the whitewashing techniques employed by many novelists in the late nineteenth century, including other apologists for industrial and capital development. He does not, for example, erase urban unrest and class insurgency from view by projecting his readers back to a preindustrial Eden. He does not romanticize the social relations, moral values, and local traditions supposedly swept away by industrial capitalism's advance across the continent, or normalize this creative destruction, however lamentable, as natural or necessary. Most important of all, he does not root American culture, dizzyingly market driven as it may have seemed to many cultural observers at the turn of the century, in some tradition or founding moment distant from commerce and its vertigo. To the contrary, Isham overtly anchors modern American history in the postbellum industrial boom. By representing his hero, the corporate titan, as the midwife ministering this birth, Isham makes a captain of finance and industry the custodian of the nation's heritage, a role the titan dramatically confirms by saving the federal government from traitors.[40]

Through both the content and structure of their narratives, pro-corporate historical romances organize a vision of the past that projects a national destiny spared of the necessity of economic panic and social trauma. Capitalist history, these novels aim to demonstrate, progresses along a steady, upward line. It does not lurch precipitously, thrown forward (or backward) by collision or crisis. As the capitalist hero of Payne's *Mr. Salt* puts it, seeing a massive crisis approaching in 1893, "So I suppose we'll have a fit or two. But the fit will pass. Great Scott, you can't stop things permanently! They've got to go on getting bigger and bigger and richer and richer! You can't stop that!"[41] Such historiographical pronouncements remind us that moments of profound change, when the future of a nation or group seems uncertain and the trajectory of history seems alarmingly off kilter, inspire fantasies not just about the future (as in *Caesar's Column* [1890], Ignatius Donnelly's terrifying countervision to Edward Bellamy's *Looking Backward* [1884]) but also about the past. Shaken by disruption, authors and audiences are desperate to latch onto traditions that serve as anchors against drift or dissolution. In addition, to revise history's plotline, to make it move again in a culturally familiar and politically satisfactory direction, authors must rewrite the plotline's beginning.

Economic crises preoccupied the historical fiction writers under discussion here because they constituted moments when the shape and concept of history seemed vulnerable to radical revision; they were hinge events on which the nation's economic and social destiny potentially turned. If, at the turn of the century, the "new industrial possibilities became political choices," as the historian James Livingston posits, then they also became literary choices.[42] Understanding that they were crafting history's narrative shape, pro-corporate panic novelists, turning to the past, worked to foreclose alternative futures (and, indeed, alternative presents) called forth by labor militants, populists, and other enemies of corporate expansion. They worked to repress anticorporate plotlines of American history and dismantle the idea that alternative plotlines even existed.

Reading and Writing Crowds

Panic novelists preoccupied themselves not only with the historical roots and ramifications of economic crises but also with the sociological and psychological dimensions of market dynamics. Like many market observers, they were fascinated and perplexed by the collective emotions that sent the market spiraling downward, wreaking havoc for everyone. What moved thousands or hundreds of thousands of investors and depositors to panic, shed their stocks, withdraw their savings deposits, and contribute to a market collapse? What explained bizarre events like the "Ice Water Panic" in 1898, when a morning headline announcing the sudden death of a prominent New York banker (reportedly after he drank too much ice water the night before) sent brokers and investors racing to Wall Street, where, in two frenzied hours of selling, $120 million evaporated from the market?

One answer implicated panic novelists themselves: market reading and writing. Financial markets, like all markets, are markets for information, and it is by reading, especially reading financial news, analysis, and gossip, that most investors at the turn of the century gathered the information, however limited, that prompted them to buy or sell a stock. A constant incitement to projection and anticipation, the stock market offered a thrilling read—literally. Crowds of investors huddled over ticker machines in banks, hotel lobbies, and brokers' offices, scrutinizing the emerging stock tape to discern price trends. Edwin Lefèvre, a respected financial journalist and fiction writer, observed during the panic of 1901 that "some men will stand by the ticker and, as if fascinated by the horror of their ruin, unable to take their eyes off the tape, gaze on unblinkingly, hour after hour, each minute seeing them poorer."[43] Everywhere across the country, market readers pored

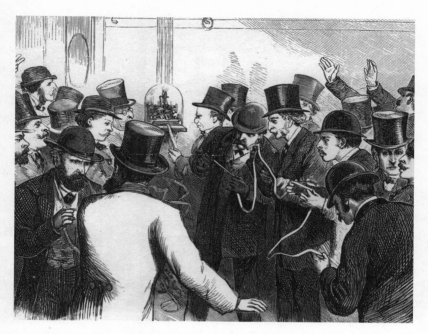

Wall Street traders scrutinize ticker tape in the early 1870s. *Frank Leslie's Illustrated Newspaper*, 13 April 1872. Reprinted in Levinson, *Wall Street: A Pictorial History.*

over financial newspapers, newsletters, and brokers' "tipster reports," anxiously imagining the possible effect of market turns on their own and the nation's future.

The stock market is constituted and sustained by these acts of reading. The market is composed of readers who are intensely aware that other investors are reading the same material at the same time and that their collective interpretations and predictions will have an effect on the market. Because price fluctuations, especially when the market is most volatile and unpredictable, are tied to collective interpretations, investors react to "what they believe will be the probable effect of facts or rumor on the minds of other traders," as one early market psychologist put it.[44] Moreover, they have to react quickly, before others do, in order to take advantage of this mass reaction, which often

Uncle Sam relaxes as panicky speculators gaze at the quotation board in a
broker's office during a slump in prices. *Leslie's Weekly*, 16 February 1905.
Reprinted in Levinson, *Wall Street: A Pictorial History*.

only intensifies its effect. In sum, writing exerts such massive influence in the market not just because it provides information desperately
sought by impatient investors in need of guidance, but also because it
generates a response among the investing public that tends to gather
mass and momentum of its own, fueled by the twin pressures of
consensus and competition.

At the turn of the century, when stock market swings affected the
nation's industry more directly than ever before, observers looked
with consternation, at times bordering on terror, at the power of mass
reading to undermine financial markets and threaten the nation's
economy. Financial observers, crowd psychologists, cultural critics,
politicians, business ethicists, and others attempted to understand
the seemingly resistless dynamics of collective reading in the stock

market, the pandemic emulation and competition among financial readers. What sociological, psychological, and cultural dynamics, they asked, explained the performance of rumor, news, advice, and other writing that incited investors to buy or sell stocks, sending prices reeling? How could these runaway effects be contained? How could seemingly virtuous forms of market writing (such as exposés targeting Wall Street corruption) be distinguished from seemingly vicious ones (such as stock operators' false, fear-breeding gossip) if both triggered the same catastrophic public effects? What role did other exciting (and inciting) forms of popular reading such as yellow journalism or reform fiction play in producing such effects? What was the relation between readerly excitement inside and outside the marketplace, and why did some mass emotions appear so threatening to the nation's economic stability while others appeared so innocuous?

The figure around whom these questions sensationally converged —indeed, the figure who gave these questions front-page urgency for several years—was Thomas Lawson, the most feared stock promoter, muckraker, and novelist in the United States at the turn of the century. In 1904, he published an announcement that triggered a panic wiping out almost half a billion dollars of market value in three days, which convinced him that he could produce a more disastrous panic that would topple the nation's financial structure. Between 1904 and 1907, using advertisements, financial newsletters, magazine exposés, and melodramatic fiction, Lawson attempted to forge an army of small investors who would, on his command, sell their stock holdings en masse and ignite a financial cataclysm. Working openly, he insisted that publicity and persuasion, the keywords of so much passionate controversy in the Muckraking Era, would clear Wall Street of the influence of villainous financial barons and disable their machinery for despoiling the public. Market terror, Lawson argued, would ensure market democracy.

Lawson's stunning campaign; his extraordinary deployment of readerly sympathy to foment financial panic; and the sensational debates he generated among his contemporaries about the proper uses of the stock market, the mass media, and reform fiction, comprise the materials for my analysis in chapter 2 of reading and writing's agency, including fiction's agency, in the stock market. I show how cultural critics, anxious to preserve the wholesomeness of "legitimate" reform but aghast at the power of Lawson's writing to shake up financial markets and foment political revolution, used the category of "fiction" to explore and ultimately map out the boundary between socially virtuous and vicious textual effects.

Preoccupied with the individual reader and novel reading, historians and other scholars of American reading practices have largely ignored the ways collective acts of reading produce demonstrable economic and political effects. Although they have sometimes concerned themselves with the marketplace as a context for reading (for example, reading's constitutive role in commercial networks, or commercial reading's role in the construction of the public sphere, or reading's role in shaping individuals' experience of money and markets), scholars have paid little attention to reading's concrete influence on commerce and markets, leaving the investigation of reading's economic effects to finance sociologists, historians of the business and financial press, and media-effects researchers.[45] Many kinds of writing, of course, aim to elicit action. Reform texts clearly aim to activate, not merely advocate, social change. But few kinds of writing—the published threats of terrorists offer the closest analogue—perform their material "work" so efficiently, reflexively, or routinely as financial writing. And none, at least in the years around the turn of the century, could so easily engender national catastrophe.

The magnitude of financial literature's influence peaked as the twentieth century began. With outside investment in Wall Street exploding, more of the public than ever clamored for financial guidance, and the reach and number of financial papers dramatically expanded. The sums of money that could be made by exploiting what insiders called Wall Street's "fiction factory" jumped precipitously with the emergence of giant industrial corporations. Panics dramatized the alarming efficacy not only of such manipulation but also of any reading and writing that frightened the public. During panics, the market was most sensitive and unstable, and outside investors, frantic to escape financial ruin, overwhelmed by rumors, and lacking clear guidance, were most suggestible. Panics offered, as one journalist put it, "unlimited opportunities for sensational and terror-breeding state-ments."[46] As Lawson repeatedly demonstrated, a few words rightly timed, successfully broadcast, and widely believed (or widely dis-missed) could trigger a panic and spread ruin—and, some feared, in its wake, revolution—across the country. In sum, collective acts of reading and writing achieved unprecedented influence in times of market crisis. Jittery markets transformed journalists, stock promot-ers, and, as in Lawson's case, novelists into national heroes or villains, investing them with huge, if temporary, responsibility and power.

Media observers and literary critics were not the only ones preoc-cupied with the suggestibility of market crowds. Political economists, crowd psychologists, New Thought "success" writers, and novelists also tried to find an explanation for the contagion of financial giddi-ness and terror that produced panics.

At the turn of the century, American stock markets offered the most sensational—and, for many observers, instructive—demonstrations of collective psychology and its economic ramifications. Stock prices were at bottom determined by what Thorstein Veblen called "folk psychology," the collective forecasts and fears of thousands of inves-tors.[47] The fact that the capital value of the nation's major industries was tied to the "indeterminable, largely instinctive, shifting move-ments of public sentiment and apprehension" terrified critics, who marveled at the public's financial ignorance and irrationality.[48] "Spec-ulation is a study of mobs. . . . It is the art of analyzing massed stupidity," wrote Frederick Upham Adams in his panic novel The Kid-napped Millionaires (1901).[49] Around 1900, the first books of what we now call behavioral finance appeared, initiating the science Adams had in mind. Written for investors, texts such as G. C. Selden's The Psychology of the Stock Market (1912) were premised on the idea that to predict and take advantage of price movements, one had to grasp the psychology of the investing public, the "mind" of the market. Finan-cial analysts, culture critics, and social scientists urgently wanted to understand this mind, the herd mentality that led individuals, once they entered the market, to be "moved by the same impulses, actuated by the same feelings, experiencing the same emotions, having the same thoughts and the same views."[50]

To comprehend the sensational contagion of market opinion and emotion, many analysts turned to crowd psychology, a science, or, more precisely, an amalgamation of sciences, including sociology, psychic research, and the study of hysteria, that emerged in the 1880s and 1890s to explain the seemingly unique forces that motivated and shaped mass behavior. Initially preoccupied with revolutionary mobs, religious manias, and other extraordinary, seemingly degenerative forms of collective behavior, crowd psychology came to study how "modern conditions of mental intimacy" exerted an apparently resistless pressure on individuals, impelling them to submit to novel fads, popular crazes, demagogic appeals, and other sensational conformations in which the ostensibly deliberate actions of the rational public gave way to the spellbound single-mindedness and suggestibility of the mob.[51] In crowds, psychologists asserted, "men become imitative beings and their actions are determined by suggestion from the actions of others," a finding soon generalized into a social theory that, updating older conceptions of sympathy, enshrined imitation as the foundation of human behavior and social organization.[52]

To explain the apparent plasticity and imitativeness of individuals under the influence of social suggestion, psychologists likened crowds to hysterical patients and hypnotized subjects. More precisely, they likened the "mob mind"—that is, the mind of individuals in a crowd as well as the mind of the crowd itself—to the suggestible mind of hypnotics and hysterics. To develop this analogy, crowd psychologists and their popularizers drew on well-known studies of hysteria in France and trance states in the United States. These studies, fueling and fueled by a surge of popular interest in entrancement, hypnotism, and spiritualism in the United States in the 1890s, showed how hypnosis awakened subjects' "second" self, a subconscious self that, ceasing to be governed by individuals' conscious will, slavishly obeyed the hypnotizer's command, abandoned itself to mimicry, and, in hysteria, gave itself over to its own automatistic imperatives.

Financial markets at the turn of the century offered crowd psychologists a fertile site for studying the psychic contagion associated with hypnosis and hysteria. Indeed, outside the clinical wards, séances, and performance halls where hypnotists operated, the pandemic imitativeness of the crowd and the consequent dissolution of individuals' psychological sovereignty could be witnessed nowhere more routinely or spectacularly than in stock and commodity markets. Market panics, these analysts suggested, were the pathological consequence of hypnotization, occasions when the second self of the market burst uncontrollably, hysterically forth.

Frank Norris's *The Pit* (1903), American fiction's most sustained examination of the psychic hazards of entrancement in—and, more precisely, by—market crowds, serves as the key text of my third chapter. I have chosen to focus on *The Pit* because it offers an extraordinary analysis of the connection between financial panic, entrancement, and market reading and writing. Whereas Thomas Lawson focused public attention on the sensational power of certain kinds of texts and their manipulation of readerly sympathies to sway the market, Norris provides a highly figurative investigation of the psychic hazards of attempting to bring the market under a single individual's writerly and readerly control. Turn-of-the-century finance fiction writers routinely depict scenes of market reading, frequently likening the imaginative clutch of the market to the narrative hold exerted by their own narratives. Norris goes further, analyzing not only the similar rhetorical appeal of markets and novels but also their comparable narrative dynamics. Norris elaborates an analogy between the wheat market and the well-crafted novel: both constitute machines that can be made to go of themselves, disastrously in the case of the runaway market and felicitously in the case of the ideal novel. Even more strikingly, Norris deploys a mesmerism plot to align the automatism of these two machines with the automatism of what French researchers called a "hystérisable" mind, a mind that could be made hysterical through hypnosis. Through such figural and narrative triangulations, Norris weds a conventional account of the panicky market's sublime incomprehensibility—a featured part of eyewitness accounts of stock and commodity exchanges since the 1860s—with an account of the notorious indecipherability of hysteria's protean symptoms. More strikingly still, Norris represents the panicky market's unreadability and unwritability as a kind of mesmeric counteroffensive performed by the market itself, one during which the sublime mechanics of the market and the subliminal machinery of the speculator-hero's mind climactically merge.

Accounting for Panics

Market crises and crowds offered writers at the turn of the century the chance to study not only the sociological problem of mass reading's material effects and the psychological problem of mass hysteria but also the ethical conundrum of aggregate accountability. The challenge of determining what produced financial crises went hand in hand with the challenge of determining who produced them. Whatever their root cause or trigger, panics required the participation of a mass of individuals acting in combination, if not collusion. Local bank runs and small stock panics erupted when enough individuals, fearing each other's fear, scrambled to protect themselves, compounding the crisis for everyone. In large financial crises, the web of causality was more complex, entangling thousands, perhaps hundreds of thousands, of individuals. Blame could, in theory, be laid on everyone—businessmen, promoters, speculators, borrowers—who fueled a boom and accelerated its inevitable collapse. Even seemingly innocent outsiders could be held at fault. Will Payne's story "In the Panic," for example, anticipating Frank Capra's film It's a Wonderful Life, highlights the moral cowardice of panicky depositors by celebrating the courage of a young immigrant woman who returns her meager savings to a threatened bank. Almost any economic actor, legally and reasonably trying to protect his or her own interests, could be charged with abetting a financial catastrophe and endangering the nation.[53]

Contemporary observers struggled to make sense of the diffusion of moral accountability across the shifting network of exchanges, interests, and obligations that made up the nation's economy. Motivating these efforts was the desire not simply to put an end to panics but also to demystify new forms of economic obligation, organization, and agency that came to dominate financial life at the turn of the century. The emergence of large industrial corporations, the centralization of financial networks, and the unprecedented scope of public participation in the stock market meant that economic distress—and, indeed, all economic effects—radiated across the business universe farther and faster than ever before, implicating masses of individuals such as stockholders, depositors, and corporate employees, none of whom had ever considered themselves direct participants or accountable agents in the economy's functioning.

To clarify the blur of causes and effects across the financial universe, finance novelists deployed a variety of narrative tools. The most important of these was melodrama. By unveiling plottings, personal crimes, and confessions, melodrama, wed to an obsolescent economic and political republicanism, allowed readers to see that deliberating, morally accountable agents were behind even the most chaotic, complex, and far-reaching economic effects. Spotlighting enclaves of human agency in an otherwise reified economy, financial melodrama exposed the links between individuals' moral character and the effects of their behavior. It reinstated a familiar means of assigning and describing personal blame under an economic regime where masses of individuals (for example, shareholders and corporate employees) appeared to participate, directly or obliquely, in economic villainy, including the setting off of financial crises. It also deployed traditional dramatic resources to conjure forth moral outrage when villainy—and victimization, too—was no longer recognizable. Sitting in corporate boardrooms, modern malefactors no longer looked or behaved like the "old-time villain," as the sociologist Edward Ross put it.[54] Able to produce economic effects (such as stock crashes) a thousand miles away, they deployed their power in alien and inapprehensible ways. To be moved to demand reform, according to Ross, the public needed conventional stagings of villainy and victimization. Financial melodrama provided these traditional sentimental triggers. It made "modern sin" (as Ross called it) personal, legible, and dramatic.

Writers also turned to conspiracism, or conspiracy belief, to make sense of the new economy's confounding matrix of expectations, intentions, and actions. Competing with emerging and more abstract analyses of social structures and group belief, including conceptualizations of what we now call hegemony, financial conspiracy theories simplified the moral tangle posed by new forms of interdependence and organization by tracing economic outcomes, no matter how embracing or diffuse, to the villainous intentions of specific groups.[55] Refusing to distribute blame across the collective or distinguish degrees of moral responsibility, conspiracism, like melodrama (its typical aesthetic mode at the turn of the century), asserted that moral accountability within these vast collectivities could be specified and contained, a possibility conspiracists as well as nonconspiracists urgently desired. It preserved familiar notions of moral agency, character, and causality, even as these notions were being rendered obsolete by corporate modernity.

One of the most interesting investigations of moral diffusion is Sinclair's *The Moneychangers*, a behind-the-scenes account of the panic of 1907 that serves as my key text in chapter 4. Although it follows conventional financial conspiracist melodramas by exposing the viciousness and omnipotence of banker titans, *The Moneychangers* offers an extraordinary study of outsiders' moral accountability. Blurring the line between conspiracy's outsiders and insiders, Sinclair exposes how middle-class individuals, especially shareholders and depositors, not only consent to their own entrapment within capitalists' vicious designs but also, for this reason, share blame for the private and public injustice capitalism itself encourages. Because they know that the modern industrial economy is overseen by a few unremittingly corrupt bankers and corporate directors, middle-class individuals can maintain their standing as virtuous citizens—and, indeed, protect themselves and others from ruin and exploitation—only by dislodging themselves from this economy and organizing themselves into a republican counterforce, one devoted to restoring the transparency and efficacy of representative government. In Sinclair's novel, an outraged, activist electorate constitutes a virtuous alternative to the market mob as well as the financial conspiracy. Republicanism constitutes financial panic's remedy and its salutary replacement.

Like many other socialist propagandists at the turn of the century, Sinclair undermines the distinction between financial conspiracy and finance capitalism, between economic sin and economic structure. Sinclair describes a moral economy that interpellates individuals both as ethical members of a national public and as cogs within a systemic machinery. In this moral economy, individuals are implicated far beyond the amount of their financial investment. The conspiracy governs a system (or "the System," as he called it) so infected and infecting, so conducive to vicious and self-aggrandizing behavior by the handful of individuals who preside over it, that to bankroll it in any way makes one a partner in these individuals' villainy.[56] Sinclair uses the idea of conspiracy to chart the transmission of personal moral accountability across the entire modern corporate landscape, from consumers to producers, shareholders to corporate directors, and all beneficiaries of the corporate order to exploited industrial workers. Sinclair's novel makes this causal web, so vast that its extensiveness can only be imagined, envisionable. Conspiracism allows Sinclair to safeguard the conceptual coherence and political relevance of citizens' moral autonomy in a universe where economic investments produce incalculable and thus uncontrollable financial, social, and political effects.

Theodore Dreiser, the focus of my final chapter, is another fiction writer who took up the moral accounting challenges posed by financial panics. However, in contrast to Sinclair and other novelists such as William Dean Howells who explored the ethical complexities of market crowds, Dreiser understood the financial universe to be completely amoral. In Dreiser's naturalist panic novel *The Financier* (1912), financial behavior, no matter how self-serving, corrupt, or predatory, does not morally incriminate individuals; it merely expresses individuals' natural drive to satisfy their wants and accumulate power and profit. If crowd psychologists saw financial panic as a laboratory for studying the psychological laws governing crowds, Dreiser sees panic as a field site for investigating the natural laws and sociological truths revealed by the wary cooperation and cutthroat competition among economic animals. For Dreiser, panic constitutes an exemplary naturalist drama.

Unlike most panic novelists, Dreiser is interested in financial panic as a cause, rather than an effect, of morally controversial behavior. More exactly, Dreiser is interested in the ways panic exposes what can—and, more important, cannot—be brought to moral account. The novel aims to show that nature's agents, individuals like the title character whose actions accord with nature's laws, cannot be comprehended or contained by conventional forms of moral accounting. In fact, in the novel, every attempt to make individuals accountable and to settle accounts—not just moral but also juridical, financial, and sentimental—either fails or backfires, producing some unaccounted-for remainder that generates more futile accounting projects, more debts, and more imbalances. What makes *The Financier* so remarkable is that the argument it unfolds about the limits of these various kinds of accounting applies to narrative accounting as well, including its own. Of all the panic novels with which I am familiar, *The Financier* is the most relentlessly self-reflexive, using its study of what can and cannot be brought to book—what literally falls inside and outside the margins of financial account books and other kinds of texts—to call attention to its own innovation and ambition: to expose how conventional narrative forms, especially biography and biographical fiction, structured by a desire to bring human plots to ethical account, can never adequately convey nature's sociology or metaphysics. Beginning with its representation of financial panic, *The Financier* experiments with a narrative form that acknowledges the irreducible openness of the universe, the inexorability of human plotting and counterplotting, and the impossibility of bringing any of these plots to a successful close.

Among the panic novelists I discuss, it is Dreiser who most fully realizes the formal implications of panic's challenge to representation, for Dreiser refuses to encompass the market's sublime excess or its endlessly ramifying social effects within a conventional narrative teleology, and he refuses to be alarmed by the dissolution of personal autonomy that scandalized other panic novelists. He is the only panic writer who sees market crowds as natural, inescapable, and productive. Indeed, he sees them as engines and conditions of literary narrative.

Rather than offering a broad survey or genealogy of panic fiction, *Panic!* focuses on several extraordinary novels written within a few years of each other. I have chosen these texts because they offer the most edifying and interesting investigations in American fiction of literary and cultural problems associated with financial panics and market crowds at the turn of the twentieth century. Instead of encompassing these texts within a monolithic argument about literature, history, and economics during this era, I have privileged the particularity and variety of these works, their narrative and rhetorical dynamics, and the problems they study and embody. There are pragmatic but also polemical reasons for this. Against studies that view contemporaneous literary expressions as homologous instantiations of a single market logic or cultural symptomatology, I want to highlight the myriad ways that fiction registers, refracts, and works on markets and culture at a given historical moment.

I have organized the chapters into three sections. The first, comprising a single chapter, focuses on competing conceptions of history convened around financial crises at the turn of the century, and it recuperates the desperate ideological battles about class and gender that panics precipitated among various political and financial constituencies in these years. The second section, consisting of two chapters, focuses on the sociology and social psychology of market crowds. It analyzes how novelists turned to literary sentimentalism, sympathy, and the sublime to figure and control the economic, political, and psychic damage wrought by the aggregate actions of these crowds. The final section, also consisting of two chapters, focuses on the ethical and epistemological challenges posed by panics and their collective dynamics. These challenges frame my discussions of literary melodrama and naturalism.[57]

Chapter 1

Panic and the Pétroleuse

What shall we call the man and the men who seduce,
but do not assassinate,—Guiteaus of political economy
who would overcome, not one, but all departments of our
government; who travel by night and under-ground to betray
trusts they have invited; who, living among us as fellow-men
and neighbors, loyal to the covenants of society, are traitors
to all the ties of honor, justice, and mercy that make the
American community possible, and the want of which
makes the Paris commune?

   Henry Demarest Lloyd on Jay Gould

The most disastrous and discouraging effects of an evil
financial system always make their appearance at the centers
of social life—the home and the fireside—the most sacred
places on earth.

   James B. Weaver, *A Call to Action*

     In an address to socialist sympathizers at Boston's Fanueil
Hall in 1903, the ex-minister George Herron called on his audience to
consider the continuing relevance of the Paris Commune of 1871 for
the revolutionary movement in the United States. The memory of the
Commune still smoldered in the minds of socialists, even after thirty
years. His audience remembered how the Parisian working class, hu-
miliated by the National Assembly's capitulation to the Prussian army
and infuriated by the French government's subsequent attempt to
disarm and subjugate the city, elected its own leaders and waged a
brief, bloody, and disastrous defense against French troops that left
thousands of Parisians dead. For Herron, as for many American labor
radicals, the Commune represented a glorious experiment in popular
democracy, a fleeting but monumental triumph for the working class,
and an inspiration for the ongoing class struggle. Aware that most

Americans remembered the French civil war only as "a time of red and meaningless terror" and that the Commune endured primarily as a catchword for anarchy and social pathology, Herron awaited the writer who would "sing the true epic" of the Communist government.[1] This writer would reveal the Paris revolution to be the source and model of the better days ahead, a future when "these evil days of capitalist misgovernment . . . shall have passed away forever."[2] Looking back to 1871, the romancer of the Revolution would confirm what Herron took to be the lesson of the Commune: socialists must accept the inevitability of class conflict and resist any accommodation to capitalism.

Frederic Isham was not the writer Herron had in mind.[3] Isham's financial panic novel *Black Friday* (1904), published a year after Herron's jeremiad, makes ample and important use of the Paris Commune, but in the novel the Commune represents the apocalyptic fulfillment of modernity's worst trends, a nightmarish vision of a lawless, leaderless society in which arson-prone mobs of women burn the ancient city, cast their vengeance on innocent citizens, and disdain whatever conserving agency history and the state might offer. Nothing in Isham's representation suggests that the Commune has anything to do with class. Indeed, nothing in the novel suggests that the Commune has anything to do with anything at all: the spasm of anarchy that marks its culmination remains unexplained, seemingly causeless.

Isham's failure or unwillingness to identify the Commune as a working-class revolt is striking, for throughout the last decades of the nineteenth century, as Nell Irvin Painter, Philip Katz, and other historians have documented, the Commune "served as the prevailing image for Americans faced with labor unrest."[4] The great wave of strikes beginning in 1877 "fixed the image of the Commune—violence, burning, and bloodshed—on the very idea of organized workers and socialists of any sort," and observers, dreading economic and social rupture, continued to identify strikes, labor demonstrations, anarchist violence, and populist insurgency with the Paris uprising through the turn of the century.[5] Isham's refusal to suggest historical causes or contexts for the violence seems doubly odd, given the novel's overt concern with history and historical explanation. Mingling established fact with romantic invention, the middle "book" or section of the novel (there are three "books" in all) offers a history of "Black Friday," the sensational financial panic of Friday, 24 September 1869, a crisis precipitated by Jay Gould's brief, bold corner of the nation's gold market. Isham accounts for the gold corner's conspiratorial beginning, its chaotic climax, and its dramatic demise when President Ulysses S. Grant steps in and ends it. For Isham, Black Friday is the first crisis to test the stability and progress of the newly united nation, and in telling its story, Isham means to shed light on the momentous years after the Civil War, a "period of wondrous awakening" and an economic "golden age" of business combination and consolidation that, in Isham's revisionary imagination, serves as historical origin and business model of the industrial trust boom in his own day.[6]

Even stranger, the Commune plot, although it directly succeeds the Black Friday plot, has no obvious narrative connection to it. The two stories, set two years and an ocean apart, constitute discrete sections of the novel, and the hero's successful efforts to quell the financial panic in the Black Friday plot play no apparent role in his subsequent adventures in Paris. Indeed, reviewers of *Black Friday* based their critique of the novel on the seeming gratuitousness of the Commune plot; they found it "bizarre" and "totally unnecessary to the story."[7] The odd fit of the Commune narrative invites a number of questions: What are we to make of the presence of the Commune in a novel that centers on a financial panic? Why give the legendary panic a detailed, if partly fanciful, history and offer no explanation at all for the equally legendary uprising? Why structure a novel—a novel otherwise committed to dramatizing causes and effects—around two plots that have only an accidental historical and narrative relation to each other?

My answer, put simply, is that Black Friday and the Paris Commune function as allegorical refigurements of economic crisis and proletarian revolution, and that Isham, anxious to preempt the imagining of class violence in the United States, represses any causal connection between the two phenomena. In truth, however, the panic plot and the Commune are not entirely disconnected. They are linked obliquely by the marriage crisis that arcs through the entire novel. In book 1 of the novel ("Fluctuations"), the hero, Richard Strong, meets and marries Elinor Rossiter, the daughter of a recently bankrupted American aristocrat. The marriage sours immediately: on their honeymoon, chilled by his preoccupation with business, she tells him she cannot love him. In book 2 ("Black Friday"), during the buildup to the fateful panic, he strikes her after he sees her accept a kiss from another man, and she flees to Paris with her father. In book 3 ("Readjustment"), two years later, he goes to Paris to rescue her from the chaos of the Commune, and his heroics move her, months after the Commune plot has concluded, to return to him. The panic and Commune plots are also linked, however tenuously, by the discomfiting presence of another woman, a French actress who, during the market crisis, attempts to subvert Strong's marriage, and who, during the chaotic last days of the Commune, appears on a Paris stage, semi-nude, draped in revolutionary garb, exciting a fevered crowd while the theater goes up in smoke, set on fire by one of the female arsonists haunting the city. The sudden and sensational reappearance of the actress invites a final pair of questions about the formal logic of the novel: Why make such a dangerously modern woman—an actress, a free lover, a Communist (as Commune supporters were called), and a proxy for the legendary "pétroleuses" (gasoline throwers) who ravage Paris—one of the two main links between the financial crisis and the class revolt? Why make a wayward but finally mainstreamed wife the other?

This chapter aims to make figural and ideological sense of Black Friday's extraordinary triangulation of financial panic, class conflict, and female independence and to illuminate the remarkable historical work this triangulation performs. I argue that Isham has two related ambitions in Black Friday, both of which merit explication and justify, I hope, the attention I am giving to a book few people have read in a century. First, he uses the financial panic at the center of Black Friday to expose, dramatize, and connect an astonishing array of cultural evils he sees transforming modern America. No other American novel equates market crises with so many distinctly cultural disorders; and no other novel deploys a financial panic to render such a sweeping and sensational judgment on American cultural decline. Although the Commune plot, following the financial plot, may make no narrative sense, it has a clear thematic rationale. We are meant to equate the Commune and the gold panic, recognize them as commensurable threats to social order, and associate both with the most dangerous developments of modernity: feminism, free love, popular culture, class mingling, the treacherous repudiation of private and public bonds, and liberalism run riot—all of which lead, in the historical narrative and analogical web constructed by Isham, to mob violence, political rebellion, and economic chaos.

For Isham, French anarchy and American financial panic stand for each other and for the social, political, and economic turmoil attending the complete "maddening" of values in Gilded Age America (BF 279). Formally, anarchy and panic serve as general equivalents, like money, rubrics under which seemingly disparate social dislocations can be brought together, compared, and substituted for each other. The connection between panic, anarchy, and money is not accidental, for Isham's novel centers on a money panic. Gould and the gold clique undermine the stability of money's value, confound currency prices, and by doing so put all values in flux. Money, the universal commodity, is the measure and "prop"—Isham's word—of all values (BF 116), and its manipulation, made possible by the absence of a gold (or any other) standard in 1869, introduces instability throughout economic and social life. It provides a metaphor for the vertiginous unanchoring of cultural values coincident with, if not also caused by, the financial crisis. "Here was chaos. Values had run mad," Isham tells us (BF 279): wives rebel against their husbands, merchants make claims upon aristocrats, and French women set their national and cultural capital aflame.

If markets, as some have argued, are arenas in which communities resolve their differences by giving individuals and groups a rational (or, at least, predictable) means of negotiating and thus agreeing on values, then panics, as in Black Friday, are occasions when the structure for resolving differences breaks down and the community's values are up for grabs. How panics are quelled, for Isham, suggests not just how markets should be made safe for investment again, but also how cultural crises, and, in particular, women's rejection of marriage obligations, might be brought to order. This may seem to be a clichéd equation of volatile markets and unruly women and an equally clichéd expression of patriarchal disciplinary authority. It turns out to be something else, however, for Isham shows, with considerable anxiousness, how independent women, unlike markets, cannot be compelled to return to their normal, natural function. They must *choose* to return to their husbands, and in their consent lies their historical and political significance.

Isham's desire to diagnose and remedy the gender trouble plaguing modern America is inseparable from his second primary ambition in *Black Friday*: to (re)construct a history of (and thus a prophecy for) modern America purged of any trace of class conflict. At bottom, Isham fears class and cultural revolution produced by economic crisis. The novel displaces this trauma by taking the narratives and buzzwords of the most sensational moments of class crisis around the turn of the century—the Haymarket affair, the silverite insurgency in the 1890s, and McKinley's assassination by an anarchist in 1901, moments many thought foreshadowed the coming apocalypse—and recasting them within a politically innocuous narrative that exactly reverses their ideological valence. These upheavals provide the "shadow narratives," to use Russell Reising's term, that organize the "massive residue of sociohistorical reference" encoded within the novel, the accreted traces of specific ideological pressures that shape all novels during their composition and often queer their narrative resolution.[8] In short, the gold panic in Isham's novel serves as an allegorical (p)revision of these crises. As such, it offers a means of re-emplotting American capitalist development in order to safeguard it, at least its imagining, from anticorporate challenges.

Isham's novel reminds us that populists and socialists (and rogue capitalists such as Thomas Lawson) were not the only ones writing sensational novels about financial panics. Friends of corporate gigantism, equally preoccupied with the dangers posed by economic upheaval, also produced alarmist panic fiction. *Black Friday* deserves special attention not because it acknowledges a threat to capitalism's progress but rather because it neutralizes this threat by locating it in capitalism's speculative fringe, not its proletarian underbelly. In Isham's historical recontextualization, we are meant to forget the Paris Commune's association with labor and populist militancy and instead focus on its identification with the volatility produced by financial speculators. In the end, we are meant to read capitalist crisis not as an inevitable or necessary collision between capital and labor, but rather as a single, decisive skirmish between capitalism's virtuous and vicious avant-gardes, between its progressive center and its radical margin, a skirmish finally won by the elite torchbearers of corporate capitalism—the progressive center—once a strong central government comes to its aid. Seemingly unrelated to this internecine battle, revolution, waged anarchically by its own torchbearers, the pétroleuses of Paris and their American equivalents, simply disappears from view, dislodged from the historical narrative and displaced by the very different kind of class rapprochement represented by the resolution of the marriage plot. In this way, Isham's capitalist romance preserves history's arrow from the possibility of any radical deflection.

The novel's remarkable cultural and ideological work operates along two interrelated and ultimately contradictory axes, one thematic (or analogical) and one historical (or causal). The first half of this chapter explicates Isham's thematic argument, an argument about gender, history, and corporate modernity sustained by parallels (and contrasts) between the novel's three major crises. The second half excavates the historical sources—the source material as well as the animating anxieties—of the novel's treatment of economic crisis and historical causation. In psychoanalytic terms, this analysis moves from the manifest to the latent historical "pretexts" of Isham's financial allegory, sorting out Black Friday's figural displacements and illuminating its historical repressions and narrative returns. Moving backward from the economic crisis of the mid-1890s to the class violence of the mid-1880s, this regression ultimately reveals how the novel's panic about history—more precisely, about one shape that history can take—shapes its history of panic.

Black Friday, 1869, and Black Friday, 1904

In 1869, Jay Gould, one of Wall Street's most notorious and daring operators, succeeded in cornering the nation's gold supply, triggering one of the most sensational financial panics in the nation's history. Since 1861, the nation had been without a stable currency.

Congress had declared greenbacks, or paper dollars, legal currency, and their value, untied to any standard, fluctuated against the price of gold. The New York Gold Exchange, the "wildest market in American history," as one financial historian has described it, served as a market for the metal, setting prices around the nation.[9] The overwhelming portion of the trading, $70–90 million worth on an average day, consisted of the betting by speculators on gold's price movements.

In August 1869, Gould formed a clique with the equally notorious operator Jim Fisk to buy up all the available gold in New York, control its price, and eventually sell it to traders and speculators who desperately needed specie to meet their commercial obligations.[10] One problem loomed from the start, however. If President Grant or his treasury secretary, George Boutwell, decided to open the vaults of the U.S. Treasury and release a flood, even a stream, of gold into the money market, the corner would disintegrate. Gould met the problem head on: he bribed Grant's brother-in-law and confidant, Abel Corbin. With Corbin in his pocket, Gould handpicked the official who would oversee the Treasury's day-to-day operations and met with the president, finally persuading him of the economic benefits of high gold prices.

Convinced that the president would not obstruct a rise in the price of the metal, Gould, Fisk, and their agents set their machinery to work. Gold prices drifted higher and then, buoyed by the force of the gold ring's buying, surged upward, reaching spectacular heights on Thursday, 23 September, when it became clear that there was no more gold for sale in New York. As the shortage climaxed, the volume of daily trading reached somewhere between $500 million and $800 million, eight times its normal level. The gold ring, having fictitiously lent $100 million in gold, more than six times the amount of the available supply in the city, could now hike its price to whatever extortionate level it chose, terrifying borrowers. Speculators who had sold gold short, desperately counting on the government to puncture the bubble, were ruined. Without gold, bankers, traders who bought or sold anything overseas, and all those who depended on them—merchants, farmers, manufacturers, shippers, and dockworkers—were paralyzed. Foreign trade stopped, and the nation breathlessly waited for the president to act.

On Friday the twenty-fourth, described by Henry Demarest Lloyd as the "darkest day in our financial history," President Grant, alerted by an assistant's revelation that Gould had tried to bribe him and spooked by Boutwell's conviction that a severe money lockup could lead to a lasting depression, finally authorized the Treasury to release its gold reserves.[11] News of the government's decision produced chaos on Wall Street. Speculators who were not bankrupted by the precipitous rise in prices were now bankrupted by gold's sudden collapse. Within fifteen minutes, according to one sensational report, "half of Wall Street was involved in ruin."[12] A mob of speculators stormed the offices of Gould, Fisk, and their brokers, demanding restitution. The New York state militia was called out to prevent the lynching of the gold-ring leaders. There were suicides and continued threats of mob violence. In the panic, a thousand tons of gold were traded. The staggering volume made settling accounts impossible: no one knew which trades were to be honored, which banks and brokers might fail. The amount of money that hung on this accounting was huge, greater than the nation's entire supply of gold and greenbacks.[13] The panic continued for days as speculators and borrowers, fearing repudiations and foreclosures, desperately sold their stocks for whatever money they could get. Only a few brokers escaped untouched. Wall Street activity slackened for months, and the wheat trade slumped for years.

As the facts of the corner and its devastation came to light, the panic came to be seen less as a financial drama than a national melodrama, a lurid tale of villainy, conspiracy, and treachery. Gould and his clique had not only thrown the country into a commercial crisis, victimizing brokers, businessmen, and farmers; they had also, even more sensationally, conspired against President Grant, the sainted military hero and savior of the Union. Gould had infiltrated and poisoned the presidency: Grant's family was implicated, and Grant himself was briefly suspected of abetting the gold plot. In the political melodrama, Gould starred as the arch villain, a rapacious swindler who sought profit without conscience. Fisk played the parvenu clown who thrived in the public spotlight. Corbin, a traitor to his family and his president, assumed the role of the clique's benighted puppet. Investigations and exposés identified other culprits—the subtreasurer,

Scene on Broad and Wall streets on "Black Friday," 24 September 1869.
Harris, *Memories of Manhattan in the Sixties and Seventies*.

the absence of a gold standard, the awesome power wielded by corporations—but for the next thirty-five years, Gould remained the focus of the story. An enemy of the state, he took advantage of the anchorless financial system and held the public's money hostage for his own mercenary ends.

Except for the involvement of his fictitious hero—a major qualification, to be sure—Isham recognizably reconstructs the events leading up to and during the gold panic. Isham puts his account to obvious ideological use, leaving little doubt about the economic viciousness of the gold conspiracy. In the novel, the high prices speciously advocated by Gould as a boon to the country and the speculative mania that accompanies them are "an untoward menace to prosperity," the "outcome of abnormal and artificial causes" (BF 216). It is specifically to discourage this unwonted inflation that Richard Strong, a railroad baron, takes up his financial fight against the gold ring. One of the nation's "builders" after the Civil War (BF 101), Strong is a model of fiscal conservatism, an uncompromising believer in "real" commercial values, stable economic growth, and financial accountability. Normally willing to let market forces determine prices, he intervenes in the gold trade only to protect the market's ostensibly natural operation from the disastrous influence of manipulators.

Strong ends the crisis by convincing Grant to open the Treasury reserves. We are clearly meant to see his activism on behalf of economic stability as a patriotic service. The gold corner is, after all, an act of national treachery, an overt attempt to undermine the federal government (Isham has the ringleaders not only place spies and corrupt officials but also kidnap the president). At stake in the crisis is the viability of centralized government itself. The president's unequivocal, if tardy, response to the panic erases any doubts about the federal government's political, economic, and moral authority. In thwarting the treachery of the gold ring and (re)assuming regulatory power over the nation's currency, Grant fulfills what for Isham is the president's moral and political obligation to safeguard the stability of the nation.

Isham's defense of federal intervention in money market crises serves as a thematic stand-in for his defense of patriarchal marriage.[14] In Black Friday, we are meant to regard husbands as the domestic representatives of central state power and compare the president's authority to end the market crisis with Strong's authority to quell domestic and social unrest. In short, the gold crisis is the centerpiece of the novel's warning against decentralization outside and inside the home.

Domestic Anarchy

The marriage crisis, the focus of book 1, occupies over half of the novel. Elinor's father invested the family's money in Confederate bonds during the Civil War; when the South lost and repudiated its war debts, these bonds became worthless, bankrupting the family. Eager to spare her parents the humiliation of having to mingle with tradesmen (the family's class decline being the most obvious of the "fluctuations" referred to by the title of book 1), Elinor reluctantly agrees to marry Strong, a plain-speaking captain of industry who earned his recent fortune through his careful stewardship of several railroads. The marriage fails her romantic ideal, and during their honeymoon, when he is distracted by news of a business plot against him, she spurns him. Isham characterizes Elinor's turn from him as a "rebellion" and identifies it repeatedly with the treachery of the gold speculators. Should we miss the point, Isham has Elinor kiss one of Gould's secret agents, a treachery doubly nefarious since he is one of Strong's employees. Isham goes further and identifies both Elinor's and Gould's treachery with that of the Confederacy. Elinor, the South, and the gold conspirators all repudiate sacrosanct "bonds." Strong makes this obvious when he explains that "a state, like an individual" might always repent the repudiation of its obligations (BF 145).

We are clearly meant to compare Strong's handling of the marriage crisis with Grant's vanquishing of the Confederate rebellion and with their joint handling of the gold crisis—and also, in book 3, with the French government's subjugation of its own civil crisis.[15] For Isham, the husband's authority and the federal government's are models for each other, both built on foundational public trusts. Obligation, duty, contract, bond: the book fetishizes these as bulwarks against dissipation and chaos. Anarchy, whether at home, in the market, or in the streets, is simply not to be tolerated.

Like the panic and the Commune plots, the marriage plot argues for the containment of rebellion and anarchy. However, crucially, unlike those plots, it repudiates fiat and force as the means of accomplishing this. The capitalist titan does not, and, indeed, cannot, strong-arm Elinor to accept his mandate. This is the source of the anxiety that percolates through the last third of the book and makes its closure seem so grudging and forced. Strong realizes that his heroic rescue mission in France is necessary but insufficient to win Elinor back; he realizes that she must make this decision herself. Indeed, it is Elinor, not Strong, who brings about their reconciliation. Believing that Elinor never loved him, and unsure what sentimental claim he has upon her (since he hit her when he last saw her two years before),

Strong leaves her in Paris once she is out of danger, resigning himself to their separation. However, months later, in the last pages of the novel, she suddenly appears at their home, confessing that she "could not help" returning to him (BF 403). Wedding public obligation and private desire, Elinor naturalizes her return to the marriage as an inner, sentimental imperative ("I could not help it . . . Ever since that night in Paris I have felt I must see you"). She tells him she always loved him but that she did not recognize her true feelings until now. By such a declaration, she retroactively establishes her faithfulness to the marriage contract, backdating it to eliminate any evidence of her breach. Her rebellion appears now simply as a failure of self-knowledge: if she had better understood her own true desires, she would have embraced the idea of being Strong's wife from the start. She writes off her rebellion as the behavior of "a very foolish, impractical girl" (BF 407). They agree that they had mistreated and misunderstood each other.[16]

We are meant to applaud both Strong and Elinor and to see their reconciliation as a salutary alternative to the final solutions of the panic and Commune plots. We are meant to applaud Strong because he recognizes that wives, like states and markets, must have some independence and that central authority should be exercised—if it can be exercised—only when this independence sufficiently threatens the safety of the nation. We are meant to applaud Elinor because, even as she acts out her semi-autonomy, she ultimately consents to central authority.

If her consent makes the new marriage relation virtuously democratic, it also makes it safely feudal. In the mawkish conclusion, Elinor, drawing Strong close, proclaims that he is her "king" (BF 408). This coronation resolves the problem that initiated the marriage crisis in the first place: her anachronistic desire to marry "some romantic . . . impractical, Prince Charming" (BF 407).[17] Back with her king, Elinor gets her royalty, but, more important, she now sees, like so many heroines in finance fiction, that her allegiance to outmoded aesthetic and cultural values kept her from recognizing the romance of modern business, a romance all the more maturing because it is wedded to the "real" concerns of the nation. Discovering that building railroads and fending off stock raids—Strong's commitment to advancing American capitalism—is romantic after all, she brings her marriage ideal up to date, finally aligning it with national progress, natural law, and economic necessity.

Elinor makes peace with modernity by, as the title of book 3 suggests, "readjusting." Modernity, in turn, makes peace with her. For Isham, everything, including the fate of the nation and the fate of history itself, hangs on her adjustment, especially on the fact that she initiates it on her own. By choosing to return to Strong, Elinor distinguishes herself from the feminists and free-love advocates who populate the book and preach the radical transformation of the marriage bond. By choosing to make Strong her king, Elinor stabilizes the traditional center of authority within the marriage relation; as importantly, she preserves the nation from the anarchic effects of this relation's overthrow. In this sense, Elinor, embracing her conventional marital role and obligation, is as much of a national hero as Strong.

Isham makes the monumental stakes of her choice clear by linking the sex revolutionaries not only with the financial mavericks who undermine the currency (and thus "all values" [BF 116]) but also, more sensationally, with the "pétroleuses" who set fire to Paris. We are meant to see the overthrow of the institution of marriage as both a parallel to and an incipient form of civic catastrophe. Elinor assumes the symbolic burden of saving civilization from destruction and preventing America from turning into France. Should we miss the chain of equations that potentially identify Elinor's rebellion with the fire-starters' mayhem, Isham, in the climax of book 3, has Elinor set upon by a bloodthirsty Parisian crowd that mistakes her for a pétroleuse (they see a bottle of medicine in her hand, thinking it is gasoline). For Isham, radicalism enables and invites such confusions.

The most obvious connection between the three plots of Black Friday is the enduring presence of the enemies of traditional marriage bonds, women excessively given over to their revolutionary theories or their spectacular bodies. Isham overtly links feminists and sex radicals with the financial and civil insurgents and, more generally, with the sensational unsettling of values that, for Isham, characterizes contemporary culture. Jim Fisk rides about New York with Lydia Thompson, the pioneer "queen" of burlesque who scandalized New Yorkers in 1868 by making the prurient display of female legs a commercial stage sensation.[18] Accompanying Thompson is Zoldene, the ubiquitous French actress who writes a fateful note alerting Strong to his wife's unfaithfulness. Zoldene's sexual magnetism is linked several times in the novel with the ruinous fascination of the gold trade, and her semi-nude performance as a Communist Zouave in a burning theater in Paris during the "Bloody Week" specifically recalls the panic inside the Gold Exchange two years before. Zoldene is "repellent," promiscuous, prodigal, and reckless (BF 256). She abandons her husband— he turns out to be the man Elinor kissed, provoking Strong's jealous violence—for the crass attention of the public; and she dies, apparently in a panic she helped inflame. She is a nightmarish symbol of cultural dissolution, a sensational caricature of the New Woman, sexually unbridled, aggressively visible, flaunting her freedom from husband and state in public—the kind of "modern Pandora" that Elinor, by returning from France to reassert her wedding vows, disavows.[19]

Zoldene represents what Elinor might have become and also, more important, the civil discord she might have unloosed if she had continued to repudiate her conjugal bonds. Such a portent is signaled in book 1, which ends with a brief, disdainful discussion of Susan B. Anthony, the "Girl of Finance" (BF 176), and other women "who leave the duties of their own sex to invade the privileges of the other" (BF 178). Thunder sounding like "the distant bombardment of a beleaguered city" accompanies the discussion, an image literalized in book 3 when Paris, set ablaze by the pétroleuses, is bombarded—that is, saved—by government forces (BF 179). In this later narrative, Elinor, nursing her traumatized father, is trapped in the city. Strong comes to Paris to find her, and through his eyes, we see how emancipated women, most notably Zoldene, have demolished civilization. He first witnesses a free-love rally inside a church where women smoke and drink and preach "the right to do anything" (BF 367). Soon after this, women arsonists toss gasoline bombs into his hotel room. Then, as if this were not enough, he sees a "gross, ragged, gibbering" throng, including prostitutes wearing legion-of-honor sashes, gathered to see the incomparable Zoldene on stage (BF 373). Drawn into the theater,

"The Burning of Paris." *Harper's Weekly*, 1 July 1871.

Strong is caught in the panic triggered by the smell of smoke. Thrust outside by the crowd, backlit by a hell scene of fire and violence, he sees Elinor, carrying the medicine for her ailing father, and the approaching crowd. He rescues her from a culture spinning apart from its center.

Elinor and Zoldene represent twin, but not identical threats. They represent contrary orientations toward history, both of which are at odds with Strong's vision of enlightened capitalist progress. Although Elinor's initial dissent points to an apocalyptic future in which marriage no longer anchors culture against its own centrifugal tendencies, her rebellion stems from her sentimental commitment to the romanticism of the past, her inability to relinquish feudal, fairy-tale fantasies. In contrast, Zoldene and her feminist proxies wish to cast off the ballast of tradition and pitch the world chaotically into the future. By returning to Strong, Elinor makes herself at home in the present. More important, she makes herself at home in a particular version of history in which Strong's cultural, political, and economic values triumph. Culturally, this history favors traditional articulations of men's and women's spheres and marriage roles. Politically and economically, this history favors ongoing but stable capitalist development, inexorable but enlightened corporate growth, and government involvement only as needed to clear away occasional obstructions slowing the economic juggernaut.

Elinor finds her place in history by retreating from revolutionary France into her home. No longer given over to fanciful feudal nostalgia, and saved by her husband from the nightmarish attacks of workers committed to a fantastic future, she embraces the new, progressive regime. This closing embrace of the real and the contemporary, validating corporate progress, nation building, and women's conjugal dependence—a rational, not radical, modernity guided by enlightened and patriotic business leaders—is inseparable from *Black Friday*'s class resolution, at least at a thematic level. The reunion of Elinor and Strong that brings Elinor up to date and into history signals the supremacy of Strong's class and validates its new cultural and national authority. At first glance, the reunion seems to represent a formulaic marriage of sterile aristocracy and virile democracy—a joining of the cultured Rossiters (Elinor's family), who are beholden to their ancestral pasts, with the parvenu Richard Strong, for whom the past is a drag on progress. In actuality, however, the reunion represents the wedding of two elite classes or class fractions, an old, moribund patrician elite and a new, emergent corporate elite. It is not a wedding of equals. Elinor's father dies, his old-world allegiances and emasculating dispositions having unfitted him for topsy-turvy New York and revolutionary Paris. Elinor, freed from her daughterly ministrations, can (re)turn to Strong. Fathering businesses, Strong represents the new paternity, the warden of progress itself. Elinor's coronation of him inaugurates the inevitable and welcome reign of the masculine industrial elite, now a protector, not a rival, of feminized and obsolescent patrician culture. In short, rescuing her in Paris, Strong rescues her from absorption into both the proletarian future and the aristocratic past. Elinor's return, indebted to this rescue and yet self-chosen, saves the nation from the sexual incendiarism of the one and the debilitating effeminacy of the other.

I have teased out these parallels and contrasts between the three major narratives in order to explicate what I take to be the major thematic work of Black Friday: a defense of the marriage relation, a defense that equates fidelity to the marriage contract with realism, patriotism, economic progress (under the auspices of the corporation), class harmony (the patrician class bequeathing its cultural authority to the business elite), and cultural stability. To make this defense, Isham overtly sutures domestic rebellion to sensational cataclysms: financial crisis, civic collapse, and (in the torching of Paris's famous palaces, hotels, and museums) the annihilation of cultural memory and heritage.

The marriage plot performs important ideological work: it refigures and represses the imagined possibility of class apocalypse in the United States. To see how this works, we must see how "behind" the marriage crisis, shadowing it, looms the threat of class revolution. We do this by turning to the historical figures evoked by Zoldene, the "Girl of Finance," the free-love radicals, and the haunting pétroleuses: Victoria Woodhull, Susan B. Anthony, and Elizabeth Cady Stanton. Around the time of Black Friday in 1869, these famous feminists provoked forms of cultural panic that Isham faithfully, even studiously, reconstructs. These historical figures haunt the marriage plot and link the novel's gender, economic, and political threats.

Introduced by one newspaper in 1869 as the epitome of "The Coming Woman," Woodhull was Gilded Age America's most scandalous feminist and most prominent free-love advocate.[20] (She makes a cameo in the novel when she, Jim Fisk, and other agents of disorder "invade" the holy sanctuary where Elinor is about to be wed [BF 54].) As every Wall Street observer knew, Woodhull was one of the few Americans actually to profit from Black Friday.[21] She was also one of America's most sensational defenders of the Paris Commune.[22] In 1871, she led thousands of marchers through New York to commemorate the Commune martyrs, and, from her brokerage house, which she established with her Black Friday windfall, she published Marx's account of the uprising as well as America's first English translation of *The Communist Manifesto*. Woodhull's associates of the period, Susan B. Anthony and Elizabeth Cady Stanton, wrote about Black Friday in their newspaper, the *Revolution*, proclaiming that financial revolution (against a masculinist gold regime) would accompany "the dawning self assertion of woman."[23] Observers repeatedly linked their feminist agitation and the uprising in France. One editorial, titled "The American Commune," observed that Anthony expressed the "immoral views and sentiments of the French Commune" that were "rapidly developing and attempting to organize under the Women's Rights standard" on this side of the Atlantic.[24]

Even if these feminists' activities and critiques had not been linked with the Paris Commune, they would clearly have frightened most Americans. By adding book 3, however, Isham specifies what gave Woodhull, Anthony, and Stanton's threat its special urgency after 1871: their association with the pétroleuses of Paris. The pétroleuse made the American women's entangling of feminist, financial, and revolutionary discourse explosive.

We can begin to recognize the remarkable historical work of *Black Friday*—its construction of an alternative modernity, a vision of American history voided of class conflict—by understanding the intensity and range of fears provoked by the sensational figure of the female arsonist. For most Americans, the image of the pétroleuse setting buildings and homes ablaze (either to delay the invasion of troops or simply to gratify her "love of riot")[25] confirmed the connection between feminist agitation, political revolution, economic conflict, and cultural catastrophe. "Pale, frenzied, . . . [and] fierce," as a poet in *Harper's Weekly* described them, the pétroleuses presented a nightmarish specter of women aggressively repudiating bourgeois norms of womanhood.[26] Many witnesses (and subsequent commentators) identified the arsonists as prostitutes, morally dizzied by their distance from domestic life, hystericized by their all-too-public vocation and their abandonment to their bodies. Most commentators did not distinguish the pétroleuses from other women of the Commune, all of whom they saw as rowdy, reckless affronts to nature. Given over

"'The Commune or Death!'—Women of Montmartre."
Harper's Weekly, 8 July 1871.

to unfeminine theorizing and public speaking, these women formed clubs where they urged the legalization of divorce and women's sexual independence. (As historians have subsequently detailed, they also smoked pipes, toted pistols, and wore revolutionary garb, delighting audiences, male and female, who thronged the clubs to see them.)[27] These feminists led marches and fought at the barricades. During the Bloody Week, they reportedly not only set fire to homes and civic buildings but also plundered the city, gave enemy soldiers poisoned wine, and murdered officers after they had surrendered—atrocities recounted in dozens of American histories, short stories, novels, poems, and plays about the Paris Commune through the turn of the century.[28]

The Communardes' desire to upend or abolish marriage only solidified their identification as anarchists fulminating against government authority, since, according to a century-old logic, any attack against marriage, with or without the flamethrowing, constituted an attack on the integrity of the nation. Preoccupied with this intersection of gender trouble and political revolution, American antifeminists viewed this spectacle of female self-assertion with unmitigated horror, seeing the influence of Communism on the U.S. woman's movement as a premonition of revolution's spread across the globe.

Americans identified the pétroleuses and the women of the Commune not only with free love, antistatism, and the undermining of traditional centers of authority but also, inseparably, with class upheaval. The obviousness of this point is crucial because Isham obscures it entirely, placing class and economic threats to the nation's political economy where no observer of the Commune would have thought to look for them: in financial arbitrageurs and effeminized aristocrats. The growing conflict between labor and capital provided one of the basic narrative and ideological lenses through which Americans viewed and judged the Commune. For years, Americans believed reports indicating that the Commune had been plotted by the International, the revolutionary body of socialists and anarchists. The New York bourgeois press, especially, inflamed Americans' class fright; the *Nation*, for example, reporting on the Paris Commune, "saw the socialist specter 'gaining among the working-classes all over the world' and declared one had to be 'wilfully blind' to 'imagine that America is going to escape the convulsion.' "[29] By 1871, the International had crossed the Atlantic, and when fire ravaged Chicago that year, many observers saw this organization's terrifying handiwork. One observer declared, "The diabolical combination of the Communists to overturn capital and revolutionize society uses fire as its most effectual weapon. The conflagrations of Paris and Chicago should be warnings to the world."[30]

Around the turn of the twentieth century, as historians and literary critics have noted, images of women were commonly deployed by writers, artists, scientists, and others to symbolize modernity and specify its dangers (and, less often, its promises). The Paris Commune played a crucial role in these figurations because it produced the pétroleuse, agent of and allegorical stand-in for the most sensational forms of jarring change and breakdown to which definitions of modernity so often pointed. The female figure epitomized by the pétroleuse was regularly identified with mobs, urban masses, and, most important for my analysis, working-class agitation.[31] In fact and in popular imaginings, the wanton women who link the economic and revolution plots of Black Friday were representatives of class insurgency. What the novel obstructs us from seeing is that in the decades connecting Black Friday and Black Friday, this insurgency was produced by economic crisis.

While Americans around the turn of the century, including novelists, anxiously traced out the intimate causal connection between class apocalypse and economic crisis, Black Friday pairs a revolution and a financial crisis—a crisis that specifically evokes economic crises of the 1880s and 1890s, as we will see—without suggesting or even considering any direct causal connection between the two. In Isham's account, only the figure of the modern woman links them (a point to which I will return at the end of the chapter).

The Gold Standard and Class Conflict

The possibility that Isham's novel, through various historical and figural mediations, raises and represses the problem of class upheaval may seem clear enough when we focus on the Commune plot and, once we recognize the revolutionary threat posed by Wood-hull and her comrades, the marriage plot, but what about the finance plot? Is the gold panic something more than a metaphor for the domestic and civil dislocations elsewhere in the novel? Reading symptomatically, not thematically, how do we get from Black Friday to class apocalypse? How do we discern a turn-of-the-century anxiousness about class violence in a narrative about a brief spasm in the money market in 1869?

Put simply, we connect the historical and rhetorical dots that begin with Black Friday in 1869, end with *Black Friday* (1904), and cross through "Black Friday," 11 November 1887, the day the anarchists convicted of conspiracy in the Haymarket bombing were executed—the culmination of the greatest red scare in America during the nineteenth century. We perform a historical reading that (re)traces the thread of historical causes, conditions, and contexts that ties the novel's key tropes, associations, and plot points to the traumatic class conflicts of the 1880s and 1890s. At the same time, we perform a series of allegorical readings that illuminate the prior historical deployments of these images and connections; we mine the "sedimented tradition of ideological usage" in which they are lodged.[32] We show how Isham's novel refigures, re-emplots, and realigns these ideologically encrusted representations for his own revanchist ends.

This excavation begins with the currency debates of the 1890s. The novel's panic plot, preoccupied with the challenge to the Treasury, the corruption of the currency, the stunning contraction of credit, and the heroic collusion of corporate leadership and executive authority, engages—and revises—the major themes of the money battles of the 1890s. Alongside the Commune plot, it exposes the massive social stakes of the debate over the gold standard.

The problem of the gold standard gained its extraordinary urgency in the depression of the nineties, when currency questions dominated national political and economic debates and threatened, many observers warned, to lead to a class war—another Paris Commune—in America.[33] Paul Kleppner summarizes the conservative panic provoked by the silver movement: to gold advocates, " 'free silver' was linked with repudiation of honestly incurred obligations, tramping armies of vagabonds, control by union dictators over the terms and conditions of work, strikes involving violence against property and persons, and a general breakdown of social order. Frightened out of proportion to the actual threat, they summed their fears by symbolically depicting 'free silver' as the inevitable prelude to anarchy."[34] Menaced by William Jennings Bryan's legendary crusade for silver, Republicans exploited the image of the Paris Commune. Theodore Roosevelt warned that if elected, Bryan would "substitute for the government of Washington and Lincoln . . . a red welter of lawlessness and dishonesty as fantastic and as vicious as the Paris Commune itself."[35] A gold spokesman predicted that "a law compelling the people of this country" to accept "fiat" dollars would lead to a "Commune in the United States."[36] In warning of another civil war, Republicans linked Bryanites not only with Communist revolutionaries but also with Confederate secessionists. When McKinley, staunchly pro-gold, defeated Bryan for the presidency, the *New York World* saw the victory as a sequel to Grant's triumph: "Not since the fall of Richmond have patriotic Americans had such cause for rejoicing. . . . Then the integrity of the Union was secured. Now its honor is preserved. It is a triumph of morality and patriotism."[37]

Such fears and connections allow us to see how Isham's Black Friday refigures the bitter sectional and political conflict over the gold standard at the end of the century. As a recostuming of the Treasury crisis of the nineties—a crisis triggered, in most people's minds, by the panic of 1893, when the U.S. Treasury, drained of its gold reserves, could no longer safeguard the stability of the currency—Isham's allegory fits imperfectly, but the underlying ideological equation seems clear. Richard Strong, vanquishing those who are "tampering with gold" (BF 278), represents the corporate elite in the mid-1890s who waged a massive public relations campaign against Bryan and the millions of farmers and small entrepreneurs who fought to place the nation on a silver standard. Strong represents the "sound money" leaders who argued that the inflation and instability produced by silver would incite ruinous speculation, invite the abuse of financial credit, encourage the private and public repudiation of financial obligations, and lead to the general derangement of values.

More significantly, Strong stands for the corporate leaders reform-ing American enterprise in the 1890s who saw the gold standard as a means of ending economic crisis and class conflict, perhaps forever. Here, most clearly, we see how *Black Friday* promotes a historically specific—and violently contested—vision of capitalist modernity. Busi-ness leaders saw the depression and class conflict of the 1890s as the consequence of an outmoded economic system in which small firms seeking advantage (or simply trying to survive) in unregulated markets engaged in reckless, wasteful, and ruinous competition. Such compe-tition, exploiting the new productive capacity of machinery, led to overproduction, falling price levels, and retrenchment that took the predictable form of massive layoffs and wage reductions that pro-voked lockouts and strikes. In short, business leaders recognized that the old unregulated competitive-entrepreneurial dispensation—an an-archy epitomized by Jay Gould, who became more notorious as a railroad baron than a Wall Street manipulator—caused "unmanage-able panics and depressions" and led to "dangerous class conflict."[38] Faced with what one banker called the "threatened division of society into two great antagonistic classes," and acting out their self-image as the protectors of civilization and providential agents of progress, cor-porate leaders set about reorganizing American enterprise and ra-tionalizing markets by combining industrial businesses into large cor-porations, an overhaul of the economy that they achieved, stunningly, in less than a decade.[39]

The gold standard anchored this restructuring. Only a gold stan-dard could support a modern investment system that depended on the long-term stability of prices, including the price of money (credit); and thus only a gold standard could support the new industrial-corporate order that depended on this investment system. As the historian James Livingston argues, large capitalists saw the establishment of this new corporate-industrial order as a moral and, above all, a social mission. They saw the fate of modern America and civilization itself hanging on the gold standard. Preserving the standard was a way—and for some business leaders, the only way—to prevent "depression, political up-heaval, and apparent cultural disintegration."[40]

Read against such threats, Richard Strong, trying to prevent the gold clique from deranging money's value, bears the symbolic burden of protecting the nation from industrial warfare and social fracture. His example is meant to convince Isham's audience (without whose investments and savings the new corporate order would fail) that corporate titans—not Bryanites, debtors, and other small businessmen wedded to an obsolescent entrepreneurial or republican ideology—should serve as the proper guardians of the nation's economic and social stability. His heroism is meant, in line with the propaganda of corporate spokesmen, to persuade middle-class Americans that concentrated economic power serves a socially conscientious purpose. Strong shows that corporate leaders, standing "at the center of all that was new," represent progress, civilization, enlightenment, and, reassuringly, destiny.[41]

Reconstructing the 1869 panic, Isham's narrative cites and engages some of the most ideologically charged themes of the political economic crisis of 1890s—themes still consuming agents and enemies of the new financial order in the first years of the 1900s.[42] *Black Friday* performs its most interesting ideological work, however, not by echoing these themes but by transfiguring them and reversing their ideological charge. Above all, Isham upends the Populist Party's indictment of the "money power" behind the gold standard. In Isham's historical and financial allegory, plutocrats, marshaling unprecedented economic power, advance the nation instead of destroying it. Industrial development benefits, rather than injures or ignores, the producing classes. What one silver manifesto called "the allied hosts of monopolies, the money power, great trusts and railroad corporations"—Strong, recall, is a railroad titan—act on behalf of the public, salving, not stirring, class conflict.[43] More pointedly, in Isham's novel, the U.S. Treasury, colluding with what one Populist spokesman called "the present rulers of the world—the great bankers, the railroad presidents, . . . the uncrowned monarchs of commerce," saves, rather than robs, the public.[44]

This last revision is crucial since it exactly reverses the Populists' most frequent and potent charge against the "money power": that the forces allied behind the gold standard—the U.S. government in sympathy with Wall Street—formed a gold conspiracy. "Wherever one

turns in the Populist literature of the nineties one can find this conspiracy theory expressed," notes Richard Hofstadter.[45] The terms
"gold conspiracy" and "gold ring" were catchphrases of the silver
campaign. In pamphlets, speeches, and novels, antigold polemicists
painted sensational images of a banker and capitalist plot, originating
in Wall Street (or London), to hoard gold, contract the money supply,
starve the producing classes, and create financial panics and economic
crises. James Goode's *The Modern Banker* (1896) serves as an exemplary
antigold novel against which we might read *Black Friday*. Goode's
novel explains how Eastern bankers try to corner the nation's gold and
infiltrate the White House, and it elaborates, with footnotes, how the
American Bankers Association created the panic of 1893, "the greatest
panic the world ever saw," to force the repeal of pro-silver laws and
tighten its stranglehold over the nation's money supply.[46] Like many
silverite tracts, *The Modern Banker* traces the history of the gold ring to
the years after the Civil War (and, moreover, sympathizes with the
Confederacy).

What makes *Black Friday* so remarkable is that it does not wholly
invert the Populist account of the gold conspiracy. Rather, by opposing
virtuous capitalists and vicious speculators and blaming the gold conspiracy on the speculators, *Black Friday* aligns itself with the Populist
narrative. Like sensationally popular antigold writers such as William
"Coin" Harvey, Ignatius Donnelly, James Weaver, and Sarah V. Emery
(and, indeed, like enemies of Wall Street since the Civil War), Isham
demonizes speculators as enemies of the state and the natural order.
However—and this is the ideological payoff of Isham's refiguration—
his condemnation of speculators functions to quarantine capitalists
like Strong from the Populists' attack. It does this by deflecting this
attack onto conspiring speculators such as Jay Gould. Such speculators, all could agree, possessed a "dark, mysterious, crafty, wicked,
rapacious, and tyrannical power . . . to rob and oppress and enslave the
people."[47] To the extent that Isham's historical revision unites capitalists and Populists as common enemies of speculators, it moots their
historical antagonism. At the same time, to the extent that Isham's
allegory aligns speculators and Populists as common enemies of the
state and corporate modernity, it identifies these—the Gould ring, the

Bryanites, the Confederacy, the Communards, and so on—as threats to capital accumulation. Either way, by demonizing the enemy of its enemy, by condemning speculators who conspire to corner gold and create financial panics, Black Friday legitimates corporate capitalism as the vehicle of democratic progress, public safety, and class harmony.

"Black Friday," 1886

Isham is not trying to win over Populists and others convinced of the existence of a Wall Street gold conspiracy. Instead, he is trying to erase these antagonists of the new corporate order from view. How he does this makes Isham's book so extraordinary. Black Friday takes the idioms and narratives of the enemies of corporate expansion, occludes their radical function, and appropriates them for vastly different ideological ends: to repress the imagined possibility of class revolution, to suppress the ambient anxiety, spiking into panic during economic crises, that capital accumulation would foster, not mitigate, working class militancy.

The most striking example of this narrative and ideological retrofitting is the book's use of the gold crisis in 1869 to stand in for the class panic that seized middle-class Americans in 1886, a panic relived and relieved by the execution of four anarchists on 11 November 1887, a day that came to be known as "Black Friday" among labor radicals and their sympathizers. More than any other event following the Paris Commune, this Black Friday shaped the popular image of class revolution through the turn of the century. We have dug down through the revolutionary percolations of the 1890s, then, to get to the Haymarket violence, the ideological wellspring of Isham's narrative.

Beginning with the Paris Commune and gaining intensity with the great strike riots of 1877, the possibility of class warfare consumed enemies as well as agents of large capital in the United States in the last decades of the nineteenth century. In the 1890s, the most sensational prophecies of class apocalypse came not from conservatives who equated Bryan's supporters with anarchist and Communist revolutionaries, but rather from the silver agitators, who typically distanced themselves from militants. Viewing bloody revolution as the inevitable consequence of the Wall Street gold conspiracy, a psychologically if not historically necessary uprising against the hegemony of the "money power," Populist polemicists and other reformers warned of fire in the streets, "terrible social convulsions," and universal discord—in short, another Paris Commune—that must follow if corporations, bankers, and speculators were not somehow stalemated.[48]

The threat of class war consumed observers during the strike-torn years of the 1880s as well. In 1884, one reform writer noted that "hardly a novel is published without its little contribution to the literature of the social problem, hardly an issue of a newspaper but has its leader on some phase of what, as the world is coming to feel, is the greatest of all questions, or some lamentation over the threatening revolution. But what sort of revolution is this which we are warned against?"[49] The answer came on 4 May, when a dynamite bomb, thrown by an unidentified anarchist, exploded near a labor demonstration in Chicago's Haymarket Square, killing a policeman and wounding about seventy others.

Two and a half million workers were jobless, victims of an economic depression. For several years, in Chicago, the most industrialized city of the 1880s and the epicenter of the American anarchist movement, members of the International Working People's Association and allied radical labor groups had been staging massive rallies that drew thousands of cheering spectators. These demonstrations—together with anarchist publications on dynamite, assassination, explosives, and streetfighting—alarmed city and state authorities, and in April 1885, police and soldiers amassed to halt the progress of an orderly labor parade. Thousands of workers, seeing they were threatened with violence, agitated for counterviolence. Their leaders pressed for revolution. Concluding that only by arming themselves could laborers obtain their rights in the face of such reaction, anarchist orators roused workers to "agitate, organize, revolt!"[50] Radicals intensified their call for revolution in 1886, calling for an American Commune, terrifying Chicago's business community. On 1 May, May Day, workers nationwide went on strike for an eight-hour workday. In Chicago, eighty thousand workers marched up Michigan Avenue. On 3 May, four strikers were killed by jittery police. IWPA flyers in German and English urged workers to "Arm Yourselves and Appear in Full Force!"[51] Thousands of laborers and sympathizers came together a day later in Haymarket Square to protest the police action. When police tried to disperse the thinning, rain-soaked crowd, an anarchist threw a bomb.[52]

A "full-blown red scare" gripped the city.[53] Citing the "infamous excesses of the Chicago rioters," the newspapers warned workers around the nation against following the "bloodthirsty wretches"—the anarchist demagogues—"who have no likeness in modern history except in the Paris Commune."[54] Police, trying to root out a communist conspiracy, raided labor meetings, arrested known activists, and interrogated thousands of laborers. Rumors of anarchist arsenals of explosives spread terror throughout the wealthier parts of Chicago. In 1887, four anarchist leaders, charged with conspiracy to murder, having exhausted their state and federal appeals, were hanged. Half a million people joined in the funeral march. Chicago newspapers predicted civil war, a complete and violent social breakdown. The trial thrust the sensational image of the fiendish, rabid, bomb-throwing anarchist to the front of popular consciousness. A companion figure to the gasoline-throwing pétroleuse, the archetypal anarchist "dreamed visions of blood and fire, of sudden death, overthrow of all law, of a revolution that was to reverse society, overthrow all social order, and open the hoarded millions of the land to the grasp of plundering hands."[55] Readying themselves for proletarian revolt, dozens of states established or revived militias.

I do not know whether Isham had the Haymarket tragedy directly in mind when he wrote his novel. I have found no biographical or bibliographical evidence to prove or disprove an intentional connection. I am tantalized, however, by the astonishing coincidence of terms: this other "Black Friday," like the gold panic of 1869, is linked with civil war, anarchism, conspiracy, revolution, and social trauma.[56] Moreover, the agitation leading up to the bombing focused on speculators; the anarchists drew inspiration from the Paris Commune and publicly identified themselves with the Communists; and they singled out Jay Gould as their arch- and archetypal enemy.

The rally that prompted the police turnout in 1885 was a protest

"The Anarchist Riot in Chicago: a dynamite bomb exploding among the police."
Harper's Weekly, 15 May 1886.

against the opening of the new Chicago Board of Trade building. For the IWPA, which planned the rally, the building served as the vile embodiment of a tyrannous capitalist system, a den of millionaire "thieves and robbers" who bet on commodity price movements with money stolen from labor.[57] Anarchist leaders talked loudly of blowing up the building and killing the business leaders gathered there for the opening. Such violence, part of a campaign to "sweep the capitalists off the face of the earth," would "make the capitalists tremble."[58] The Paris Commune played a featured role in this talk. At anarchist rallies, vituperations against the Board of Trade and its members were met with shouts celebrating the Paris Commune, and laborers sang the "Marseillaise" as they marched toward the Board of Trade building on their way to Haymarket.[59] Jay Gould, by many accounts the most hated man in America, also figured in the violence. Anarchists scorned Gould, not for his speculative scheming on Wall Street (as insurgent Greenbackers had in 1869), but rather for his legendary ruthlessness toward labor as a railroad owner and monopolist. "The best thing one can do with such fellows as Jay Gould and Vanderbilt is to hang them on the nearest lamp-post," counseled the anarchist terrorist Johann Most, perhaps the most feared man in America.[60] Albert Parsons, the prominent anarchist editor and orator, invoked Gould's name just before the Haymarket bomb blast.[61]

Hayden White, glossing Claude Lévi-Strauss, points out that historical explanations are "determined more by what we leave out of our representations than by what we put in."[62] There is no mention of class violence in Black Friday and no mention, as I have noted, that the Paris Commune was a workers' revolt. However, what is repressed from the novel is less determining, and less striking, than what returns, refigured, within the novel's financial narrative. In the same way that he remaps the fault lines of the Populists' conflict with Wall Street gold conspirators, Isham preempts the imagining of class revolt by figuring the enemies of Gould not as anarchist revolutionaries but as capitalist avatars. This is the novel's most astonishing work: it recasts the Haymarket anarchists' animus against Gould as Strong's defense of capital.

We are not allowed to see anarchist violence as a legitimate or even possible threat. In the novel, the anarchist revolt in Paris is ephemeral and unrelated to Black Friday, which also is ephemeral, quickly contained by Strong's heroics. For this reason, capitalist crisis in Black Friday appears not as an explosive end-game between labor and capital (or producers and plutocrats), but rather as a fleeting, historically accidental skirmish between vicious and virtuous forms of capitalism.[63] To bring its ideological work into relief, we might compare Black Friday to another panic romance, Will Payne's Mr. Salt (1903), published a year earlier, which also juxtaposes a financial panic narrative and an anarchist plot but which presents these as historically and narratively linked features of the crisis of the 1890s. Payne's novel makes no distinction between the capitalist hero's progressive industrial vision and his machinations on Wall Street. The depression of the nineties, beyond any individual's control, ruins him and sharpens his exploitation of his workers. An anarchist plot to kill him is foiled, but the conflict of labor and capital still smolders, even as he turns anemically from finance to philanthropy at the end.

In Isham's novel, Gould, the arch capitalist, is allied with the pétroleuses who are burning down Paris; both represent obvious threats to economic stability, national progress, and state authority. At the same time, the speculators whom Gould ruins are allied with Haymarket anarchists: the speculators' shouts after the panic recall Parsons's diatribe against Gould before the Haymarket explosion, and the speculators' march toward Gould's office, threatening violence, recalls the anarchist procession to the Board of Trade. These realignments of historical antagonisms constitute the ideological perversion of the novel: to the extent that the Haymarket revolutionaries represent the enemies of Gould, they are identified with Strong and Grant, corporate capitalism and centralized federal authority. To the extent that they represent the enemies of centralized state authority, they are identified with Gould and gold arbitrageurs, capitalism's most regressive and radical arm. In short, Isham establishes ideological equations where we would expect oppositions, and vice versa. Without our noticing, revolution simply disappears, replaced by its opposite, and whatever revolutionary trace might remain dissipates in the last line of the novel, when a minister feebly tells Strong that "the poor, sir . . . we have always with us" (BF 409), a sign of the impossibility, not the inevitability, of revolution.

Queen of the Anarchists

I have suggested that Black Friday refracts history in multiple ways, that its narrative of events in 1869 and 1871 re-emplots and refigures crises of the 1880s and 1890s, and that these crises manifested (to observers in those decades, at least) the revolutionary threat latent in, and possibly endemic to, modern American capitalism.

These crises constitute the specific historical determinants of the novel's anxiousness, and I have suggested that they also serve as covert, if possibly unconscious, referents of the novel's allegory. If we wish to specify more immediate sources of the book's class panic and more immediate "pretexts" of the book's allegory and bring our historical and figural connect-the-dots full circle, we need to look no further than the assassination of President William McKinley, "the willing tool of Wall Street," by an anarchist in 1901—an act, the killer claimed, inspired by Emma Goldman, the reincarnation, for most Americans around the turn of the century, of the pétroleuse.[64]

"The appalling crime of September last brings the nation face to face with the problem of anarchy," began the January 1902 issue of the *Arena*.[65] The assassination threw the country into a panic. "Not since 1887 had there been evidenced such lust for blood, such savagery of vengeance," Goldman recalled. "The press, the pulpit, and other public mouthpieces were frantically vying with each other in their fury against the common enemy."[66] Mobs attacked anarchist newspaper offices. Encouraged by new state and federal anti-anarchist legislation, police raided anarchist meetings and arrested anarchist lecturers, despite their condemnation of the assassination. Publishers and editors rushed books and articles about anarchism and socialism into print.

Goldman's alleged involvement electrified the nation. At the turn of the century, she was the most famous anarchist in America. Nine years before McKinley's assassination, her lover had attempted to murder Henry Clay Frick, whose Pinkerton agents had killed nine steel workers during the Homestead strike. When McKinley's killer confessed that Goldman's lectures inspired his violence, her name appeared in headlines across the nation, and authorities waged a nationwide manhunt for her, finally arresting her in Chicago. (She barely recalled meeting the killer, and the police, lacking evidence, dropped their charges against her.) In an article that appeared only three weeks after the president died, she expressed sympathy for the killer (later likening him to "our brave Chicago martyrs"),[67] incurring the savage condemnation of mainstream editors and distancing many former associates.

Goldman brings together the primary class and gender threats that *Black Friday* represents or refigures. From the start of her incendiary career in America in the early 1890s, she lectured on the Paris Commune; through the 1890s, she excited mass support for anarchism at Haymarket commemorations; and in 1901, at Eugene Debs's invitation, she spoke at the inaugural convention of the Socialist Party. Crucially, she mixed her lectures on labor militancy with speeches on feminism, prostitution, and, most provoking of all, free love. More than any figure since Woodhull and the pétroleuses, Goldman popularized the connection between class insurgency and gender revolution. She radicalized what many antifeminists in the mid-nineties, tormented by visions of another Commune, saw as the vicious and portentous entanglement of free silver and female suffrage.[68] "A wave of panic about the future of the family swept over many middle-class Americans at the turn of the century," observes Mary Jo Buhle, and Goldman's advocacy of free love inflamed the already widespread fear that socialism and anarchism would lead to "the destruction of the family and the ruination of women."[69] Goldman, who began to reach out to mainstream audiences in the months before Isham published his novel, embodied this protean menace.

Black Friday registers and responds to Goldman's threat by replacing one Goldman, the revolutionary anarchist, with another gold man, Gould, the bête noire of Wall Street. The novel wrests the Black Friday of 1887—"our Black Friday," Goldman called it[70]—from the radical labor movement and replaces it with the Black Friday of 1869, safely contained by Strong's heroics, by its narrative distance from the Commune plot, and by its historical remoteness. If Goldman, dubbed the "Queen of the Anarchists," stands behind Gould, she also, more obviously, stands behind Zoldene, who appears now not as a "May-day queen" (BF 256)—the queen of the springtime festival—but rather, more ominously, as a May Day queen. This resignification, this tense blend of monarchial and revolutionary valences, informs the novel's close, when Elinor coronates Strong. Becoming Strong's queen and subject, Elinor, serving capital and conserving marriage, reoccupies the place corrupted by these radical queens.

Black Friday writes modern American history as corporate capitalist history, legitimating capitalist modernity and rendering alternative modernities invisible. Strong is an agent of history not only because his actions materially aid the forward march of America's economy but also because he views the economy historically, seeing daily Wall Street fluctuations, even the gold crisis, through the long lens of industrial expansion and empire building. We are meant not simply to identify with his vision but also to see it as the only vision possible: history, for Isham, simply *is* corporate capitalist progress. Within this historical narrative, the panic of 1869 is innocuous and, more important, dispensable. It is an accident, irrelevant to the logic of accumulation. By privileging this monocular vision of history in which panic is fundamentally irrelevant, *Black Friday* wards off the reader's apprehension of an alternative vision of history in which economic crisis is theoretically fundamental and historically inevitable.

It has become commonplace to observe that all historical narratives construct versions of the past, that past history exists as a body of contending scripts, and that historians, insofar as they offer narrative explanations, must privilege certain ways of emplotting the past above others. The narrative forms historical accounts take, however, constitute not only interpretative statements about the past but also arguments about the future. The grand patterns overtly or covertly structuring narrative accounts of the past establish specific trajectories for the future. History as tragic decline, entropic breakdown, comedic triumph, teleological unfolding, revolutionary *Aufhebung*, and other master narratives place obvious limits on the possible forms the future's unfolding will take. Also, because they can rewrite or delete particular historically fateful moments, historical accounts can imaginatively re-determine the future that follows from those moments. Science fiction and popular movies such as *Back to the Future*, retroactively changing some "nexus" or critical event, have made the conceptual premise of this kind of "alternate history" familiar to us.[71] Historical romances, undermining what once constituted a meaningful distinction between history and fiction (what did happen and what could happen), experiment not only with possible pasts, then, but also with the possible futures determined by those pasts.

For Isham, Black Friday—the gold panic of 1869 and "behind" it the anarchist violence of 1886—functions as such a "nexus" event. Its re-emplotment annuls a vision of history that focuses on commercial crisis and forecasts revolutionary conflict, a vision outlined in Marx's *Communist Manifesto* and glossed repeatedly in socialist propaganda at the turn of the century. In its place, *Black Friday* establishes a vision of history in which such crisis and conflict are historically and theoretically irrelevant.

As I have indicated, agents as well as enemies of capital accumulation saw Haymarket and, more broadly, the three decades since the Paris Commune, as a historical watershed for the United States. To many observers, the proletarian upheaval of the 1880s and the Populist insurgency of the 1890s were projecting the nation toward class warfare. In book after book with titles such as *The Coming Climax*, *The Coming Revolution*, and *The Impending Crisis*, reformers warned that the antagonism between capital and labor must be relieved and economic crisis must be prevented to avert social apocalypse. One of the most widely read warnings about the future came from the silverite Ignatius Donnelly, a three-term congressman from Minnesota, whose novel *Caesar's Column* (1890), a lurid countervision to Bellamy's best-selling *Looking Backward* (1888), follows the war between the capitalist gold conspiracy and the oppressed poor to its nightmarish finale, set in 1988. In Donnelly's climax, the insurgent poor, radiating outward from the Treasury building on Wall Street, illuminated by bomb explosions and fires, sweep over New York, unleashing their fury on the rich, a quarter million of whose corpses are ultimately cemented into a titanic column commissioned by the revolution's leader—a horrifying memorial to the death of modern civilization.

Black Friday displaces the warnings not only of reformers such as Donnelly but also of socialists committed to the overthrow of the bourgeoisie. To understand the urgency behind Isham's repression, we need only to view it against Jack London's own Commune novel, *The Iron Heel* (1907), one of the most sensational accounts in American fiction of the class war that must (for London) consume the nation.

Published three years after Black Friday, London's novel shows how the looming conflict between the capitalist oligarchy and the revolutionary proletariat escalates, suddenly, horrifyingly, into Armageddon-like warfare during an economic crisis in 1917. The capitalist "Iron Heel," rising from the ruin of a Wall Street panic, and colluding with the U.S. Treasury, learns of the revolutionaries' preparations for a Chicago Commune and successfully casts its overwhelming military and technological might against the city's working class. The final chapters, modeled on Donnelly's narrative as well as on descriptions of the Paris Commune, present a sublime panorama of the Iron Heel's punishing destruction.[72] During the three days of the Commune, waging urban war against the revolutionaries, the Iron Heel's forces massacre demoniacal hordes of unorganized workers who swarm the battle zone, bomb and machine-gun hundreds of thousands of warring laborers and mercenaries, exterminate the revolutionaries, and ride tanks over streets mountained with corpses.

The Iron Heel serves as a useful counterpoint to Black Friday not only because London portrays the bourgeoisie's panic about anarchists and socialists; and not only because he sensationalizes the haunting imminence and awful necessity of class war; and not only because London deploys so differently the figures and narratives that consciously and unconsciously preoccupy Isham—financial panic, revolutionary conspiracy, civil war, the Haymarket explosion and trial, reactionary cooperation between large capitalists and the federal government, and so on; but also because London styles his novel as a history. The Iron Heel takes the form of a private document penned in 1932 by the wife of an American revolutionary leader, but found and edited around the year 2600, well after capitalism has been superseded, overcome at last by centuries of revolutions. The revolutionary events she recounts take place between 1912 and 1917. The putative editors provide the manuscript, which breaks off mid-sentence, with a historical introduction that points out the narrator's ideological and historical blind spots; they also add footnotes that, remarkably, gloss texts and cite historical "facts" from these revolutionary years (as well as events before 1907, including the Haymarket explosion). From the start, because of this fictional scholarly apparatus, we not only know what will happen within the narrative, but also, looking back from the enlightened future, we see how the premature uprising of 1917 fits within the dialectical history that leads to capitalism's overthrow. With seven centuries' hindsight and with a scientific understanding of the economic laws and class forces shaping history's progress, we are told, or reminded, that the Chicago Commune was just one of many violent crises in the evolving, irreconcilable antagonism between capital and labor.

Both *Black Friday* and *The Iron Heel* are genesis tales that equate modern American history and modernity itself with the intensification and extension of industrial capitalism. However, *The Iron Heel*, with its much longer historical perspective, insists that capitalism, inevitably imploding under its own contradictions, ultimately obstructs, rather than serves, history's forward movement. *The Iron Heel* insists on causal and fundamental, not thematic and accidental, connections between capitalism's advance, economic crisis, and class apocalypse. For this reason, because it is lodged within a Marxist eschatology seemingly confirmed by future historical events, *The Iron Heel* can pretend to suture its own formal rupture: framed by the editors' totalizing history, the manuscript's incompleteness does not betray (to the audience after capitalism) any ideological edginess or confusion. In contrast, *Black Friday*'s fragile closure and the near-total narrative irrelevance of the Commune plot attest to Isham's difficulty in coming to terms with the revolutionary history he continually, if unconsciously, evokes.

Black Friday and *The Iron Heel* both aim to establish continuity between the past they represent and the (ostensible) present of their publication. But whereas Isham makes an industrial titan the agent of this bonding and represents anarchists, and especially anarchistic women, as agents of rupture and amnesia, London privileges a revolutionary woman as the lone interpreter and preserver of the past. In *The Iron Heel*, until they discover the narrator's manuscript, the historians of the future have no account of the rise of the Oligarchy. She alone makes this historical moment available, securing its place within the uniform vision of history plotted by the future's historians. A final contrast: whereas Isham's heroine comes back from the brink of domestic anarchy and revolution to be reconciled with her capitalist king, London's heroine, the narrator, born into the upper class, chooses to join her husband, a socialist leader, and become a revolutionary. Indeed, her conversion and marriage qualify her to become history's literal agent and amanuensis. She is useful to the postcapitalist historians because of her privileged post observing the revolutionary leadership, and she is useful to London's readers because her bourgeois eyes have been opened to the justice and inevitability of revolution.

Conclusion: Women and Revolution

Isham's two primary ambitions in Black Friday are to portray the cultural dangers—above all, the feminist threat—facing modern America, and to purge modern American history, including future history, of class conflict. How are we to connect these two aims? One way that I have suggested is to treat the marriage crisis and the political economic crises—Black Friday and the Paris Commune—as thematic analogues, commensurable threats to law, order, and central authority. In this reading, Black Friday's wayward women, treacherous speculators, and frenzied arsonists are homologous figures, co-representatives of "anarchy" (loosely defined) and parallel symptoms of the worst kind—an entropic, not progressive, kind—of modernity. There is ample historical precedent for such a reading. Antifeminists had equated threats to the marriage relation and economic and political threats to the republic for well over a century. In the Gilded Age and Progressive Era, as I have noted, many antifeminists specifically linked female suffrage, free love, socialism, and anarchism, their panic crystallizing around the figure of Emma Goldman. To many, the dissolution of patriarchal marriage led to communism, and vice versa. They feared what Elizabeth Cady Stanton warned of in 1888: that "women will strike hands with labor, with socialists, with anarchists, and you will have the scenes of the Revolution of France acted over again in this republic."[73]

How do the insurgent women in the novel help purge American history of class conflict, then? I have argued that Isham preempts the imagining of revolution by rendering the causal connection between economic crisis and class insurgency invisible. He does this by disconnecting the panic and Commune plots, by voiding the Commune plot of any revolutionary context, and, more remarkably, by rewriting the anarchist and Populist insurgencies of the 1880s and 1890s as an ephemeral, reversible, and ultimately inconsequential financial panic. Thematically paired with the financial panic and the Commune, the marriage crisis also clearly represents some form of return of the repressed, but its ideological or therapeutic work rests on its *not* being easily quelled. Because husband and capitalist cannot control her, Elinor represents the truly serious, if figurally oblique, class threat. Because Strong cannot force Elinor to return to him—because she is emphatically *not* like a manageable or manipulable market—her actions become invested with whatever latent and lingering fears about economic crisis and industrial warfare the financial plot cannot close off.

This is why Elinor's choosing to return to Strong is so important. By saying she "could not help" but come back to Strong, Elinor not only annuls whatever threat she posed to marriage relations but also dissipates whatever revolutionary anxiety endures after the gold panic and Commune have been contained (BF 403). More exactly, by re-embracing her normative role as wife, Elinor converts the revolutionary threat into a gender threat that she herself neutralizes (and which, at bottom, may not be so threatening since it rests on and reinforces an apparently natural gender difference). By channeling latent and lingering fears of revolution into the marriage crisis, Isham recasts this anxiety into a more personal, individual, and cognitively manageable form.

Seen in this way, the marriage resolution restores the formal coherence that gives ideological closure to the novel. Elinor's return works to repair the narrative gap between the panic plot and the Commune plot, the gap that most obviously signals Isham's desire to disconnect economic crisis from revolution. Elinor's return retroactively rationalizes the Commune plot's narrative relevance, for she claims that Strong's heroics in Paris impel her to come back. She explains, "Ever since that night in Paris I have felt I must see you" (BF 403). This line, easy to miss, makes the Commune plot directly serve the marriage plot. The line is important not only because it subordinates the revolutionary crisis to the marriage crisis but also because it displaces a causal relation between economic crisis and revolution, replacing it with a more oblique, safely private link between Black Friday and the Commune: the marriage crisis and, more exactly, Elinor's return. In short, the sentimental necessity of this return renders invisible the causal logic that haunted American business leaders and reformers. It also replaces the scientific inevitability of class warfare prophesied by Jack London, George Herron, and other Marxian socialists.

Elinor provides a causal connection between the panic and the Commune so that Zoldene will not. Zoldene transparently serves as a figure for the Commune, a proxy for the pétroleuses, and for this very reason, Isham keeps her from signaling anything more than a thematic relation between the Black Friday and Commune plots. Because her character bears such charged revolutionary associations, Isham must prevent Zoldene from reminding us that revolutions follow from economic crises. This is why her reappearance in the Commune plot, while sensational, is also accidental. Strong's chancing upon her during the Commune two years after Black Friday reinforces the fact that there is no intrinsic connection between the panic and the Commune, between economic crisis and class conflict. As characters, Zoldene and Elinor thus serve parallel ideological ends, but in converse ways. The most revolutionary woman, the Communist free-lover, represses class apocalypse by dislodging revolution from any historical narrative that might explain or predict its imminent possibility. The least revolutionary woman, the re-dedicated wife of the capitalist titan, represses class apocalypse by converting its imminent possibility into a declaration of faith in a capitalist future, a future without crisis, and thus a future without panic.

Chapter 2

I Can Do Anything with Words: Thomas Lawson's Frenzied Fictions

To speak to the world and to have the world listen—and
shiver or exult as the speaker willed—that was worth while.
Edwin Lefèvre, *Sampson Rock of Wall Street*

Between 1904 and 1907, Thomas Lawson, the nation's most feared stock manipulator, financial reformer, and novelist, threatened to produce a cataclysmic market panic that would topple the financial structure of the United States and free Wall Street from the control of Standard Oil's financial barons. He carried out a sensational trial panic in 1904 and, consolidating his massive readership into a market army, appeared poised to unleash economic catastrophe when the massive panic of 1907 struck, preempting his campaign. Never before or since has an American writer been able to wield such power over the stock market, and never has an American's writing been so closely identified with financial panics and their production. Indeed, Lawson serves as our most sensational example of the writer *as* panic bringer.

This chapter examines the capacity of Lawson's advertisements, exposés, and fiction to produce market terror and turmoil. It also studies his critics' struggles to comprehend and quarantine these effects. The national controversy surrounding Lawson's writing brings together several of the Progressive Era's most pressing anxieties about the molding of public opinion: first, his contemporaries' fears about the scope and effect of public persuasion in the marketplace; second, their fears about the new powers of publicity made available by the mass media, including stock advertising; and third, their fears about the power of fiction to arouse economically and politically dangerous kinds of emotions. Lawson vexed his contemporaries, even those sympathetic with his ideals, I argue, because he confounded what they considered to be the most threatening with the most legitimate forms of persuasion. On the one hand, as a stock promoter, Lawson openly exploited the power of words—exposures, rumors, stories—to arouse the investing public and sway the stock market, using his published warnings to cripple stocks and incite panics. On the other hand, as a muckraking journalist, he marshaled the power of publicity to expose and counter the influence of a group of financial titans who, he claimed, used the stock market to pilfer the public's savings. Astonishingly, he combined these two activities, ultimately identifying market manipulation itself—his own panic mongering—as a legitimate reform tool.

Historians focusing on the Muckraking Era have discussed Lawson's explosive Wall Street exposé, *Frenzied Finance*, and his meteoric career as a financial reformer, but they have paid little attention to his career as a stock promoter and no attention at all to his brief career as a novelist.[1] The one or two financial historians who have mentioned Lawson's 1907 stock market novel, *Friday, the Thirteenth*, have ignored what I see as the most remarkable feature of the novel and of Lawson's writing generally: its potentially catastrophic agency in the marketplace. To many of his contemporaries, Lawson was the most influential writer of his era because his mere utterance, even his silence, set off market panics. The effect of his promotional and reform writing on the stock market makes his turn to fiction striking, since his novel not only describes the effect (or, more precisely, the efficaciousness) of words in financial markets but also constituted a weapon in Lawson's panic campaign. Incredibly, the novel, a weepy melodrama filled with scenes of personal ruin, is a sentimental weapon. Lawson hoped that his readers' sympathetic identification with the novel's hero, with himself, and with each other would move them to march into the stock market and spread terror there. The only writer to employ fiction to precipitate a financial panic, Lawson saw market manipulation and economic devastation as felicitous effects of readerly compassion.

The Sensation of Thomas Lawson

Lawson is remembered today for *Frenzied Finance* and for his brief career as America's most controversial muckraker.[2] Beginning its twenty-month run in *Everybody's* in the summer of 1904, *Frenzied*

Finance made Lawson famous overnight, and for almost three years he stood squarely in the national spotlight. One of the most sweeping indictments of Wall Street ever written, the series detailed the operations of a "System" governed by Standard Oil's financiers for using the public's bank and insurance deposits to rig the stock market and artificially produce booms and panics. Just as sensationally, it elaborated Lawson's own role in the System's most devastating manipulation, the sale of Amalgamated Copper stock in 1899, the largest securities swindle up to that time in U.S. history. Never before had anyone with such privileged access and authority outlined Wall Street's corruption. According to Lawson's fellow muckraker, Charles Edward Russell, Lawson "told a story that for lurid details exceeded the imaginations of the wildest of shocker writers. . . . Every paragraph contained material for a libel suit. . . . The country gasped and wondered and gasped again. For a time it talked of nothing else."[3] Crowds fought at newsstands to get copies; they included "the financiers whom Lawson exposed, eager to end the suspense in which during thirty days of every month they wondered what ghastly secret of the underworld of high finance Lawson would tell next."[4] Propelled by the wild popularity of the exposé, *Everybody's* quadrupled its circulation and became the nation's best-selling magazine.

The series galvanized and polarized the nation. Lawson's supporters celebrated him as an "idol of the American people," a "game and competent old fighter" who alone was willing to stand up to Standard Oil's financial strongmen.[5] Citing its rhetorical force, narrative appeal, and potentially revolutionary influence, they likened *Frenzied Finance* to Harriet Beecher Stowe's *Uncle Tom's Cabin*. Lawson's enemies, in contrast, characterized the series as a dangerous mingling of truth, falsehood, and invention, a threat to the work of "true investigators and reformers" such as Ida Tarbell and Lincoln Steffens.[6] They charged that *Frenzied Finance*'s exquisite balancing of confession and condemnation was simply another example of Lawsonian market manipulation, this time disguised as a reformed reformer's jeremiad, a claim even his supporters found hard to dismiss when Lawson angrily quit reforming after the panic of 1907 and announced his return to stock manipulation to recoup the money he had spent on his public crusade.

"'The Golden Calf'—Mr. Tom Lawson as Moses." *Life*, 16 February 1905.

No financial writer has incurred more savage criticism. "No man in America is more hated and despised," wrote an interviewer in 1907, who justified his lengthy series on Lawson, the longest up to that time on a living American, by noting that Lawson was "damned from one end of the country to the other as a charlatan, impostor, lunatic, trickster, faker, egotist, thief, liar, and perjurer."[7] At the height of his influence, ministers preached sermons against him, and newspapers labeled him a public enemy. One rival editor—one of several critics who threatened publicly to shoot him—characterized Lawson as clinically insane, a judgment seconded in a lengthy published diagnosis by a reputable psychologist.[8]

Trying to make sense of the Lawson sensation, historians of the Progressive Era have generally focused on *Frenzied Finance*, but it was actually his advertisements and newsletters and their effect on the stock market, not his reform articles, that made Lawson the most controversial writer of his day.[9] Running his own financial news bureau, he spent thousands of dollars every day on advertisements, and he telegraphed lengthy pronouncements to financial editors throughout the United States and Europe, a strategy that allowed him to spread

rumors, deflect attacks, and shape a day's market activity.[10] Thousands of small investors subscribed to his newsletters, and hundreds of thousands of readers pored over his ads. Claiming inside knowledge of corporations' plans, Lawson warned of potential swindles and impending slumps in stock prices. His "panic shrieks" ("TRL" 819), urging his readers to sell their holdings immediately, were set in huge, bold type and sometimes covered an entire newspaper page. His promotional ads were only slightly less stunning. He claimed access to secret documents and conversations, announced potential earnings as if they were settled facts, and invoked whatever authorities he could muster or invent to substantiate his pronouncements. Driven by Lawson's "brass-band-and-hurrah work" ("TRL" 106), mobs of investors fought in the nation's financial districts to get hold of new stocks that he insistently promoted.

The most infamous of these manias, the sale that brought Lawson national attention as a swindler and later as a reformer, was the promotion of Amalgamated Copper stock in 1899. Copper, a staple of the new electricity industry, had been the nation's hottest stock for several years. Lawson's idea was to buy up dozens of copper companies and create a massive trust that would control the price of the metal around the world. Lawson claimed that he brought the idea to Standard Oil (the only company with enough money to finance such a venture), persuaded its financial officers of the viability of the scheme, and became attached as a promoter for the new corporation. The mere rumor of such a trust backed by Rockefeller's money machine created a national frenzy. Crowds clamored for information about the new corporation, and Lawson obliged with sensational ads. "It was like the crusades of the middle ages, a popular movement," observed the *New York Times*. "People in the Lake Superior region, like the people of Boston, bid against one another for shares—mortgaged their houses, borrowed money, went to all extent to secure the precious stuff."[11] On the day of the sale, Lawson's offices in Boston were mobbed, and crowds rushed the National City Bank in New York, Standard Oil's bank, to get at the subscription desk. In just two hours, assured by Lawson that $100 shares could be resold at once for $150 or $175 and that an investment of $5,000 could net $75,000 in a matter of days, the public subscribed for almost half a billion dollars worth of Amalgamated stock, a staggering record at the turn of the century.[12]

What made Lawson so infamous was that the stock promptly collapsed. Copper values shrank $200 million, the greatest drop the Boston market had ever seen, and Amalgamated shares plummeted from $130 to $33. In *Frenzied Finance*, subtitled *The Crime of Amalgamated*, Lawson charged that Standard Oil orchestrated the crash from the start in order to buy back the company's shares at panic prices. He claimed that he had been personally hoodwinked by Standard Oil's financiers; that in place of his public-spirited, everyone-gets-rich stock offer, the System had instituted its own treacherous scheme; and that he had been obliged, against his will, to continue promoting the swindle.[13] Never before had the public been bilked out of so much money by a single scheme. Clarence Barron, whose respected financial newspaper warned against Lawson and Amalgamated from the start, memorialized the swindle in parodic verse:

"A mariner thou?" the broker cried;
　"Now sure thou mak'st pretense!"
"Nay, sir; three months I sailed the coast
　In the good scow Impudence—

"Till I wrecked her—pulled her all apart
　To store the copper in her;—
'Twas a blithesome task—on sea and shore
　As a wrecker I was a winner!

Now list—for big-type ads. are past,
　Don't take,—in fact, have moss on—"
The broker swears at thought of his shares—
　He knows there stands a Loss on.[14]

Even more damning than "Loss on's" role as publicist for the copper trust was the allegation made by Barron and others that he profited personally from the panic. This charge—that he molded public opinion in order to take personal advantage of the huge price fluctuations his pronouncements caused—dogged Lawson throughout his career. His shrillest critic, the newspaper publisher C. F. King, wrote a history of modern finance specifically to show that Lawson "had become a millionaire by grace of the misguided, blind following of his siren voice on the part of thousands of deceived victims."[15] Most Americans acknowledged that Lawson *might* be humbugging them and gulling the thousands of small investors who followed his market counsel. They had good reason to be skeptical: Lawson conducted several sensational and ruinous advertising campaigns in companies he himself controlled, even while he blasted market manipulators in *Everybody's*. In each case, Lawson boomed the stock, sending its price up as investors swarmed to buy it; then urgently warned against its imminent collapse, creating a panic and decline; and then, with an audacity that stunned even his critics, boomed it again—each time, it

"Tommy." Fales, *The Life of Lawson*.

was charged, buying and selling before the fateful reversal, profiting at the expense of the public. The *New York Times*, citing his sway over tens of thousands of investors, labeled him a "Moses of destruction."[16]

Lawson defended himself and his mistaken predictions publicly. He professed that "in stock affairs I have been as square with the public as it is possible for a human to be," but his critics feasted on his self-aggrandizing and contradictory explanations.[17] He charged that his predictions were so often wrong—one article investigated whether Lawson was *ever* right—because the System, bent on destroying his credibility, used its vast wealth against him in the market. Although he readily admitted that he lied to "the other fellow in the game," as was expected when one manipulated stocks, he insisted that he never lied to the public.[18] He admitted making false promises, but he argued that they profited the public more than the System's lies. He also maintained that he never knowingly misled the public except in the service of the public's own good, a stunning qualification. Beginning in 1904, he went further and claimed that the ruinous panics he produced were in fact reform weapons, deliberate attempts to subvert the System that held a vise grip on the public's money. In financial cataclysm, he now argued, lay the answer to financial tyranny.

Most Americans found Lawson's confounding of market reform

and market manipulation bafflingly paradoxical. He railed sensationally against Standard Oil, but, to many, Lawson still appeared to be
"the most active, the most transparent, the most brazen representative
of the terrible system."[19] His motives and activities appeared so contradictory that, as one contemporary observed, anticipating the conclusion of later historians, "no character analyst could by any skill or
wisdom determine how much of Thomas W. Lawson was business
acumen, how much megalomania, how much love of the spotlight,
and how much a sincere desire to expose and correct great evils."[20]

The Panic Monger

It does not seem far-fetched to claim, along with several
of his contemporaries, that Lawson was the most influential writer in
the United States between 1900 and 1907.[21] Lawson frequently boasted
that he could "do anything with words," and his market activities
seemed to confirm this ("TRL" 702). Critics and supporters repeatedly
offered accounts of his successful—and ruinous—influence. One critic
charged that Lawson's public statements had prompted investors all
over the country to sell their stocks and withdraw their bank deposits;
that he had single-handedly ruined many small banks; that he had
paralyzed the insurance industry; and that "so far as Wall Street is
concerned, legitimate business is practically dead, and you have, for
the time being at least, killed it."[22] According to one magazine pro-
file, his published stock warnings made "the markets of the world
tremble" ("TRL" 664).

None of Lawson's warnings had more sensational effect than his
half-page advertisements in early December 1904, the warnings that
convinced Lawson he could use panic mongering as a reform tool.
With these ads, Lawson created one of the most remarkable panics in
Wall Street history. "Not since the day of 'Jim' Fisk has Wall Street seen
anything so impudent, audacious, and spectacular as the performance
of the Boston plunger posing as the guiding genius of the storm that
has prostrated Wall Street," remarked the *New York Herald*.[23] For a week
leading up to the crash, Lawson had convinced the public through a
series of extraordinary announcements that Amalgamated stock prices

would rise dramatically. On 6 December, he suddenly reversed himself and urged his readers to sell the stock, declaring that he had just learned that Amalgamated's directors had been misleading him about the company's financial condition and that a crash was imminent. For two days he flooded the papers with feverish warnings: "Every holder of Amalgamated owes it to himself to sell his holdings at once. In the next few days there must be a terrific break"; "Sell Steel, sell Sugar, sell Southern Pacific, Union Pacific, Atchison; sell all the pool stocks. It would take one hundred Morgans, one dozen Standard Oils, and a few Banks of England to take what will be sold this trip" (quoted in "TRL" 868). Two days later, frenzied by his alarms, the volume of selling became overwhelming, and the market crashed.

All major stocks, led by Amalgamated, tumbled. According to the *New York Times*, it was "the worst freak panic that ever struck Wall Street."[24] When the crisis seemed to subside a few days later, Lawson unloosed more ads. He threatened to "strike again, suddenly, sharply, sensationally, and in a way that will produce effects upon prices and upon markets, so much more destructive, that the effects and the destruction of last week will appear by comparison as milk to vitriol. . . . The result must be terrible for Wall Street and the 'System,' and nothing can avert it" (FF 519). Prices, barely recovered from his first attack, plummeted again.

In three days, almost half a billion dollars of market value disappeared. The rural and middle-class investors whom Lawson claimed to be protecting in *Frenzied Finance* were ruined. The "savings of a lifetime of many honest investors have been swept away by the false-hoods that you have spread abroad through the public press" (quoted in "TRL" 869), charged the copper promoter Colonel W. C. Greene, who then publicly challenged Lawson to a duel, setting off a front-page "Bowery melodrama" the next day ("TRL" 869).[25]

The Lawson panic amazed and divided Wall Street. By all accounts, it was a spectacular and bizarre performance. The market recovered immediately. The panic came like "a bolt from the blue" and disappeared as suddenly when Lawson disengaged himself.[26] No one could quite figure it, or Lawson, out. Conservatives dismissed Lawson's influence, blaming the flurry on a policy announcement by President Theodore Roosevelt. Others argued that Lawson must have conspired with more powerful partners to "scare and drive the public to the financial slaughter."[27] But many observers took the panic to be Lawson's own handiwork and recognized the historical significance of his performance. The *New York Times*, no friend of Lawson, observed: "This man, having succeeded in charming thousands of people by his stories of frenzied finance into the belief that whatever he said 'went,' and, using that power, did what no market manipulator had heretofore been able to do: he broke the price of the security which he was openly attacking without any apparent outside help, and incidentally caused a sharp decline in the market which stirred the entire financial community."[28] A year later, on its front page, the *Times* underscored again the importance of Lawson's achievement: never before had a panic been announced, anticipated, and executed in the open, and never through the lone agency of an individual's writing.[29]

Remarkably, the financial historians who have commented on the Lawson panic have paid little attention to the fact that the crash occurred when the serialization of *Frenzied Finance* was in full swing, that when Lawson performed his spectacular panic, he was the nation's most conspicuous reformer. The tendency among the historians who have discussed Lawson has been to study his market activities and his reform activities separately. However, it is impossible to separate his two writing careers, and indeed, most of his contemporaries sensed that his incendiary exposés were in some way entangled with his market activities. In fact, after the panic, the *Journal of Commerce* insisted that Lawson had been working for "months, with a popular magazine at his service, upon the nerves of ill-informed investors and making them timid by his onslaughts," apparently with "some other purpose in all this besides enlightening the American public and rescuing it from the iniquities of promoters and stock jobbers of whom he has been one of the most agile."[30] The editors of *Public Opinion* were more specific: "There is very little doubt that Mr. Lawson's 'Frenzied Finance' is a part of a far-reaching and comprehensive plan of stock-manipulation, in which the public is expected to do as it is bidden by this financial Moses."[31]

Lawson answered these charges by insisting that his market operations aided his reform work, not the other way around. He claimed that the panic was a reform experiment, a test of his rhetorical power. He triggered the panic to see whether his articles had aroused the public sufficiently to challenge the System in the market, the only place, Lawson now claimed, where the System could be damaged. The experiment worked: "The power of publicity ha[s] been triumphantly vindicated," he crowed, surveying the devastation (FF 517). The panic showed that thousands of small investors followed his word. Dismissed by many as a crank before the panic, Lawson now appeared as an economic force to be reckoned with, for, as one magazine writer asked, "had he not done what he had promised to do—shake the market to its very foundations?"[32] The panic gave him his mandate and proved the influence of his and, perhaps, all reform writing. It also won him a new body of recruits. As the *Independent* noted, "The transient speculators who stand by the ticker the livelong day incline strongly to him, aye, believe in him and are confident that he is a man with a mission, that he is telling much truth and that in the end he will carry the people with him in his fight against the 'unrighteous system' of which he was so long an integral part."[33] The panic proved that the public, driven by Lawson's writing, could set market prices and challenge the System's financial hegemony.

Convinced that major panics were within his power to create and that they represented a genuine threat to the System, Lawson vowed to produce more of them. Appealing personally to the public, something no promoter had ever done, he sought to recruit the millions "who have been tricked, robbed, and insulted" by the System.[34] Confident that these followers would sell at his signal, with or without an explanation, he warned, "If I am allowed to make certain statements a destructive panic will be with us."[35] No one could afford to dismiss his threat, for merely by warning of a panic, Lawson had shown that he could bring on a wave of frenzied selling and produce a terrible crash. Relishing the seemingly titanic power of his words, he began to threaten ruin in the melodramatic, terroristic style that became his signature over the next few years. Days after the December panic, Lawson warned: "I am only in the mild, preliminary stages yet. While waiting for the next move, make no mistake. When the real work begins Wall Street and the 'System' will look like a last year's straw hat in the swirls of Niagara" (FF 520). He began to give sensational accounts of his following and their readiness to march into the market and do battle for him, always stressing the cataclysmic potential of his writing. In a telegram he sent around the copper market in 1905, he threatened: "If at liberty, I could publish ten lines and [a market] break would be reality. So sensational will be the smash believe it will carry the entire nation into panic" ("TRL" 24).

He took seriously the idea that a doomsday panic offered the surest antidote to the System's evil, and in the summer of 1905 he outlined his panic remedy in fiery speeches throughout the Midwest, working up his "new holy war" as a business plan.[36] Sharing the stump with William Jennings Bryan and Clarence Darrow, he argued that if the American people sold their corporate stocks and withdrew their savings from the banks and trusts on a certain date—to be determined by Lawson and announced sometime in the future—the System would be starved of vital funds, setting in motion a cataclysmic crisis. Such a massive withdrawal would cause "the failure and destruction of one-half the banking institutions of New York" and spread commercial catastrophe throughout the nation. He insisted that "nothing could justify it but the absolute necessity for uprooting and eradicating the 'System'" (FF 547). "Let the American strike in time with Lawson's baton," summarized the *Outlook*, and "the grim, grey Dark Tower in Broadway [Standard Oil's headquarters] will fall in resounding ruin."[37] When that happened, the revolution would be complete. The System's "dollar-making mill" (FF 41) would be destroyed, and the whole nation would benefit.

Lawson cultivated his public image as a revolutionary leader, a financial messiah providentially chosen to guide Americans out of financial slavery. He repeatedly warned of a crash in copper, each time exhorting his followers to sell their stocks and get out of the market before the collapse. He maintained that Amalgamated and other System stocks were criminally overvalued, sustained only by huge infusions of Standard Oil's—that is, the public's—money. A massive panic would expose the System's fraud, purify the market, and make stock values credible again. When, despite his warnings, stock prices continued to rise in 1905 and 1906—the biggest bull market up to that time in American history—Lawson argued that the System rigged financial markets specifically to discredit him. His threats became increasingly grandiose. By the summer of 1906, eighteen months after his first strike, he was predicting, to the day, worldwide commercial catastrophe. The public was tiring of his panic shouts, however.[38] When a massive panic prostrated the nation in October 1907, Lawson's readers ignored his plea to finally turn the tables and finish off the System; instead, they lionized J. P. Morgan and the other bankers who bailed out Wall Street. Damning the public as "a joke—a System joke," he gave up his career as a reformer and returned to Wall Street to manipulate the market for his own profit, insisting that he owed the public nothing.[39]

Up to its end, Lawson's panic campaign horrified Wall Street insiders. As a means of reform, it was reckless; as an instrument of progress, it was too costly; and as a tool of justice, it was indiscriminate. The idea that the stock market could be used to promote social goals; that it could be plied in such a way by a reformer; that Wall Street—forced into financial disaster, no less—was a tool to be used by the "masses" against the "classes": all this was entirely new. It turned the free market on its head, transforming speculation itself into an instrument of moral and financial revolution. Indeed, Lawson's market activism upset the axiom that moral sentiment had no business on the trading floor of the stock exchange. When Lawson added panic mongering to his reform arsenal late in 1904, the financial editor of the New York Times attacked him, asserting that the "stock market is fit only for appraisal of values, and if diverted to other objects, such as the adjustment of personal grievances, is impaired in its true functions."[40] The editor was not arguing that the stock market should be left alone. Although the New York Stock Exchange had always resisted external discipline and resented Roosevelt's extraordinary willingness to investigate it, regulatory sentiment worked against Wall Street from the outside. It compelled the Exchange to enforce higher standards of fairness and openness, but it left the basic mechanism of stock trading alone, never imagining that this mechanism would be moved by anything but profit seeking. Regulation could never change *why* stock prices moved.

Lawson pioneered the idea of conjoining investors' desire for profit with their desire for moral action. He transformed price movements into direct expressions of his own and his followers' moral agency. In doing so, he upended the moral claims that reformers had for two centuries made against stock speculation. Lawson urged entanglement in the marketplace, not withdrawal from it. He embraced and exploited the viciousness of the market to reform—and, some claimed, destroy—it. Regulation was not revolutionary enough to free the market from the System's clutch, so Lawson turned to the collective dynamics of the marketplace itself, dynamics he could shape through his writing.

Persuasion and the Stock Market

Lawson's mingling of market reform and market manipulation distressed his contemporaries, even those sympathetic to his aims. Erman Ridgway, *Everybody's* publisher, lamented, "I shall never cease to believe that if you had kept out of Wall Street after you began the series with us, you would be the biggest man in the country to-day."[41] Seeing no way to reconcile Lawson's paradoxical status as critic and conspirator, many editorialists labored simply to determine whether the social good of Lawson's exposures outweighed the harm caused by his panic ads and promotions. According to the *Nation*, Lawson aided the public as a whistle-blower, but "it [was] preposterous to suppose that [as a reformer] he [could] lead it."[42] What seemed preposterous, however, was not that Lawson could lead the public, but that he could lead it responsibly, without taking advantage of it, for he had already proven his ability to command the public, win and sustain its attention, shape its opinion, and guide its actions. More to the point, he had amply demonstrated his knack for leading it to slaughter.

Lawson's reform writing came under attack for many reasons, but its purported dangers boiled down to its effect on his readers and, more specifically, his readers' effect on the stock market and the nation's economic and political stability. Lawson's contemporaries took his threats seriously for two reasons. First, Lawson wrote in and for the stock market, where public utterances, especially by a financial writer with such a loyal following, exercised uncanny agency. Second, Lawson's financial revelations inspired a wave of sensational exposés that whet the public's desire for sweeping economic and political changes—changes, Lawson's critics feared, his market ads might easily set in motion.

Financial sociologists and market psychologists routinely observe that "it is human volition which fuels the dips and recoveries of Wall Street, motivated by individuals' attitudes about opportunities for gain and caution."[43] Anything that sways the calculations, hopes, and fears of investors sways the market, since stock prices are, at bottom, an expression of investors' opinions and moods. Profiteers have always taken advantage of the stock market's sensitivity to the rumors, reports, and other market pronouncements that shape these attitudes. In the United States, attempts to spread false information and influence stock prices were prosecuted at least since the 1830s, and in the last half of the nineteenth century, critics eager to curb stock speculation (as well as apologists anxious to protect it from overzealous regulation) commonly denounced the evil and ease of such manipulation. Throughout the century, powerful cliques of stock operators relied on the financial press to incite public interest—and also destroy public confidence—in specific securities. Financial news bureaus and Wall Street newspapers were commonly used, and sometimes paid, as organs of specific speculative interests. "The 'points,' the 'puffs,' the alarms and the canards, put out expressly to deceive and mislead, find a wide circulation through these mediums, with an ease which admits of no possible justification," observed Henry Clews, whose own investment bank employed journalists from nineteen newspapers and included a press suite.[44] By 1900, stockbrokers' "tipster" reports constituted a regular feature of financial newspapers.[45] Market insiders repeatedly confessed their amazement at the willingness of the public to take substantial financial risks on the basis of these manufactured tips. Histories of Wall Street, biographies of its major figures, and contemporary accounts of the stock exchange are filled with examples of such manipulation.

In *Frenzied Finance*, Lawson anatomized how the System used its media organs to manufacture news, mold public opinion, and "lead the people toward the shambles" (FF 219). For Lawson, however, publicity, "the most powerful weapon in the world" (FF 532), could also neutralize the System's press machine. So long as the public owned a critical mass of the System's stock, he repeatedly proclaimed, popular opinion would determine the System's well-being. Indeed, Lawson represented his struggle against Standard Oil, in plainest terms, as a rhetorical fight, a propaganda battle between him and the System for control over public opinion. For Lawson, stock prices reflected this opinion; rather than investors' fear or greed or financial judgment, they expressed the intensity of Americans' reformist sympathies, their outrage at the System's larceny. Stock prices reflected the public's loyalty to him and his campaign. They registered, more exactly, his persuasive power.

Persuasion has always been considered dangerous in America. The confidence men, mesmerists, and seducers who appear throughout eighteenth- and nineteenth-century American literature register the longstanding fear that Americans, free to make up their own minds about their leaders and their vocations, guided by experience but lacking a usable past, driven by private interest and dependent on credit, might easily be misled by wily rhetoricians. Of course, not only individuals but also groups, classes, and "the public" itself might be duped and swayed, if not by confidence men or politicians, then by the press. Indeed, at least since the 1830s, critics lamented the press's seemingly tyrannous capacity to manufacture and mold public opinion. They feared that the power of the press would undermine democracy itself. Since the country was governed by public opinion, it was frequently noted, whoever controlled public opinion in fact governed the country.

Such fears spiked in the decades around the turn of the century. Media networks for the first time extended across the country, and cheap magazines with national circulations found their way into the homes of the majority of American families. Never had such powerful and centralized influences been brought to bear on the public's mind. Many observers were alarmed by the efficiency with which big business manipulated the broadcast media and, exploiting new publicity tools such as press agents, swayed public opinion.[46] Even more alarming was the popular influence of the sensational newspapers of William Randolph Hearst and Joseph Pulitzer and their imitators, who were charged with transforming the public into a mob and "scatter[ing] the seeds of sedition, class hatred, discontent or the fruits of prejudice."[47]

Journalists countered these corporate and demagogic threats through their muckraking. Personally affronted by the criminal practices—graft, exploitation, fraud, monopoly—that everywhere seemed to poison democracy, the early muckrakers, most famously Ida Tarbell, Ray Stannard Baker, and Lincoln Steffens, sought to furnish the public with information about covert corporate and government crimes, information on the basis of which the public would demand legislative remedies. Their investigations and exposures served as models of legitimate moral and political suasion. Emphasizing verifiable evidence, these journalists assumed the role of scientists and historians, relentless fact gatherers who weighed, sifted, and followed up evidence and let their findings determine their conclusions. Previous generations of reform writers, attached to specific political parties and movements, "had behind them much hot faith and fury," as the journalist Will Irwin put it, but "little cold fact."[48] Above all, the exposés of the muckrakers exemplified restraint. Intent on analyzing specific social ills, tracing their genesis and comprehending their ramifications, these writers were "concerned only with facts, not with stirring up revolt."[49] "We were journalists, not propagandists," observed Tarbell, who considered herself a historian, not a reformer.[50]

The *American Magazine*, launched in 1906 by the former staff of *McClure's*, gives one a sense of this spirit of restraint in its mission statement. It advertised itself as a journal that "keeps its temper, gets things somewhere near as they are, loves mankind, never attempts to puncture anything which it is not convinced is a sham, and then does it with good nature and precision."[51] By proclaiming its even-temperedness, the editors of the *American Magazine* meant specifically to distance themselves from Lawson and his violent sensationalism.[52] Lawson, to say the least, lacked the "air of enforced calm" of the earlier muckrakers.[53] In fact, he had no patience with the conscientious restraint of Tarbell and others investigating the crimes of big business. In his incendiary foreword to *Frenzied Finance*, Lawson claimed that for all their "facts, statistics, and evidences," Tarbell and others failed to "bring to the hearts, minds, and souls of the men and women of to-day that all-consuming passion for revenge, that burning desire for justice, without which no movement to benefit the people can be made successful" (FF xii). His own stories, in contrast to Tarbell's, would be "scarleted, yellowed, and blacked to the limit," for if the people were to be "aroused to a fierce blind-to-fear, deaf-to-favor passion," they had to be turned from "their present diminishing meal of syndicate-skimmed milk, corporation-kneaded bread, and trust-churned nine-ounces-to-the-pound butter" toward "a raw-meat, cayenne-peppered, green cactus diet."[54]

By 1906, less than three years after *McClure's* made muckraking a featured part of mainstream magazines, public sentiment, goaded by Theodore Roosevelt's public condemnation of the "hysterical sensationalism" of the literature of exposure, had turned against muckraking.[55] Encouraged by the success of Lawson and others, an "epidemic of exposure" had taken hold of the press. Fueled by popular demand, sustained by editors' need to outsell competitors, and propelled by a sense that corruption could be found wherever one looked for it, exposés had become more sensational, less concerned with analyzing social ills and aimed more at unveiling an underworld of vice and fraud. Lamenting the increasing luridness of magazine muckraking, the editor of *Collier's* complained in March 1906 that "the harshest yellow journalism is being imitated in numberless periodicals. Each would fain outbark Lawson, Hearst, or Russell."[56] A month later, Roosevelt gave his momentous muck-rake speech castigating the investigative journalists who concerned themselves only with the negative aspects of society and whose vituperativeness was "one of the most potent forces for evil."[57] Roosevelt clearly had Lawson—as well as David Graham Phillips and Upton Sinclair—in mind. He denounced

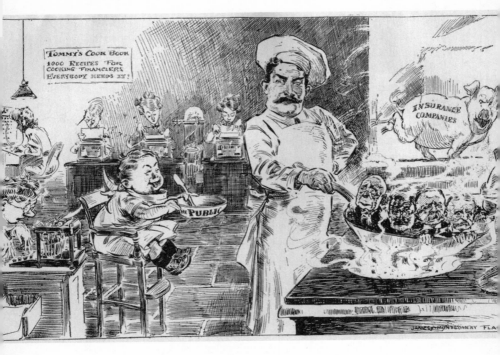

"Frying Frenzied Financiers." *Life*, 12 January 1905.

these writers' "indiscriminate assault upon men in business," warned against their slanders, and railed against their opportunism.[58] He damned, in particular, their rhetorical recklessness. These were jittery times. Socialism seemed a credible threat; violent labor strikes plagued the nation; and demagogues found favor with the public. Hearst, a radical, was running for New York governor. Roosevelt warned that "sensational, lurid, and untruthful" attacks might do "more damage to the public mind than the crime itself."[59] Sober factualism, it seemed, had given way to "hysterical, unbalanced," "melodramatic and cheap" diatribe.[60]

The conservative press condemned Lawson and the others as "sensation-mongers" and "reckless falsifiers."[61] To these critics, the political dangers of such reckless writing seemed obvious. Ray Stannard Baker (who complained to Roosevelt that the muck-rake speech failed to distinguish between his own brand of writing and Lawson's) lamented that sensationalism "increased the unrest and indignation" of the public without providing "the soundly based and truthful information" required for effective action in a democracy.[62] According to Roosevelt, even Congress was "Lawson-ized, so to speak . . . so jumpy, even about reform, that it is difficult to get coherent—that is, effective—action from them."[63] He might have added "proper" action, since the danger of sensational journalism, all agreed, was that it was too effective at gripping the public mind and moving it to action. For critics, such writing replaced the reasoned appeal of painstaking investigative work with a dangerously efficient and apparently resistless emotional force. The new kind of journalism (reform writing, the literature of exposure, and yellow journalism were commonly lumped together) exerted a shallow, vulgar, unhealthy, and addictive appeal. It not only thrived on but also actively produced "morbid and vicious public sentiment," stimulating rather than satisfying the public's appetite for sweeping changes.[64] In short, it threatened to take reform too far.

When critics cited the "vast appetite for horrors" whetted by such literature, they clearly had socialism in mind.[65] *Frenzied Finance* and the exposé journalism with which it was associated were widely seen as fomenting class hatred and political revolution. "The honest man, hysterical with anger at the crimes of high finance," and everyone else who was convinced that corporations were irremediably rotten were "following the lead of the statesmen of the yellow press toward the ruinous experiment of straight-out socialism," warned Ellery Sedgwick, soon to be editor of the *Atlantic Monthly*.[66] As the most incendiary of the muckrakers, Lawson confirmed the worst fears of conservatives when he was embraced by the socialist press, despite his admission that he colluded with Wall Street's most nefarious insiders, manipulated the stock market, and raised hell on behalf of bourgeois investors. Writing about *Frenzied Finance* years later, Lawson emphasized that he aimed to preempt, not provoke, revolution—he wanted to purify capital markets, not do away with them—, but during *Frenzied Finance*'s sensational run, the socialist press credited him with doing "more than any other one individual" to rouse public indignation against the financial establishment and to make its systematic larceny common knowledge.[67] Socialist newspapers even advertised *Frenzied Finance* and reprinted parts of it. "Keep it up, Mr. Lawson!" urged *Wilshire's*, the largest socialist magazine. "You will help make something drop and the something is going to be a great deal bigger than you think it is! You are doing more for Socialism, Lawson, than is *Wilshire's*."[68] Other socialist papers offered more guarded assessments of Lawson's usefulness for the coming revolution, but all acknowledged Lawson's extraordinary power to ignite and mobilize the public's—including the working class's—anger.

Indeed, Lawson carried enough prestige among socialists that Upton Sinclair, early in his revolutionary career, sent Lawson a manuscript draft of *The Jungle* and nervously asked to visit him in Boston. Sinclair's father reportedly wrote Lawson a letter on Upton's behalf, claiming that the famous stock operator could "do more than any living man" to advance his son's cause and career.[69]

Lawson's critics agreed about what made him most dangerous: through his exposés and his panic warnings, Lawson was leading stockholders astray—astonishingly, toward socialism. His writing threatened to arouse revolutionary sentiment among his millions of readers, a readiness to unite in some form against the capitalist kleptocracy that systematically diminished the purchasing power of their incomes. Remarkably, to explain his power, Lawson's critics focused on *Frenzied Finance's* novelistic appeal. They cited Lawson's melodramatic writing style and his capacity to generate suspense, his mastery of "the art of the serial story writer" who always "keeps his readers eager for the dramatic climax."[70] In comparing his exposé to fiction, his critics were doing more than offering a facile, if vague, explanation for how Lawson held and swayed his readers. Alarmed by the political and cultural effects of reform fiction, they were also seeking to mark out what made his reform writing illegitimate: its breathtaking destructiveness and resistlessness.

Because Lawson ultimately linked panic mongering, reform, and novel writing, I want to spend a moment discussing the perceived effects—more exactly, the apparent capacity to produce effects—of fiction in this age of mass persuasion. "Fiction has been one of the most effective weapons" in the reform fight, claimed a reviewer of *The Jungle*; "he who would reach and sway the reason of the masses must appeal to it through the imagination and by . . . an appeal that should move the sympathy while convincing the reason."[71] Benjamin Flower, radical editor of the *Arena*, claimed that David Graham Phillips—who went on to write over twenty novels—was doing his "greatest work for the cause of democracy" not by his journalism but by his fiction writing.[72] Phillips agreed; like Bellamy and other reform novelists, he thought more readers would heed the warnings and lessons of his novels than his investigative articles. For Phillips, novels were uniquely able, through their narrative and imaginative hold, to make the reader "see, feel, and understand" the plight of society's victims.[73]

This capacity to evoke sympathy and provoke disorderly sentiments gave the reform novel its terrifying power. The *American Magazine*, despite advertising the "unusually lucid and picturesque story-telling power" of its journalists,[74] lambasted "the artist who preaches," warning of his poisonous influence:

> For the necessities of his art,—the need of picturesqueness, of seizing his audience, of the appeal of his characters for sympathy,— [he may] make complications in his treatment of sociological ideas, suggestions, and remedies, and may obfuscate even his own intentions—may create an emphasis to the destruction of scientific exactness. He is in danger of being entrained by the urge of his imagination into misleading statement, or morally confusing dramatic effect,—into unconscious impulsive appeals to some amiable, but possibly unsound sentiment. He is likely to . . . render himself liable to the charge of falsifying life, and of inculcating incorrect and destructive conduct on the part of those who are carried away by the passion of his expression, or [those who] . . . give themselves to a course of action in which wholesome restraint, useful and educative self-control, and the ennobling discipline of self-sacrifice, are set aside.[75]

Reform fiction endangered the country not simply because it "lied" or distorted life but because it aroused feelings that might easily express themselves in socially, politically, and economically unwholesome and unaccountable ways. In short, reform fiction exercised an exceptionally dangerous kind of agency on the reader and in the world. It could move the public to overthrow the government or, more immediately, to overturn the nation's financial markets.

Frenzied Finance stood at the center of the cultural firestorm over the virtues and hazards of reform writing and fiction. Critics condemned the exposé (as they had Lawson's promotional work) as "fiction" in the older sense of being wholly or partly false. According to Denis Donohoe, the first financial critic to offer a sustained critique of *Frenzied Finance*, "Facts there are unquestionably in Lawson's story, but facts so strangely contorted that in his hands they have assumed the outward appearance of grotesque fiction. Commonplace incidents, those of the most trivial character even, have been subjected to a process of gaseous distention, until, swollen out of all resemblance to their natural selves, these goblin portents are turned adrift to affright the timid and fill the credulous with vague foreboding."[76] Lawson labored to refute such charges, arguing in the preface to *Frenzied Finance* that "while it is true that fiction is expressed in the same forms and phrases as truth, no man ever lived who could shape 400,000 words into the kinds of pictures I have painted and pass them off for aught but what they were" (FF v). But *Frenzied Finance* was also charged with being fiction, and, indeed, successful fiction precisely because Lawson could pass off his invention as fact. As Norman Hapgood put it, "Building on what he knows and wishing, like the novelist he is, that his story should be complete, [Lawson] fills in with as much plausibility as is consistent with excitement and suspense."[77]

More troubling than its distortions and fabrications, I want to suggest, was this last claim, that *Frenzied Finance* had the "excitement and suspense" of a novel. *Public Opinion*'s lengthy series countering *Frenzied Finance* began by charging that "Mr. Lawson is essentially and temperamentally a writer of fiction. The pen of the romancer is strongly evident in his story. He loves dramatic effects better than he loves truth—and he has no scruples in sacrificing both truth and dramatic effects when he sees anything to gain thereby."[78] On the one hand, Lawson's series was seen as helping move the literature of exposure away from the facile appeal of fiction. It was included among the works helping to transform the literature of exposure from "cheap entertainment" to an "efficient instrument of civic and national reform."[79] On the other hand, "plausible, powerful, amazingly original and always interesting," it was undeniably gripping reading, and its novelistic appeal, cheap or not, clearly could not be separated from, let alone contrasted with, its efficiency as a reform instrument.[80] Filling each installment with striking plot twists, dramatic accounts of audacious crimes, and promises of further revelations and explanations, Lawson told his story "in dime-novel style, and thereby gathered a great audience" ("TRL" 146). So "miraculous" was the "facility and force of expression" of his articles, that many doubted Lawson authored them, alleging they were the work of a "literary hack."[81] In short, his novelistic hold over the reader seemed to account for his influence, virtuous or vicious, over the public. Indeed, the New York Times answered the query "How Lawson Makes People Do What He Wishes" by citing his novelistic power: he held his audience "with the dramatic power of Dumas, the imagination of Kipling, and the humor of Twain."[82]

Understanding this, Lawson's followers sent letters to Everybody's urging him to write a novel. "Why do you not produce a great and popular book, a great novel that will strike the right chords in the hearts of the masses, and do for the present generation what 'Uncle Tom's Cabin' did for the last?" wrote a reader from Minnesota, who cited the coercive, if nutritious, force of fiction: "Are not our writers breaking their heads to invent sensational plots to feed a public crazy for a sensational stage and sensational library? You, Mr. Lawson, do not have to invent—feed the sensation-loving public with the real 'stuff,' and if they cannot swallow and digest it, as spread before them in EVERYBODY'S, they will swallow it when poked down their throat by the means of drama and novel."[83] Lawson took up the suggestion in December 1906, not, however, because a novel would make his facts more palatable to the public, but rather because a novel would free him from having to rely on facts at all. He left the "field of fact narrative" for that of "fiction story telling" because storytelling, not facts—indeed, storytelling freed from facts—would enable him to carry out his market revolution.[84]

I will turn to Lawson's novel in a moment. For now I want to suggest that Lawson's critics used the invidious label "fiction" to mark out and quarantine the characteristics of Lawson's muckraking that seemed most dangerous—that is, most resembled his panic mongering and stock manipulation. However differently they engaged their readers' emotions, Lawson's writing against the market and his writing in the market both sent "the human herd stampeding . . . blindly toward certain disaster"—toward the Scylla and Charybdis of socialism and financial cataclysm.[85] "Fiction" signified this unwholesome and uncanny efficaciousness.

The label functioned to protect the purity of "legitimate" reform.[86] During much of the nineteenth century, literary tastemakers performed a similar sort of boundary work when they compared certain kinds of emotionally exciting fiction to addictive substances. As Nancy Glazener observes (writing about the 1870s and 1880s), such a comparison served "to contain and exorcise whatever was dangerous about any emotional experience provided by [this] reading."[87] The association between sensational reading and addiction is instructive because it specifies what most alarmed critics about the power of Lawson's writing: its apparent resistlessness. I do not mean the resistlessness of its emotional and somatic effects on individual readers, something commonly associated with sentimental and sensational literature in the eighteenth and nineteenth centuries, but rather the irreversibility of its material force in and on the marketplace. At bottom, Lawson presented such a threat not simply because his "fiction" compelled his readers, but rather because it compelled them in and into the stock market, where public statements, predictions, exhortations, and warnings produced immediate, dramatic, and seemingly uncontrollable effects.

Lawson's writing seemed resistless specifically because of the dynamics of collective reading in the stock market, the pandemic emulation and competition among market readers that I discussed in the introduction. Lawson commanded a critical mass of investors, and his power over them, sustained by his muckraking's novelistic appeal, produced seemingly ineluctable effects. By warning of a panic, Lawson created a panic, which activated an automatism of its own: not only investors but also banks, holding stocks as collateral, failed; and businesses, tied to banks by a web of credit obligations, also went down, the collapse of one precipitating the collapse of the next. Not addiction, but infection, a keyword in the emerging discourse of social psychology, characterizes Lawson's effect on readers. Sympathetic contagion—not investors' feeling for each other, but rather investors' feeling like each other, all fearing each other's fear—gave Lawson's writing its awesome efficiency.

The popular currency of accounts of Wall Street's "terrible nerve-devouring excitement" at the turn of the century might explain the intensity of Lawson's critics' alarm: perhaps they feared that his spellbinding exposés awakened an appetite for excitement his readers might seek to fulfill in the stock market, where, in any case, he was pointing them.[88] However, even if we allow that some readers' cravings for more stimulation sent them rushing to their stockbrokers and not, say, to stage melodramas or amusement parks, where sensation itself was packaged and sold, and even if we grant that some investors' desire for excitement outweighed their fear of financial ruin, Lawson's followers, at least those who obeyed his market directives, do not seem to have been carried away by a craving for excitement, an addiction to recklessness, or a desire to abandon themselves to what one early Wall Street historian called the "perpetually fresh sensations of the free market."[89] What unnerved critics, in fact, is that these followers were extraordinarily disciplined, carrying out their general's commands immediately and efficiently. Lawson's followers were dangerous precisely because their actions and desires were prompted and guided not by market imperatives but rather by Lawson's directives. Moreover, their speculations did not demonstrate their loss of self-control or their dispossession by the market; their speculations showed, instead, their collective sense of power as an insurgent class. If they were unusually excited, it was because they imagined themselves assuming control over the vast, capricious machinery of the marketplace, a privilege only the System, and before it, the most powerful financial barons, had enjoyed. What frightened critics most was the mingling of volition and chaos that Lawson's writing produced in the market. Financial disaster, should it come, would not be a result of either his readers' discipline or the market's automatism alone; these factors threatened calamity by operating sensationally together.

Panic Fiction: Sympathy and the Stock Market

A week after the Lawson panic, the financial editor of the *New York Times* addressed the stock manipulator, commenting, "As an advertiser you are the best on earth. If you had not been born to be a stock rigger . . . you would have shone as a litr'y feller."[90] However, Lawson was already a "litr'y feller." As a promoter and a reform writer, Lawson showed how breathless melodrama and a "picturesque, pungent and attractive" style exerted real and potentially catastrophic effects in the marketplace.[91] And he was a novelist. His novel *Friday, the Thirteenth* appeared in four monthly installments in *Everybody's*, beginning in December 1906, and it came out as a book soon afterward.

Friday, the Thirteenth recounts the sensational career of a stockbroker, Bob Brownley, who discovers that he can produce catastrophic stock market panics simply by "opening and closing his mouth" and pretending that he has more stock to sell than his opponents can buy (*Friday* 108). Brownley uses his discovery—that words alone can sway the market—to wreak vengeance on the nefarious "System" of financial wreckers who, by viciously prompting a panic, nearly bankrupted a young woman, Beulah Sands, whose family fortune Brownley had promised to rescue and with whom he falls in love. To recoup her loss, Bob creates a colossal panic (on Friday, the thirteenth) that produces ruin and despair across the country. Beulah learns of the panic at the same moment she learns that her father, ruined by the System's panic, has killed himself and the rest of her family. Overwhelmed with grief, she breaks down, losing her memory and becoming eerily childlike. Brownley continues to produce panics for several years, overturning the market with seemingly magical ease when the mood suits him and becoming the world's richest and most powerful man. Aggrieved and enraged by the personal and economic trauma wrought by the System, he promises to destroy it and its newest weapon, the Anti-People's Trust, a caricature of Amalgamated Copper. In the novel's climax, he brings on an apocalyptic panic (again on Friday, the thirteenth), convinced that only such direct and massive action will put an end to the System's tyranny. This panic causes unprecedented devastation, but before the panic can undermine the world's economy entirely, Brownley delivers a stunning speech to the New York Stock Exchange. He reveals his trick for controlling the market and itemizes the reforms that must be made if the Stock Exchange is to be protected from others using this trick. His speech instigates an epic market fight that will determine whether Wall Street will be ruined or reformed. At this moment, Beulah, now his wife, miraculously recovers, but when she reads headlines about Bob's latest panic and the sudden death of his rival's family, she recalls the news stories that triggered her breakdown. Overcome by the memory, she dies.

Lawson claimed that "seventeen experts pronounce it the greatest fiction ever written. Booth Tarkington and others say so."[92] Fans wrote him letters predicting he would one day be recognized as "one of the greatest story writers of the age" (Friday, appendix, n.p.). Critics were decidedly mixed about it. Some found it "sensational and stirring," "unquestionably entertaining"; others found it unbearably vulgar, sentimental, melodramatic, and implausible.[93] The Outlook, finding little in the book but "cheap fireworks," concluded: "In the two respects of screaming vulgarity of mind and what can only be called drunkenness of imagination, Friday the Thirteenth is probably the most remarkable novel that was ever offered to the public above the level of those who read The Police News."[94] Some saw it as downright dangerous. The Bookman grouped Lawson with Upton Sinclair and Thomas Dixon, calling them "lurid prophets of incendiary fiction."[95]

Friday, the Thirteenth is one of the most sensational treatments of financial panic in American literature. It was certainly the most highly anticipated. Perhaps no first try at fiction has ever received more attention or encouragement. Lawson's announcement of his intention to write fiction made the front page of the New York Times, and over 25,000 copies of the book were sold before it reached stores. Lawson's announcement terrified Boston high society, which feared that Lawson, snubbed and vengeful, would write a novel exposing its meanness. (Lawson would leave this to David Graham Phillips, whose novel about Lawson, The Deluge [1905], denounces the Boston smart set.) By contrast, his fans around the nation, some of whom claimed to have walked miles in the snow to get hold of his reform articles in *Every-body's*, enthusiastically supported his new endeavor, and they wrote waves of letters wishing him luck as a novelist.

The mostly handwritten letters, facsimiles of which Lawson included in an appendix to the novel, make it clear that the public was interested in Lawson's performance as a writer and that his popular support was secured in large part by his literary gifts. His readers wanted to see what this new literary form could do, if it would "annihilate Wall Street stock gambling" and "pull down the pillars of the Wall Street structure," as Doubleday, the book's publisher, advertised. They clearly saw his fiction as a reform tool, one that would carry on and intensify the work of his exposures. "In this form the facts go home," wrote one reader after he or she had read the first installment of the novel; "now they live and palpitate" (*Friday*, appendix, n.p.). Lawson's readers genuinely wanted his fiction to succeed, to exert a demonstrable reform influence by arousing and stirring the public. "May the sweep of your pen sway millions," encouraged one reader (*Friday*, appendix, n.p.).

Such comments are striking, for Lawson's pen had swayed, and was at that moment swaying, millions to risk and lose money in the stock market. When the novel came out at the start of 1907, Lawson was busy executing his most vicious and, according to some observers, desperate market campaigns. He may have been preaching panic as a progressive tool to free the public from the tyranny of market insiders, but when *Friday, the Thirteenth* came out, he was routinely producing "cruel, conscienceless, and pitiless" panics in his own dummy mining companies, panics that stunned and ruined those who followed his market advice.[96] As a result of this blatant and apparently ruthless manipulation, Lawson found himself discredited and reviled by many who had once supported him. Just when literary reviewers were turning to Lawson's novel about a stock operator's titanic agency, ministers were preaching against Lawson's disastrous power.

In his most complete statement about the reasons for his turn to fiction, a few paragraphs addressed directly to his readers in *Every-*

body's in November 1906, Lawson explained that he wanted to "hold and even increase my audience," to disable the normal operations of the New York and Boston Stock Exchanges, and ultimately to "rip out the foundations and tumble in the walls of the Stock Exchanges."[97] He did not say directly that he was using his fiction to trigger a market panic, but the previous summer, when he was outlining his terror campaign in speeches throughout the Midwest, he told his publishers that his stories would "help ripen the conditions" for his promised cataclysm; he argued that "some huge illustration of its practicability be given at the moment it is promulgated."[98] By illustrating the practicability of a panic attack, *Friday, the Thirteenth* would seem to be priming the public for his market strike.[99]

Given Lawson's sensational career as an incendiary phrasemaker, it should come as no surprise that *Friday, the Thirteenth* is preoccupied with the catastrophic agency of words. The market plot hangs on Brownley's realization that mere utterances can exert seemingly magical leverage over the market. He discovers that under existing Exchange rules, creating a panic is ultimately "only a question . . . of a man's opening and closing his mouth and spitting out words" (*Friday* 109). Bob uses his discovery and repeatedly booms and plunges stock prices, selling to the System at the top and forcing the System to sell back to him at the bottom so that by the end of each panic, he has enriched himself and impoverished his enemies without forfeiting (or possessing, for that matter) a single stock. His speech from the Exchange rostrum at the end—on which the "welfare, not only of Wall Street, but of the nation, perhaps even of the civilised [sic] world" depends (*Friday* 195)—produces even more sensational effects. He explains his discovery, and he observes how, broadcast now around the world, the trick will undermine "the whole stock-gambling structure" (*Friday* 215). The moment his speech ends, and on his signal, the traders begin frenziedly selling, desperate to get what they can before the promised cataclysm, initiating the apocalyptic battle that will decide whether Wall Street is to be regulated or ruined. His speech, in short, creates the conditions that make the end of conventional stock gambling inescapable.

The romance plot hangs on equally catastrophic and resistless rhetorical effects. Beulah goes mad after the first panic and dies during the final panic because on each occasion she reads and relates two headlines, one announcing a horrific family crime (first, her father's murder of her mother and siblings, and later, the suicide of Brownley's nemesis after his family dies in a car crash) and the other announcing the financial wreckage caused by Bob's market work. Lawson connects the fateful market speech and fatal news headlines overtly: the System's newspapers, fanning the flames of a boom that eventually ruins Beulah's father and triggers his murderous rampage, "pointed to a killing" (*Friday* 118).

What about this lurid tale would prompt readers to follow Lawson into the market and set off the apocalyptic panic he had been promising for so long? One possible answer has to do with the novel's sensationalism and the performance of sensationalism within the story. While the novel clearly laments the personal ruin wrought (and represented) by the newspaper's sensational headlines, it also suggests that this ruin, itself sensational, can work to inspire reform. Beulah's psychological fracture provokes Brownley's campaign against the System. Brownley attempts to redeem and redeploy sensation's agency in the market, to enact there the same tyrannous effects the sensational news enacted on his lover's mind. It is tempting to imagine that Lawson, keenly aware of sensation's agitating power, intended the sensationalism of the novel, Beulah's demise, in particular, to arouse his readers in the same way Brownley was aroused. However, sensation by itself hardly seems powerful enough to incite his readers to insurgency. If sensation were all that was required, he would not have had to turn to fiction, since *Frenzied Finance* offered sensation in abundance.

Instead, what his novel evokes, and what Lawson counts on to mobilize readers to follow him into the stock market and bring Standard Oil to its knees, is sympathy. Unremittingly sentimental, *Friday, the Thirteenth* works up and works on the reader's sympathy for Brownley. Brownley transparently stands in for Lawson, and by sentimentally justifying Brownley's campaign against the System, Lawson intends for his readers, united by their sympathy for Bob, for Lawson, and for each other, to come together as a market army and avenge the suffering of the System's victims in and outside the novel.

Before elaborating on these transfers of sympathy, I want to observe that in engaging its readers' private emotions in the service of public goals, *Friday, the Thirteenth* fits squarely within the rhetorical tradition of the nineteenth-century novel. As Glenn Hendler notes, the nineteenth-century American novel was "most often conceived of as a public instrument designed to play in a sentimental key."[100] *Uncle Tom's Cabin* (1852), the most famous and successful example of this sentimental activism, aimed to bring an end to slavery by moving readers to feel sympathy for slavery's victims. Whether evoked in the privacy of the reader's home or evoked in public spaces (such as temperance meetings, to take one of Hendler's examples), sympathy was commonly viewed as a public and political resource. What makes *Friday, the Thirteenth* extraordinary—unprecedented, to my knowledge—is that it puts readerly sympathy to work directly in the marketplace. It aims to arouse readers not simply to enter the stock market, itself an unprecedented kind of sentimental work, but more astonishingly to throw their weight behind a known stock manipulator and to produce a nightmarish panic that will ruin innocent investors and cause unimaginable collateral destruction. It deploys readers' tears to generate market terror.[101]

Exploiting literary sentimentality to activate (and unloose) market sentiment, Lawson brings together two kinds of sympathy rigorously separated in nineteenth-century sentimental fiction: personal sympathy, or compassion, such as the reader is expected to feel for the grief-stricken Brownley, and market sympathy, the emotional contagion that moved stock prices and fueled financial panics. This second notion of sympathy refers to the emulativeness of investors, the way market actors, either because they are uncertain which way the market will move or because they wish to act more quickly than other investors, constantly watch each other, imagine how others will respond to potential market movements, and "base their opinions on the prevalent attitude of others like themselves."[102] It refers also to the pandemic quality of this imaginative projection and imitativeness, the way emotions in the stock market reproduce themselves and spread, gathering mass and momentum.

In Lawson's day, financial observers and market psychologists, acknowledging their debt to crowd psychologists and sociologists who studied the forces that motivated and shaped mass behavior, were preoccupied with sympathy, emphasizing its exceptional efficaciousness in the marketplace. Explaining the contagion of irrational exuberance that caused booms and panics, the economics professor Edward Jones observed, "States of mind, hopes and beliefs, are communicated from one to another by means of what is best described as sympathy."[103] Sympathy was not a salutary means of bringing an atomized community of economically self-interested individuals together, however, as it was for Adam Smith and his followers. Instead, sympathy signified the hazardous ties that produced a mania or mob mentality. The sympathetic spread of unrealistic opinions and untempered emotions continually threatened the economy. For Jones, "the force of sympathy and imagination in the propagation of opinions is not an intelligent one and in economic matters it makes for the support of opinions dangerous to the stability of industry." The "more intimate the association, the more will the common thinking processes be influenced by the sympathetic force," and never (he wrote this in 1900) had economic association been more intimate.[104] Intensified by financial centralization, the speed and spread of economic information, and the scope of economic transactions, "sympathetic force" exerted unprecedented leverage on prices, making financial crises more likely than ever.

Lawson signals the importance of the link between feeling for other individuals and feeling with other investors early in the novel. Explaining why his initial attempt to win back Beulah's father's money failed, Bob confesses that when he took that ruinous plunge, he had not yet experienced the agony suffered by the System's victims. Because he had looked upon stock speculation as a game and because the System had never crushed his heart—although he knew it crushed millions of other hearts—he had been insufficiently moved to appreciate the magnitude of the System's trickery (*Friday* 77). Thwarted by the System, however, he now agonizes with Beulah over the loss of her father's money. Having also lost his own money, and aggrieved that she suffers on his account, Bob sobs on Beulah's breast, and his "hot, blinding tears" motivate him to avenge her and her father's misery (*Friday* 81). Feeling another's pain as his own compels him to return to the market, study the System's trick, and use it against the System.

The scene is crucial not only because it shows how Brownley's sympathetic tears lead him to activate the sympathetic machinery of the market, the pandemic emulation that fuels the panics he orchestrates, but also because it shows how Bob personalizes the heartbreak of anonymous others. Bob's sympathy for his lover transforms his conception of the market and the ties that bind investors: Bob now sees the stock market as a sentimental community, a vast aggregation of hearts "systematically skewered" together (*Friday* 77). After he sets off his first panic, he wanders through the financial district and the "misery-infested" slums around it (*Friday* 142), asking victims of the panic to tell him of their anguish. Their stories clearly double for *Friday, the Thirteenth* itself—the lachrymose tales are supposed to evoke our hatred of the System—but they also convey that Beulah's anguish, which we experience up close, is typical of the suffering of thousands of other market victims we never see. Because hearts in the market are "skewered" together under the System's regime, Bob's sympathy (and thus also the reader's), extended to one victim, is extended to all. We are meant to see, however, that sympathy by itself will not transform anything (this marks a difference between Lawson's sentimental politics and Stowe's). Bob's turn to the market shows that sympathy must be wedded to concrete, direct, and collective action. Personal sympathy will pay off only when it is directed toward the market and unloosed within the marketplace.

We might expect *Friday, the Thirteenth* to work on readers by evoking their sympathy for Beulah, moving them to cry over Beulah's financial loss at the hands of the ruthless System and her grief on reading how this loss affects her beloved father (a grief she suffers twice, no less, once after each major panic). However, Beulah does not actually suffer after her breakdown. She becomes a blithe child without any memory of her loss, and so for most of the book the reader's sympathy is in fact directed toward Bob, whose suffering drives him to seek vengeance in the market. The reader is supposed to feel for him—that is, to pity him—and also to feel with him—that is, to feel his sympathy, grief and anger; and ultimately to sympathize with his panic operations. Beulah's inability to share in Bob's grief puts the burden of orienting the reader's feelings on Jim, Bob's best friend and business partner. As the narrator, Jim witnesses all the key scenes of Bob's suffering; and should we ever doubt how we are supposed to feel about Bob, Jim continually breaks down weeping, his "all-consuming agony of pity" provoked by Bob's enduring anguish (*Friday* 189). We read the novel, in short, through Jim's sympathetic tears.

To compel the reader to feel Bob's grief and sympathize with his market operations, Lawson deploys the "cheap" melodramatic "fireworks" and the fevered sentimentality the novel's critics found so unbearable. ("I'm glad you believe in sentiment," wrote one reader. "Your characters appeal to me so that I live with them, every nerve alert to the straining point" [*Friday*, appendix, n.p.].) Jim's weepy gaze on Bob's traumatic discovery of Beulah's breakdown, the discovery that commits Brownley to market warfare, makes this sentimental machinery plain:

> Bob was kneeling at the side of her chair, his hands clasped and uplifted in an agony of appeal that was supplemented by the awful groans. His face showed unspeakable terror and entreaty; the eyes were bursting from their sockets and were riveted on hers as those of a man in a dungeon might be fixed upon an approaching spectre of one whom he had murdered. . . . Beulah Sands was a dead woman; not dead in body, but in soul. . . . There still resounded through the room the awful guttural groans. Beulah Sands smiled, the smile of an infant in the cradle. She took one beautiful hand from the paper and passed it over Bob's bronzed cheek, just as the infant touches its mother's face with its chubby fingers. (*Friday* 143–44).

The lurid tableau, especially the creepy sentimental touch at the end, leaves Jim "sick at heart and horrified" (*Friday* 149). As if more were needed to wring tears from the reader and marshal emotional support for Bob's cause, Bob reminds us that Beulah—to whom he was about to propose marriage—is now not simply a child but also an orphan: "She has no father, no mother, no sister, no one to protect and shield her. The 'System' has robbed her of all in life, even of herself, of everything, Jim, but me. I must try to win her back for herself" (*Friday* 150). Bob will do this by trying to win the market back for itself. The sentimental injunction is clear: to fail to support Bob in the market is to forsake this pathetic orphan. Only in the market, through market manipulation of the most ruthless sort, can this poor girl gain the care and love of a parent. Only in the stock market can sentimental obligations be fulfilled.[105]

Bob's sentimental turn toward the stock exchange represents a striking turn in the history of fiction about speculation and financial panic. There was nothing new about a character's speculations causing grievous domestic damage or even leading to madness, murder, and suicide; such consequences were conventional in fiction since the 1830s, although typically it was the speculator himself who succumbed to the worst of fates, not his lover. Nor was it new for an author to evoke sympathy for the speculator himself, since in fiction innocent speculators were occasionally victims of events or actions beyond their control (such as conspiracies and panics). Lawson, however, sends the ruined speculator back into the market and, indeed, intensifies his operations there; more important, he evokes sympathy for the speculator precisely to justify the punishment Bob metes out there. Indeed, Bob's pain is crucial not because it arouses him to make war against the System but because it licenses the massive damage his war causes. If the tragedy of Beulah's dispossession had not gripped Bob, we are led to believe, he would have abandoned his panic campaign and left Wall Street altogether. Only such personal agony as he experiences when he discovers Beulah's trauma could overcome the moral revulsion he feels at the financial devastation his panics subsequently wreak. The sentimental license Lawson grants to Bob is clearly meant for the reader as well. Lawson acknowledges the awfulness of Bob's panic operations, but the reader's sympathy for Bob's private grief more than counterbalances whatever moral squeamishness the reader might feel about the commercial and social disaster that attends Bob's panics.

Lawson clearly counted on his readers to identify Brownley's market operations with his own panic campaign, a campaign, as I have mentioned, that Lawson had put on hold and was itching to restart when he wrote the novel. The parallels between Brownley's market manipulations and Lawson's are obvious. Less clearly, Lawson may have counted on his readers to identify Brownley's anguish with his own, since Lawson's wife died of heart trouble in August 1906, half a year before the novel appeared. Her death made the front page of the *New York Times*, and Lawson was widely recognized as a doting husband; many of his readers, we can assume, knew what a devastating blow this was to him. ("You are Bob Brownley, I *know*" [*Friday*, appendix, n.p.], confides one reader at the start of her letter.) In actuality, Lawson's bereavement presented a sentimental spectacle more horrifying and sensational than anything he put into his novel. Brent Walth, in his biography of Lawson's grandson, Governor Thomas McCall of Oregon, reports that Lawson "ordered his wife's unembalmed body stretched out on a pool table, where it grew gamy in the heat. He believed her death was God's revenge for the people he had ruined by his Amalgamated scheme. He stalked around the mansion, pistol in hand, threatening suicide."[106] According to Walth, Lawson continued to have a place set for his dead wife, and he waited for her every night at the train station before collapsing in tears. Whether or not his readers were aware of his loss or the gothic extremes of his grief, Lawson expected that his readers would transfer their sympathy for Brownley (and his campaign) to himself (and his own panic project). Perhaps intensified by their own prior victimization by the System, their compassion would prompt Lawson's readers to take up arms in his market war.

If readers had only Brownley or Lawson himself to feel for, it is hard to imagine how Lawson could bring his weeping readers together as a market force or how he might convince them that such a loopy plan—a novel bringing down the financial structure of the nation—would succeed. This, I am assuming, is why Lawson published his readers' letters along with the novel: readers would see that other readers felt the same way they did about Bob, about Beulah, about Lawson's reform work, and about sentiment itself. Through their identification with Lawson's stand-in, readers in fact identified with each other and came together as a group, an army, loyal to Lawson. Sympathy unified them, made them aware of their potential market power (for only as a bloc could they wield force in the market), and justified their militancy. The appendix to *Friday, the Thirteenth* provided concrete evidence of a community of feelers and followers. This concreteness was essential, since Lawson's investors, living far from each other and often far from news stands, banks, and post offices, knew (and knew of) each other only in the most abstract and mediated ways as fellow readers and investors. The published fan mail gave tactile actuality and sentimental urgency to this imagined community. In short, the fan letters transformed the marketplace, and, more remarkably, the market itself, into a sentimental activist sphere. In the novel, Jim laments that New Yorkers are so emotionally isolated that they must read the newspaper to learn about the death of a next-door neighbor (*Friday* 161). Intimate and sympathetic, Lawson's market community serves as an alternative to, rather than an extension of, the atomizing and uncaring city. Unlike the newspaper reminding readers of their anomie, Lawson's book actively forges the ties that bind and guide its readers.

To appreciate the novelty of this sentimental mobilization, it helps to understand how hostile American sentimental writers before Lawson were toward financial speculation and how fearful they were of financial panics. Throughout the nineteenth century, sentimental writers routinely dramatized how speculation encouraged recklessness and rewarded avarice. Speculating attenuated individuals' moral and spiritual values, especially their capacity to feel for others. (The most emotionally impoverished speculators in nineteenth-century fiction were slave traders whose lust for profits and fixation on price changes kept them from acknowledging the humanity of the slaves they bought and sold.) Even more than speculation's moral effect on speculators, sentimental writers lamented how speculation ruined families and destabilized middle-class homes, the putative sign and site of middle-class identity. Frequently compelled by debt to act rashly, the speculator squandered his family's savings on bad investments; and even when his speculations seemed safe, he was the victim of market forces beyond his control.[107] Financial panics, not only the major crises that beset the economy every twenty years or so but also the smaller panics that jarred the nation's financial districts several times a year, made stock speculation a chancy, potentially disastrous game. Repudiating this tradition, Lawson weds sentimentality and speculation. He transforms financial panic into a sentimental achievement. Market manipulation, rather than vitiating his reader's compassion for Bob's suffering, or Lawson's, perfects it.

Sympathy was not simply a force that inspired Lawson's readers to go into the market. As I noted earlier, sympathy was also a force his readers would activate in the market to achieve their financial and political aims. When called upon, Lawson's readers, sentimentally interpellated as members of a market army, would strike the stock market in unison, selling their holdings en masse, causing terror among investors. Just as in the novel, stock prices would plummet as each investor's desperation to sell intensified the desperation of every other investor, and stock prices would drop until the bottom fell out and banks and businesses, swept in the panic's current, collapsed. Fueling this disaster was an excess of sympathy: not simply an overwhelming intensity of emotion, but more specifically an overwhelming intensity of fellow feeling, a sentimental contagion that, fueled by the socio-logic of market behavior, spread uncontrollably.

We might think that this unloosing of sympathy in some way extended and intensified Lawson's readers' emotional attachment to Bob. Fomenting panic, we might hypothesize, offered readers a chance to transform a temporary emotional fling with an imaginary person (Brownley) into an exchange of emotion with real, if anonymous, individuals (other investors), an exchange with profound practical consequences that gave meaning and force to the sympathy elicited by the novel. However, what Lawson's readers gained in the market (or hoped to gain, since Lawson never carried out his plan) was in fact *relief* from the violent and demoralizing effects of market sympathy. Once told when and how to strike, Lawson's followers would have inside knowledge of sympathy's destructive course and would know how to protect themselves from the sentimental contagion. They would compel others to feel sympathy, but they would not themselves suffer sympathy's effects. They would force others to imitate the crowd and feel terrified by the crowd's terror. In short, they would force others—Lawson's enemies or outsiders not bound to his cause—to let their emotions be determined by the logic of the market. In the market but not of it, unmotivated by profit, Lawson's followers could both enjoy sympathy's pleasure and avoid sympathy's danger. They could enjoy temporarily giving their feelings over to a fictional character, and they could avoid allowing their feelings to become inseparable from and thus hostage to the feelings of actual others.

Preoccupied with the content of popular writing about economic crises, historians and literary critics have paid little attention to the material effects of financial texts, their capacity to roil markets and jar the commercial world. Lawson's fiction reminds us that novels perform work that is not merely cultural or ideological. They do more than inculcate beliefs, construct identities, legitimate social agendas, or "articulat[e] and propos[e] solutions for the problems that shape a particular historical moment," Jane Tompkins's still-influential description of what works of fiction do.[108] In the stock market, they can also produce, or at least credibly threaten to produce, public catastrophe.

Lawson himself ultimately abandoned his faith in fiction's consequentialness. Indeed, Friday, the Thirteenth represents a turning point in Lawson's conception of the relative effectiveness of writing about the market and writing in the market. Exposition and argument outside the marketplace were crucial, but, as Brownley suggests, reform must come "through [the] machinery of the Stock Exchange" itself (Friday 200). Indeed, six months after he published the novel, Lawson concluded that direct market action was the only way to redeem Wall Street. When Lawson angrily quit his writing crusade after the panic of 1907, declaring that he would devote his time solely to stock gambling, his announcement (and his vituperations against the public) stunned his publishers, who could not grasp how Lawson could reform the marketplace from within, how he would end stock manipulation by manipulating stocks or purify the market by becoming as vicious as his enemies. In a remarkable exchange of letters published in Everybody's, Lawson responded by noting that his market manipulation did far more damage to the System than his reform writing. Only in the marketplace did the System feel pain. "The groove-eyed public may think it was only my exposures that inflicted the damage on the System, but you should see my work in a different spectrum. One of my 'Withdraw Savings, Buy Stock,' 'The Crash is Coming,' 'Sell Stocks, Sell Them Now,' 'Buy Thus and So, Buy It Now, and Upset the System's Coming Coup,' did more real harm after exposure had blazed the way than did any of my pen pictures by themselves. Many, many times have the System's masters said to me: 'We know how to offset the effect of your articles, but your advertisements and market operations play the deuce with our plans,' and they did."[109] Neither novel writing nor speechmaking, nor even legislation, was the answer. Stock promotion and stock speculation were easier, more efficient, and more effective.

Lawson claimed that the crisis of 1907 was caused by his exposures of the System's creation of counterfeit wealth; he maintained that "the people, having been shown how this could be done and had been done, demanded, and are demanding, and will continue to demand, real money for the real money deposited by them."[110] More powerfully than any of his reform writings, the panic exposed the falseness of the System's proclamations and revealed that the nation's finances rested on fictitious accounting and illegitimate credit that, like a house of cards, might easily collapse. For Lawson, however, the crisis of 1907 was insufficiently rigorous as an exposé. Only an apocalyptic panic of his own making could perform the "final exposure." When it came—and "come it must," he declared—"the destruction [would] be more terrible."[111] His final panic would serve as the ultimate agent of truth, an antidote to the market's frenzied fictions.

Chapter 3

Frank Norris and the Mesmeric Sublime

As the oracle gave place to the astrologer, the astrologer
to the alchemist, the alchemist to the witch, the witch to the
magnetizer, the magnetizer to the clairvoyant, the clairvoyant
to the medium, the medium to the mind-reader, upon whom
now shall the spirit of the mind-reader fall?

George Beard, "The Psychology of Spiritism"

In *The Shadow World* (1908), his second novel about his experience as chief investigator for the American Psychical Society in the 1890s, Hamlin Garland describes a medium who plays a piano without touching it. He observes how "invisible fingers seemed to drop to the strings beneath" the closed lid of the instrument and played a tune according to the investigator's request.[1] No scientific law, he says, can account for this "invisible musician" (TSW 138) and her "occult force" (TSW 139). Garland's investigations aimed to shed scientific light on such "supernormal" (TSW 113) activities: Did the invisible hand guide itself? Were mediums—those not discounted as frauds—truly the instruments through which departed spirits communicated and demonstrated their powers? Or was the invisible hand guided by the medium's mind? No skepticism could match the suasive force of directly experiencing such powers, according to Garland: "A man will stand out against Zöllner, Crookes, Lodge, and Myers, discounting all the rest of the great [psychic] investigators, and then crumple up like a caterpillar at the first touch of The Invisible Hand when it comes to him directly" (TSW 103).

Such invisible hands and their uncanny independence from conscious control preoccupied psychic investigators in the decades before the turn of the century. Spectral hands tapping at parlor organs during séances, immaterial hands spelling out messages from the dead on planchette boards, hysterics' hands mechanically scribbling out letters and novels while the patient slept or talked—all these phenomena seemed to be signs and instruments of an agency lurking beneath or beside consciousness. The autonomy of these hands, it was assumed, eerily demonstrated that the hegemony of consciousness was tenuous, that under certain conditions other selves and other energies could usurp control of the mind, that there was a mechanism churning just below consciousness that might sometimes be given over to its own uncanny automatism.

Psychic researchers, of course, were not the only ones at the end of the century preoccupied with invisible hands and their sovereign behavior, for political economists and financial writers were also trying, as they had for over a century, to fathom the mysterious movements of the invisible hand of the marketplace, to read the inscrutable, possibly divine, agency behind the force apparently coordinating the manifold, often contradictory, desires and decisions of market participants. Like psychic investigators, late nineteenth-century American economic observers studied abnormal behavior—crises and convulsions and epidemics, moments when self-regulation manifestly failed, when the seemingly latent automatism of the market ran out of control. And they studied moments when the invisible hand, as in Garland's novel, became suddenly visible and stunned them. Indeed, the preoccupations of economic and psychic researchers converged at the turn of the century. Many financial writers turned to the study of hypnotism, hysteria, and second selves to make sense of financial manias and panics. Relying on the findings of crowd psychologists, these economists considered the extraordinary emulativeness of investors and businessmen in a crisis to be the effect of mass hypnotism; when a panic occurred, that emulativeness became a kind of hysteria. The market was an aggregation of minds, and in panics, driven by the consensus of investors, it acted like a single mind. The second self of the market, psychologists claimed, like that of the entranced medium or hysteric, came forth pathologically and expressed itself uncontrollably.

In his best-selling novel *The Pit* (1903), the story of a Chicago speculator who attempts to corner the wheat market and ultimately "crumple[s]," like Garland's psychic investigators, under the awesome, unmediated touch of the invisible hand, Frank Norris, like psychologists and economists, turned to the New Psychology—the clinical study of

entrancement, hysteria, and second selves—to comprehend and represent financial panic.[2] In this novel, panic threatens the psychic autonomy of the artist in two related ways, twin features of what I call the
mesmeric sublime: first, market panic invites but defies comprehension and literary representation; and, second, the pressures of the
speculative marketplace, confounded in The Pit with hypnotic emulation, disintegrate the boundaries that distinguish and protect the mind
from the market.[3]

My analysis of The Pit takes a few turns that might be helpful to map
out in advance. In short, Norris links the two central symbols of the
novel, the wheat market and the musical organ owned by Curtis Jadwin, the speculator hero. Norris figures both of these as aesthetic
machines inviting but ultimately repudiating Jadwin's control. Jadwin's relation to both machines enacts and complicates the relation
between the ideal novelist and his text that Norris posits in his critical
writing. This artist fable, I argue, doubles as a mesmerist tale; Norris,
drawing on contemporary accounts linking the market, the mind, and
mechanical automata, figures Jadwin as a hypnotist and the market as
his mesmerized subject. More remarkably, he shows how both Jadwin
and the market become hystericized as a result of Jadwin's manipulations; Jadwin's mind and the wheat market, like Jadwin's organ and
the ideal novelist's text, become ungovernable machines. This narrative—the hypnotist fatefully identifying with his medium, the speculator giving himself over to the runaway automatism and semiotic excess of the panicky market—offers an extraordinary expression of the
sublime, one that connects the world of finance, the new discipline of
clinical psychopathology, and popular mesmeric romances. Norris's
representation of the sublime, I argue, registers his fascination and
uneasiness with new, proliferating forms of economic imitation and
identification at the turn of the century, the purest instances of which
featured hysterics mimicking other hysterics in hospital wards and
speculators mimicking other speculators during market panics. Indeed, Norris's notion of the sublime aligns him with contemporary
sociologists and crowd psychologists who studied how mass suggestion and emulation threatened the idea of a sovereign self, the self-
determining subject of classical political economy. Linking Norris's

fixation on processes and forms of figuration (such as his equations of organs, markets, minds, machines, mediums, and novels) to his fascination with theatricalization, I conclude by suggesting that the image of the theater offers Norris and his readers a way to circumvent the hazards of the sublime.

This chapter extends the analysis of market emulation I began in chapter 2. There I analyzed how Thomas Lawson's novel, *Friday, the Thirteenth* (1907), produced forms of sentimental identification among his readers that united them into a stock market army; this army, when called upon, was supposed to unloose an epidemic of fear among the nation's shareholders that would cause a catastrophic financial panic. In my analysis of *Friday, the Thirteenth* and its intended effect, I focused on market "sympathy," a term routinely employed by economists and crowd psychologists at the end of the nineteenth century who studied financial crises. Turning now to *The Pit*, the second novel in Norris's uncompleted trilogy about the U.S. wheat trade, I focus on sympathy's scientific cousins, hypnotism and hysteria, cognate forms of psychic identification. Here, again, I am interested in forms of mental contagion that bind investors to each other and bind readers (and writers) to texts. However, rather than focusing on the political and economic service that imitation in the market performs, I train attention on the psychological threat that it poses (or is seen to pose) to individuals and the notion of an individuated or sovereign self. And rather than focusing on the social effects of reading in the market, I examine the psychological effects of reading the market itself, particularly when it violently defies interpretation.

The Hands on the Board

Norris sketched the constituent features of the mesmeric sublime in "Inside an Organ" (1897), an apprentice piece for a San Francisco weekly in which he describes his encounter with a huge, new pipe organ at a local church. From the start, Norris is awed by the organ's magnificence. A "great engine of music," it unleashes a "tempest of sound that roars through the church till the windows quiver."[4]

Drawn throughout his fiction to spectacles of influence, Norris is here led into "the very heart of the organ itself, in the midst of all those myriad of shouting, clamoring pipes." Trying to take it all in, he is taken in, literally: entering through a little door in the side of the organ's great case, sliding down a narrow passage, and finally climbing a ladder in the darkness of the machine's interior (and all the while deafened by a sound like "the noise of machinery"), he ascends to the solo box, "the center and heart of the organ, its very vitals." There, for a moment, he is witness to the mechanism producing the effects. His gaze offers a spectatorial mastery—he stands "high up in this tiny swell-box" with a prospect over the organ's mechanism. At the same time, he sees only secondary and tertiary signs of the organ's musical power, the half-hidden movements of indicators, the opening and closing of valves. As he lingers, the machine (as well as the rhetoric he uses to comprehend it) becomes more grandiose, and Norris's advantage, his sight *over* the machine, dissolves under its emerging magnitudes. Amid "a world of pipes," he discerns that he is dwarfed by one "as large as a liner's smokestack."

The musical effect of the organ miniaturizes him and finally, climactically, overwhelms his powers of representation: "There was no 'tune' that one could distinguish. . . . It was just sound, sound, sound—waves upon waves of it, sound that you could feel thrilling the air about you. . . . To be here, here high up in this tiny swell-box, alone with this thundering monster, struck one with a feeling of awe, of positive, downright fear—the intuitive fear of all things huge. . . . It was the thunder of artillery . . . the prolonged crashing of a Niagara, terrific beyond words." Norris's experience of the organ offers an exemplary expression of the sublime: the terror, the inability of the single mind to master and recuperate such sensory excess in language, the engulfment and absorption, the contagion of rhetorical effects. It is also a typically Norrisean figuration. The sublime object here is literally an art machine. As his characters often do, Norris stands inarticulate before the production of aesthetic effects. This sublime encounter is also, crucially, an entrancing one. Once the great rush of sound subsides, Norris feels "as if [he is] recovering from a trance."

We are to understand Norris's fixation on the organ, his subjection to the machine's automatism, and the sonic vertigo all as features of entrancement.

I have described Norris's visit to the organ in some detail because he clearly had it in mind when he wrote The Pit. In the novel, he uses key images and exact phrases from "Inside an Organ" to describe the wheat market, and one of The Pit's central symbols is Jadwin's mammoth mechanical organ, which first appears in chapter 7, when Laura, Jadwin's wife, allows Corthell, an artist, to play the instrument for her. Laura is "transfixed, all but transported," as the organ overwhelms her with "resistless power" and leaves her "quivering and breathless."[5] It is a revelatory experience. Under the spell of the music, Laura "felt all at once as though a whole new world were opened to her. She stood on Pisgah" (P 221). As the music subsides, she murmurs that it is "wonderful, wonderful. . . . like a new language—no, it is like new thoughts, too fine for language" (P 222).

We are meant to contrast Laura's passive subjection to the organ with Jadwin's aggressive subjection of the other great signifying board of the novel, the Chicago Board of Trade. Only a few pages after the organ scene, Jadwin experiences his own epiphany when he discerns that he can corner the world wheat market. In a scene echoing the beginning of Faust (Laura and Jadwin meet at a performance of Gounod's Faust), Jadwin realizes that "the event which all those past eleven months had been preparing was suddenly consummated, suddenly stood revealed, as though a veil had been ripped asunder, as though an explosion had crashed through the air upon them, deafening, blinding" (P 235).[6]

The juxtaposition of epiphanies highlights two basic postures that, for Norris, the individual can take toward the sublime. Whereas Laura reclines vulnerable and mute before the organ, overwhelmed and enthralled, and whereas she delights in being carried away by the music and in suffering its enormity, Jadwin actively engages and, for a time, dominates the market. Like romantic theorists of the sublime before him, Norris understands both kinds of engagement, the stupefaction and the countervailing aggression, as aesthetic responses. Jadwin brings the market under his control so that it is responsive, like the organ, to his lightest touch. Even when he stands before the market "terrified" (P 187) (as Laura is before the organ) or when he realizes that he is up against "the Wheat," which is "like a tidal wave . . . rising, rising . . . huge beyond possibility of control" (P 326–27), or when at the novel's end "something, some infinite immeasurable power, onrushing in its eternal courses, [shakes] the Pit in its grasp" and "deafen[s] the ears, blind[s] the eyes, dull[s] and numb[s] the mind, with its roar, with the chaff and dust of its whirlwind passage, with the stupefying sense of its power" (P 339)—when, in short, he suffers the possibility of annihilation—Jadwin charges into the "thick of the confusion" and tries to assume "direct, personal" control of this colossal mechanism (P 343).

Norris signals the fate of Jadwin's bid to master the market by focusing our attention on Jadwin's hands. In the same way that Laura's subjection to the organ music is initiated by her lingering, enchanted gaze at Corthell's "long, slim hands" on the keyboard (P 219), Jadwin's corner is inaugurated by his recognition that he can play and ply the Board of Trade with his hand. Viewing the market as a vast, engulfing maelstrom, Jadwin wonders if "the great Result which was at last to issue forth from all this turmoil was not yet achieved. Would it refuse to come until *a master hand*, all powerful, all daring, gripped the levers of the sluice gates that controlled the crashing waters of the Pit?" (P 228, my emphasis). Jadwin makes this "master hand" his own. He gains control of the world's wheat supply and becomes "as completely master of the market as of his own right hand" (P 302), which he uses to dictate wheat prices: "His hand was upon the indicator of the wheat dial of the Board of Trade, and he moved it through as many or as few of the degrees of the circle as he chose" (P 291). Indeed, during his brief apotheosis, Jadwin's hand and the market's hand become indistinguishable, for this "indicator" is a "marking hand" that moves with the price of wheat, "fluctuating with the changes made in the Pit" (P 82–83).

Despite Jadwin's power, what preoccupies Norris in the novel is the *failure* of the corner, which is represented in the final panic scene by Jadwin's losing control of his hands. Having at last attained the security of a monopoly, Jadwin becomes dizzy and suffers "vertigoes and strange, inexplicable qualms" (P 305). His "body felt strange and unfamiliar to him. It seemed to have no weight, and at times his hands would appear to swell swiftly to the size of mammoth boxing-gloves, so that he must rub them together to feel that they were his own" (P 306). Jadwin's anesthesia, the dispossession of his hands, signals a re-possession of the market by the hand that normally determines how the wheat moves and how this movement expresses itself in price quotations: the invisible hand of supply and demand, operating through the aggregate choices of countless consumers, farmers, and traders. In the same way that the adultery plot in the novel concerns the battle for the hand of Laura, pitting Corthell's magnetically charged fingertips against Jadwin's imperial grasp, the market plot ultimately concerns the battle for the hand of the price dial, pitting Jadwin's spectacularly visible hand against the resistless invisible hand of the market. Jadwin loses the battle: "For months, he had, by the might of his single arm, held [the Wheat] back; but now it rose [and] . . . broke upon him" (P 343). In the climactic panic, Jadwin goes mad, falling to and literally into the wheat pit.

Throughout the novel, Norris figures the market as a mechanism through which nature and its laws speak. They express themselves in wheat prices, and these prices, in turn, become legible in the movements of the mechanical hand above the trading floor. Jadwin stands before this machine, discovers its hidden principles, and, for a time, makes it signify according to his singular design. Inevitably, Jadwin's hand surrenders control of and is finally surrendered to this machinery. A similar coincidence of control and abdication is enacted by Jadwin's organ. A mechanical attachment allows the organ to play itself or be played manually. When Jadwin shows his business partner his organ, he says, "Look at this organ here. . . . Here's the thing I like to play with" (P 177). But he really does not play with it at all, for it produces music mechanically by itself while Jadwin desultorily places his fingers on the keys and eyes the moving stops and the sliding strip of paper.

The organ stands as a figure for the wheat market. Its own mechanism functions like the "cogs and wheels of the whole great machine of business" (P 168). Both the organ and the market's latent machinery are activated by Jadwin and for a time, at least, move in perfect concert with his imperial hand. Like the market that Jadwin believes will "go . . . of itself" wherever he wills (P 304), the organ is subject to a mechanical determinism that, until the panic in the end, perfectly coincides with Jadwin's manipulation.

That Jadwin's hand stands as a figure for a writer's hand seems clear enough from Norris's descriptions elsewhere of the novelist and his task.[7] In "The Mechanics of Fiction," for example, he describes the novel as a machine (a train that literally transports the reader) and the novelist as an engineer who understands and harnesses its mechanism. The writer painstakingly employs a "system of fiction-mechanics" to build up narrative tension.[8] Jadwin, who controls not only the "cogs and wheels" of the "great machine" (P 168) of the market but also sets in motion the "wheels, cogs, [and] disks" of his own mechanical organ, embodies the writer-mechanic who oversees the "wires and wheels and cogs and springs" ("Mechanics" 1163) that move the novel forward.[9] (Adam Smith, to extend this series of mechanical figurations, took the trope of the invisible hand from a description of the theater by Bernard de Fontenelle that bears obvious relevance to The Pit; the trope refers to the "Engineer in the Pit" of the theater, who, invisible to the audience, manipulates the "Wheels and Springs" of the stage's machinery.)[10]

In Norris's account of the mechanics of fiction, the writer-engineer cannot finally control the latent mechanism of the signifying machine. The novelist's most significant act, for Norris, is a release of control. To achieve the stunning effect he seeks from his narrative, the novelist must at some point let go of "the brake to permit for one instant the entire machinery to labor, full steam, ahead" ("Mechanics" 1161). The success of the novelist depends on his abdicating authorial agency and giving the machine over to its own automatism.

Fascinated by this exchange and conflation of agency, Norris was interested in those instances when the artist activated the latent powers of the signifying machine. He was interested, more exactly, in those precise moments when the artist's hand quite literally held the machine, when his fingertips lingered on keyboards or price dials or brake levers and, through a manipulation that was at once a mastery and a capitulation, loosed the machine and its significations from his control. The panic that concludes The Pit is that kind of release.

Mesmerizing the Market

Such a release also constitutes what clinical psychologists in the 1890s referred to as hysterical "automania," the mind's surrender to its own latent machinery, a widely recognized consequence of hypnosis. As I have observed, Norris's pairing of Corthell's and Jadwin's hands at their respective boards invites us to read Jadwin as an artist and the market plot as an artist fable. It also suggests, I want to argue now, that the market narrative is a hypnotism tale—for Corthell is a mesmerist. Norris modeled him after Emile Gallé, a major spokesman for the identity of art and hypnotism at the turn of the century, and also after Svengali, the mesmerizing musician and villainous seducer in George Du Maurier's runaway hit novel, Trilby (1894).[11]

Norris develops the analogy between hysteria and market panic explicitly. As several critics have observed, he pairs the psychic fracture of Jadwin's wife and the climactic fracture of the market.[12] Laura suffers from nerves "so torn and disordered" that "a kind of hysteria animated and directed her impulses, her words, and actions" (P 351). Her breakdown follows the prevailing clinical model of hysteria: she is possessed by a "second self," a "strange personality" conjured from her "troublous, unknown deeps" (P 121). The novel, echoing numerous popularly published cases of hysteria and multiple personality, figures this second self as reckless, emotional, and suggestible.[13] Awakened by Corthell's intimacies, it allows her, for a few dizzying moments toward the end of the book, to be seduced and lured away from her marriage. To preserve her marriage and her sanity, she recognizes she must bring to order these "capricious and riotous, elusive and dazzling" (P 273) impulses that "whip" (P 357) her on in Corthell's presence. For a time, she succeeds, even at the cost of paralyzing her psyche, for Laura "had staked everything upon a hazard, and, blind to all else, was keeping back emotion with all her strength, while she watched and waited for the issue" (P 348).

Such descriptions of control and containment connect Laura's private efforts to master the tumultuously anarchic caprices of her second self with Jadwin's public efforts to master the equally tumultuous and anarchic caprices of the market. Like Laura, Jadwin is afraid to "let go a finger" (P 331) for fear that his corner will dissolve and the wheat will burst from his grasp. His control, like hers, leads to an unnatural paralysis. Like her, most obviously, he climactically "stakes everything upon a hazard," withholding the wheat with all his financial strength just as she, on the verge of a similar surrender and fracture, tries to keep her emotions from bursting forth.

The comparison between Laura's breakdown and Jadwin's failure to control the world's wheat is remarkable not because it likens market volatility and a woman's rebelliousness or moodiness (such an analogy was traditional enough), but, rather, because it equates the etiology of hysteria and the mechanics of the market's rupture. Both Laura's hysteria and the market's panic result from hypnotization. That hypnosis could unchain the subliminal self from conscious control and unlock "the closely bound chamber of hysterical crises" was well established by the turn of the century.[14] Whether hysteria was "a disease of the hypnotic stratum," as some argued, or, conversely, hypnotism was an "artificial hysteria," both phenomena represented a splitting off of consciousness, a surrender to the subliminal mind's own automatistic imperatives.[15]

Corthell's mesmeric manipulations provoke Laura's hysterical irruptions just as Jadwin's manual passes over the Board of Trade provoke the wheat market's eruption in the climactic panic. The pairing of these narratives registers a particular confluence of the sciences of the mind and of the market late in the nineteenth century.[16] In the 1890s, the hypnotic rapport between doctor and patient—or mesmerist and subject—became a model for the mental contagion that drove people's actions in crowds. A suggestible mind such as Laura's, what the psychologist Hippolyte Bernheim called a "hystérisable" mind, or a mind that could be made hysterical through hypnosis, became not only the model for minds of individuals in groups but also a synecdoche for the collective mind of the crowd itself.[17] Crowd behavior, especially the behavior of investors and traders in a single market, was "individual hypnotization written large."[18]

For most of the nineteenth century, economic observers, fiction writers, ministers, and investors struggled to find a vocabulary that made sense of financial panics and mitigated the fears that panics produced and that produced panics.[19] Financial crises periodically wrecked the nation's economy, but they were protean, anarchic, and contradictory phenomena that often seemed to come from nowhere and dragged unsuspecting individuals and communities along their ruinous, unpredictable course. Uncannily, they came during periods of optimism and prosperity, and, from within and without, they seemed awesome and perplexing. Norris followed the economists at the end of the century who understood that "the malady of commercial crises is not, in essence, a matter of the *purse* but of the *mind*."[20] Panics, more frequent and contagious than ever before, were "psychical phenomena" explicable only in light of the new set of "psychological facts" furnished by the new science of hypnotic suggestion and second selves.[21]

The New Psychology, as this science was called, was linked to late nineteenth-century conceptions of financial crises by the notion of suggestibility and the phenomena with which suggestion was consistently associated: imitation and contagion. Imitation, by its nature, spread, and hypnotic suggestion was then recognized as the cause of the hysterical epidemics that passed in waves through the public. As Boris Sidis noted in *The Psychology of Suggestion* (1897), "If, now, something striking fixes the attention of the public—a brilliant campaign, a glittering holy image, or a bright 'silver dollar'—the subwaking social self, the demon of the demos, emerges, and society is agitated with crazes, manias, panics, and mental plagues of all sorts" (PS 311). Gustave Le Bon, Gabriel Tarde, and other early crowd psychologists had discussed the mobbish behavior of the market, and Sidis devoted a full chapter to financial "crazes" in his *Psychology of Suggestion*. Whether engineered by prescient manipulators like Jadwin, triggered by some unwonted event, or set off by rumor, psychologists understood the pandemic emulation in the marketplace to be an example and effect of mass hypnosis. "The sympathetic influence we are considering is doubtless allied to hypnotic influence," observed the economics professor Edward Jones in *Economic Crises* (1900).[22] "Both in panics and in speculative manias we observe again a species of hypnotization," noted G. T. W. Patrick, the author of "The Psychology of Crazes."[23] The Board of Trade was a vast hypnotic arena.

Panics were the pathological consequence of hypnotization. Investors in crises, as Norris's panic scenes illustrate, showed the "impulsiveness, irritability, incapacity to reason, the absences of judgment and of the critical spirit, the exaggeration of the sentiments" of the hysterical mob.[24] Suggestibility ran amok: "Every one influences and is influenced in his turn; every one suggests and is suggested to" until "every soul is dizzied and every person is stunned" (PS 303). The hysterical mind and the market in crisis shared the same anarchic manifestations: "violent fluctuations," abnormal "convulsions," unnatural dependencies, a runaway automatism, and a catastrophic rupture of reference. Like the second self unmoored by its unwonted identifications, the market in crisis seemed "extremely unstable, ephemeral, shadowy in its outlines, tend[ing] to subside, . . . becom[ing] amorphous . . . [and] rising to the surface" (PS 246).

Only a few critics have considered the relevance of entrancement and psychic powers to Norris's works—almost always in an effort to explain the mysticism of the character Vanamee in The Octopus.[25] None has noted The Pit's critical place in a long, popular tradition of mesmeric romances. But Jadwin is a mesmerist. Norris pairs Corthell's entrancing influence on Laura and Jadwin's magnetic influence over the wheat market. Like Corthell, Jadwin controls the "tremendous forces latent" in his medium, the Chicago wheat market (P 247). Like Corthell's fingertips, from which seems to flow "invisible ether" (P 219) when he plays the organ for Laura, Jadwin's hand registers and exerts an occult influence. His "impassive hand on the great dial" (P 231) charges the Pit with "a veritable electricity" (P 236). Under its "unseen and mysterious" control (P 236), the price of wheat rises, "resistless" (P 302). His hand acts as an "invisible, inexplicable magnet" (P 285).

Norris's contemporaries routinely equated the speculative titan and the mesmerist. This pairing became something of a cliché among muckraking novelists who sought to expose the unregulated power of Wall Street banking barons between 1900 and 1910. (Alfred Crozier's

The Magnet (1908), for example, literalized the "inscrutable and myste-rious" hypnotic power of Wall Street titans in its title and throughout its text.)[26] The identification of the hypnotist and the businessman also preoccupied the preachers of New Thought, Emerson's disciples in the last decades of the century (several of whose works Norris re-viewed as a journalist). Offering a popular brand of Swedenborgian business psychology, these "success writers" announced that the mind could control the forces of nature and that spiritualism and economics were not opposites but partners, changeling twins in the heart of the marketplace.[27] Although New Thought was predominantly associated with the power of the mind to cure bodily illness (it had its origins in mesmeric medicine and faith-healing in the 1860s), it devel-oped a set of beliefs about the power of the individual to think, will, and utter into being economic prosperity and abundance. In the 1890s, mingling spiritualism, psychic research, and political economics, New Thought re-costumed Emerson's Seer, even Whitman's yawping bard, as a hypnotist and businessman and placed him squarely in the mar-ketplace. Wall Street operators functioned as mesmerists, their "supe-rior element of thought" acting "in the domain of finance on other minds far and near."[28] Success writers studied men like Jadwin and the influence they communicated. The author of one success book, *Busi-ness Power*, even quotes *The Pit*.[29] Jadwin's "magnetic" influence over the market and the speculators, his apotheosis into a medium of mar-ket laws, and his overweening ambition to corner the market and halt the flow of money and wheat all enact central concerns of the New Thought economics.

New Thought is important to our understanding of *The Pit* not only because it can be read as a New Thought novel, drawn to and critical of the movement's idealist excesses, but also because New Thought writers elaborated what is at stake in the novel's fusion of the mes-meric and the economic sublime: the integrity of the boundaries dis-tinguishing and protecting the mind from the market. New Thought would have understood Jadwin's magnetism as a kind of mediumship, and his access to a fund of psychic power as a kind of "intake" or afflatus. This "self-surrender" (one of New Thought's key phrases) registers the psychological and economic paradox of *The Pit*: To succeed in the market, one must, through force of will and concentration, become divine, but to become divine makes one a passive conduit of natural laws and forces, an instrument, not an actor. One must forcibly gain access to transcendental knowledge only to regulate oneself in strict accordance with the laws it reveals. Freedom, Emerson's disciples repeatedly observed, meant obedience. In various forms, this paradox stood at the center of novels like Trilby and attacks against mediumship in its various guises throughout the last half of the century: To gain influence, the medium needed to surrender. Control, in the final analysis, meant submission. By subjecting themselves to higher powers, mesmeric subjects, psychic mediums, mind-cure patients, mystics, and idealists all risked being seduced or swallowed.[30]

Fears of mediums' dependence, endemic to political republicanism and economic liberalism (indeed, long-standing themes of the nation's literature), were matched by fears that mediums, whether opening themselves to Swedenborgian "currents of being," New Thought's "divine supply," healers' incantations, or mesmerists' plying hands, would yield to their own dangerous impulses and desires. "Suggestion from without," observed one psychologist, "must for the most part resolve itself into suggestion from within."[31] Mediumship, if risking enslavement to some higher force, also risked self-absorption, monomania, and anarchy. Laura's affair with Corthell and Jadwin's seduction by the market both demonstrate this confusion of spiritual ends and riotous democracy (and, in Laura's case, perhaps, an incipient feminism), for both characters, in receiving revelatory and magnetic powers, turn out to be surrendering to the anarchic guidance of their second selves. Both are unable to maintain a grip on control itself, to sustain, as it were, a corner over their latent and reckless impulses. To relax, for both characters, invites dissipation, hysteria, and panic.

Jadwin surrenders to the automatism not only of the market but also of his own mind. Norris signals this equation by identifying the market and Jadwin's mind in the figure of the mechanical organ. The instrument's machinery, the "cogs and wheels of the whole great machine of business" (P 168), and the "cogs and wheels of the mind" (P 283) are figures for each other. They are all machines that run under and beyond his control. And at the end of the novel, in the climactic panic, these machine figures become fatefully indistinguishable: "Something snapped in [Jadwin's] brain. . . . The strange qualms and tiny nervous paroxysms of the last few months all at once culminated in some indefinite, indefinable crisis, and the wheels and cogs of all activities save one lapsed away and ceased. Only one function of the complicated machine persisted; but it moved with a rapidity of vibration that seemed to be tearing the tissues of being to shreds, while its rhythm beat out the old and terrible cadence: 'Wheat—wheat—wheat, wheat—wheat—wheat' " (P 343). The compulsions of the wheat market, now in his mind and inseparable from his mind, tear his "being to shreds" (P 343).

In various forms, the individual's possession by mechanistic and deterministic forces within and without the self preoccupied American naturalist writers in the 1890s. However, Norris took his description of Jadwin's psychic identification with the market from medical and popular accounts of entrancement and its hazards. These accounts circulated widely during Norris's career, including his student days in Paris, when the French infatuation with Jean-Martin Charcot's research was most acute; his apprentice years, when he studied hypnotism and the New Psychology for the *Wave*; and his years of friendship with Hamlin Garland, John O'Hara Cosgrave, Gelett Burgess, and Bruce Porter, all of whom were fascinated by, even professionally devoted to, psychic research, New Thought, and hypnotism.[32]

The equation between Jadwin's mind and musical organ exploits an image routinely used by these investigators. As one New Thought writer put it, the mind was "the central organ" of man's power.[33] Jadwin's great mechanical organ is itself a psychic instrument "through which mind plays," both subject to and indifferent to the player's control, its two configurations endowed, like the dual mind, "with separate and distinct attributes and powers."[34] The self-playing attachment of the organ embodies what Frederic Myers broadly called "automatisms," a term covering the range of subliminal "emergences" into ordinary life, "messages" from the subliminal to the waking self. "We set the machine to work, and it goes itself," wrote another psychologist, describing a piano player who plays his scales and roulades while reading a book: "Such actions are performed automatically."[35]

Here and elsewhere in the writings of the New Psychologists, the subliminal mind is viewed as a self-playing machine.

Such a figuration helps us see that Jadwin is entranced in the market. Indeed, Jadwin is a textbook example of a man in the higher phases of trance, a man in whom "a new and superior personality comes to the surface and takes control."[36] At first, surrendering to this second self gives him his uncanny influence: "Now he had discovered that there were in him powers, capabilities, and a breadth of grasp hitherto unsuspected. He could control the Chicago wheat market" (P 247). The "unspeakable crumbling and disintegrating of his faculties" (P 306), however, registers what the New Psychology understood to be the potential danger of entrancement: an instrument of titanic powers, Jadwin is ultimately only their instrument. Usurpation by subliminal powers leads to nervous disorder, exhaustion, delusions, amnesia, numbness, and tingling, the litany of "strange symptoms" (P 305) that the speculator suffers by the end of the novel. Obsessions such as Jadwin's corner, signs of the genius's powers of concentration, also signal the telltale irruptions of hysteria.

The Mesmeric Sublime

Jadwin becomes hysterical in the market, but, more significantly, he becomes hystericized by the market. Jadwin suffers the fate of the magnetizing impresario who falls under the influence of his medium and cannot resist her hysterical rebellion. The market is not simply a *mechanical* medium but also a mechanical *medium*, and like trance mediums in mesmeric romances since the 1850s, the wheat market falls ruinously subject to what Henry James (in his own mesmeric romance, *The Bostonians*) called the "eloquence of the hand."[37] Like the market in Norris's novel, trance mediums were described as organs, "marvellous machine[s]" subject "to the will and the suggestion of the operator."[38] The most famous mesmerizing medium of the period, Trilby, was "a singing-machine—an organ to play upon."[39]

The market panic is the moment when this medium resists the hegemony of the artist-mesmerist and speaks anarchically, excessively, and monstrously. When the wheat breaks from Jadwin's control, the hand on the price dial rocks "back and forth, like the mast of a ship caught in a monsoon" (P 339). No one on the trading floor can discern or even guess the price of wheat since it fluctuates so wildly from moment to moment. It is chaotic and disorienting for the traders in the Pit, incomprehensible for the spectators crowded in theater chairs in the gallery, and overwhelming for the official reporter whose job it is to record and make sense of the scene. Jadwin breaks down before this unwritable excess.

The Pit's emphasis on the fate of the sign and on the hero's attempt to bring the confusion of mediumistic expression to order suggests that it is less Svengali and other mesmeric villains against whom Norris means for us to read his hero than the most famous clinical disciplinarian of hysteria's symptomology, the great French doctor Charcot. Jadwin's campaign to conjure forth and control the market's mediumistic powers, his effort to harness its sublime significations, finds its most instructive analogue in Charcot's efforts—like Jadwin's, they are sensational, theatrical, and masculinizing—to bring the famously protean symptoms and undeterminable causes of hysteria to nosographic order. (Indeed, it is only a few pages after the market's spectacular and catastrophic rupture of reference that Laura wonders whether she is possessed by hysteria [P 351].) Hysteria was famous for precisely this refractoriness. As Pierre Janet, Sigmund Freud, and others emphasized, hysteria was a malady of representation, its predominating symptom being the variability of its expressions, its superabundance of signs without any determinable etiology, foundation, or reference.[40]

What preoccupies Norris, however, is the possibility that such supervisory power and hermeneutic mastery—Charcot's, Svengali's, Jadwin's—might easily give way to seduction, subjection, and finally mimicry. The Pit records how the satisfactions of such detachment and control are constantly threatened by the epidemic or colonizing nature of suggestion itself: if one relaxed, one might become subject to and identical with the very thing one's manipulation and gaze was meant to withstand. Despite its celebration of Jadwin's aesthetic bravado, the novel emphasizes his capitulation to the monstrous automatism he has activated.

"The Mechanics of Fiction" adumbrates precisely this sublime subjection and contagion in its description of the reader struck with awe by the runaway automatism of the text. Norris figures the rhetorical climax of the "master-work of fiction" as a spectacular ejaculatory release into the reader's face: "The action [of the novel] is speeding faster and faster, the complication tightening and straining to the breaking point and then at last a 'motif' that has been in preparation ever since the first paragraph of the first chapter of the novel suddenly comes to a head, and in a twinkling the complication is solved with all the violence of an explosion and the catastrophe, the climax, the pivotal event fairly leaps from the pages with a rush of action that leaves you stunned, breathless and overwhelmed with the sheer power of its presentation" ("Mechanics" 1163). The sight of the text's giving-over to its own erotic imperative produces a similar sexual surrender in the reader. The text works to "rouse the flaccid interest of the reader" ("Mechanics" 1163), and it fulfills its task by bringing itself sensationally to orgasm. The oppressing automatism of the text incites a mimicking response in the reader.

The ravished reader of Norris's machine text becomes the speculator-artist in The Pit. If Jadwin, at the height of his power, represents the writer-engineer described in "The Mechanics of Fiction," then he becomes, during the panic, that fiction's hystericized reader. Jadwin suffers the reader's precise fate when, just as it breaks from his control, the "undiked Ocean of the Wheat" strikes him "fairly in the face" (P 343). The coming of the wheat reprises the engorgement and ejaculation of the successful work of fiction. The wheat "towered, towered, hung poised for an instant, and then, with a thunder as of the grind and crash of chaotic worlds, broke upon him" (P 343).

Jadwin's subjection, unlike the reader's, is ruinous, and we might explain the difference by noting that the specular contagion of homoerotic desire in "The Mechanics of Fiction" avoids the oedipal entanglements of actually penetrating and spilling one's seed in the maternal market or, at the very least, sacrificing one's ascetic reserve of vital seed to the sexualized and feminine body of the wheat market.[41] However, the more obvious difference is that the novel, unlike the essay, specifically studies the dangers of sublime subjection, the psychic hazards of coming face to face with a hysterical transcendence, a mediumship so given over to itself that its utterance is indecipherable, oppressive, and finally contagious. In *The Pit*, the psychic identification with the sublime object's automatism proves to be catastrophic.

Mimetic Desire

Jadwin's psychic crisis—figured variously in the novel as hysteria, engulfment, seduction, and dissolution—fits easily enough with the romantic experience of the sublime. Jadwin tries to appropriate and contain an excess—semiotic, feminine, natural, mechanical, even religious—that defies and overwhelms his powers of representation. This surfeit possesses, terrifies, and finally maddens him. *The Pit* also offers American naturalist fiction's clearest expression of an economic sublime, the idea that commercial events or operations, because of their speed, complexity, or abstractness, terrify and oppress the individual who witnesses them.[42] I have been suggesting that Norris's novel, linking the subliminal and the sublime, also elaborates a mesmeric or hysterical sublime, the entranced mind's fatal surrender to automatistic forces at once within and without.

The novel enacts the remarkable convergence of these various traditions in order to study the vulnerability of a certain notion of selfhood to pressures specific to late nineteenth-century economic culture. This threat, adumbrated in the novel's theater scenes and in Laura's subjection to the mesmerist, and represented most explicitly in the panic scenes, is that the self finds itself given over to mimesis, not only of an other but also of the countless others whom this other mimes. In market panics and hysterical crises—as in Jadwin's and Laura's plots, particularly as they unfold in the Board of Trade and the theater—self-identity becomes completely up for grabs since one's own beliefs and desires become wholly confounded with the beliefs and desires of others. These scenes and narratives provide the paradigmatic instances of pandemic emulation: the desires that forge the self from without are themselves prolific, unanchored, and evanescent.[43]

The New Psychology's most damning evidence against the idea of a coherent and autonomous self was the discovery that the self's own motives, beliefs, and desires were not always spontaneous but, rather, imitative. Hypnotized subjects patently mimicked the hypnotist, "appropriat[ing] the latter's thought, . . . feel[ing] everything the experimenter desires him to feel, obey[ing] every wish and every caprice the experimenter entertains";[44] and hysterics consistently emulated the behaviors and desires of those around them. Hysterics had an "irresistable passion for imitation," an "impulse to mimicry," their mimeticism becoming more thorough the more deeply they were entranced.[45] Scientific accounts routinely characterized hysteria itself as nothing more than a constellation of simulated symptoms. For many writers, the psychology of imitation seemed a more apt description than the psychology of suggestion.

Social critics and social psychologists in the 1890s, seeing hypnotic emulation at work in every aspect of social life, came to regard this mimeticism as an essential aspect of human being and social relations: "We are all born imitators"; "The propensity of man to imitate what is before him is one of the strongest parts of his nature"; "Our faith is faith in some one else's faith, and in the greatest matters this is most the case."[46] Gabriel Tarde's *The Laws of Imitation*—first translated, significantly, for American audiences the same year that *The Pit* appeared—offered the most influential articulation of this psychology in the United States. For Tarde, the idea of an autonomous, spontaneous self was a self-flattering fiction that masked the radical and foundational nature of mimetic desire. "The social like the hypnotic state is only a form of dream, a dream of command and a dream of action," Tarde noted. "Both the somnambulist and the social man are possessed by the illusion that their ideas, all of which have been suggested to them, are spontaneous."[47]

Outside the clinical wards, séances, and performance halls where hypnotists operated, the self's emulative, dependent nature revealed itself most obviously in crowds. And outside the Salpêtrière, Charcot's famous clinic, the pandemic emulation of crowds could be witnessed nowhere more spectacularly than in the speculative marketplace. The opinions that made market values fluctuate "were not formed by reason, but by mimicry."[48] Market sentiment "spread by sympathy and the imitative faculty from one mind to another."[49] A trader, wagering on a rise or decline in the price of wheat, tied his fortune to the crowd's valuations. In panics, when all the objective predictors of market prices became meaningless, a trader could guide his actions only by the actions of others. His economic being became wholly subject to the crowd's self-generating expectations and desires. As among a collection of hysterics, the trader's self-identity became conjured entirely from without, a simulacrum among simulacra.

Never had the marketplace been so conducive to psychic contagion. In *Economic Crises*, Edward Jones, citing Sidis, Lombroso, and other crowd psychologists, noted how the rise of the stock and produce exchanges intensified the efficacy of psychic contagion: "The more intimate the association, the more will the common thinking processes be influenced by the sympathetic force."[50] Whether eyeballing each other's bids on the congested trading floors of the nation's exchanges or divining each other's intentions secondhand through price quotations, gossip, and newspaper reports, competitors came in closer contact than ever before, and competitive emulation, accordingly, became more fevered.

The dangers of runaway mimeticism help explain not only Norris's decision to pair a mesmerism plot and a market plot (his choice, even more specifically, to set a mesmeric romance in the marketplace) but also his preoccupation with second selves. *The Pit* demonstrates both the cultural topicality and the ideological effectiveness of the clinical construction of the hidden self as a place to preserve the Self—that is, the sovereign, self-determining subject anchoring classical political economy—against the threats most purely and potently represented in market panics and hysteria. Here I am drawing on the analysis of Jean-Michel Oughourlian, a psychiatrist and collaborator with René Girard, who has read the New Psychology as a defensive metaphysical project committed to hiding the Self's fundamental dependence on and constitution by others' desires. In particular, Oughourlian argues that abnormal psychology's clinical construction of a private, noumenal second self functions to introject "inside" the Self those desires and forces that the Self emulates but that, in fact, operate "outside" it (such spatializations, at least as old as Cartesianism, being part of the obfuscatory logic of the psychology of the subject). Hypnosis, for

Traders pack the floor of the Chicago Board of Trade, circa 1900.
Chicago: Yesterday and Today.

Oughourlian, furnishes the paradigmatic example of such mimeticism, and hysteria the paradigmatic example of the Self's efforts to
misunderstand and displace its subjection.[51]

Oughourlian's analysis helps make sense of the interdependence of
The Pit's psychological narrative and the market plot. It also helps us
understand Norris's peculiar confounding of the machine forces that
beset Jadwin from inside and out. The novel identifies Jadwin's and
Laura's second selves as corollaries to hypnotic entrancement, sometimes the consequence of the characters' self-abandonment and at
other times the cause. We might view them more specifically as ac-
commodations to the dangers of hypnotic emulation, constructions
serving to protect the Self's private ownership of itself—its monopoly
or corner—against forfeiture and dissolution. Hypnosis and hysteria,
in short, are market positions. The major plots of the novel trace
how others' desires become the protagonists' own, but the novel also
shows in its climaxes how the protagonists mistakenly attempt to

transcend mimesis and dependency, Jadwin through his reckless decision to perpetuate his corner and Laura through her facile (and immaculate) "conception" of a "new force that was not herself, somewhere in the inner chambers of her being . . . identity ignoring itself" (P 354–55).[52]

We can read Jadwin's loss of feeling in his hands, the anesthesia that signals the speculator's demise, as an enactment of this dissociation. The fact that he must rub his hands "together to feel that they [are] his own" (P 306) is not only a recognizable symptom of Jadwin's entrancement but more specifically a dramatization and embodiment of his subjection. The hand, earlier a metaphoric visualization and a metonymic replacement of the invisible hand of the market, now appears as a synecdoche for (and, more specifically, a synecdochization of) Jadwin himself, a re-placement of his Self with and within his own body, a restaging of his Self's forfeiture to the market. Like Laura throughout the novel, he spectates on his own Self's performance, here played by his hand. Such theatricalization internalizes the threat of self-abandonment and thus protects Jadwin from facing its full consequences.[53]

Read this way, Jadwin's amnesia after the collapse of his corner ("Something happened. . . . I don't remember" [P 360]) functions as an attempt to make up for the failure of his benumbed hand to obscure the loss of his Self. Amnesia is simply a more desperate strategy to protect his Self's integrity. Unlike anesthesia, it does not render—or rend—the Self's otherness into a manipulable sign. Rather, it preempts any representation at all of the Self's otherness.[54] It allows the Self to be unaware that it ever was dependent. Rather than a consequence of Jadwin's corner, amnesia is its continuation. It preserves the illusion that the Self has always owned itself in its entirety. (The woman caught in the panic in the stairwell of the Board of Trade building who cries, "My arm! oh!—oh, I shall faint" [P 335], thus anticipates Jadwin's own forfeitures on the trading floor.)

Norris symbolizes such displacements in the other self-alienating organ in the novel, the great musical organ with the self-playing attachment in Jadwin's house. I suggested earlier that the organ symbolizes both the market and the mind, each something played on that also plays itself. We can now read the organ more specifically as a figure for the Self divided by the recognition of its own contingency. Played manually, it is like the hypnotic self, capable of acting only in accord with the player's desires. It confirms the autonomy and spontaneity of the player, offering the illusion that the player's Self "owns" the notes and is responsible for their production. The organ performs the Self, representing the Self to itself.

Played mechanically, the organ might appear to repudiate the Self's spontaneity and originality, but in fact it mimics and represents them to the Self. Indeed, the uncanniness of the mechanism is not that it fails to represent the Self, but rather that it represents the Self too perfectly. The machine plays perfectly and thus serves as the model the player strives to copy. The organ, played mechanically, exemplifies the mimetic other not only because the player emulates it, and not only because the player's desires are from the start constituted by this emulation, but also because the mechanical music is itself a pure instance of mimicry—all the machine can do is mime others' playing. In fact, all it can do is mime other machines. The player, in miming the performance of the machine, is at the same time miming all the performances the machine is miming. He is like the speculator in the marketplace whose economic selfhood is constituted by the endless field of others' imitative desires and expectations.

Leaving the Scene: Reading Panic

Norris's interest in dramas of signification explains why *The Pit* is so relentlessly and obviously metaphorical. In the novel, figuration and theatricalization work together. On the one hand, Norris's insistent repetition and elaboration of similes and metonymies (for example, the organ, the whirlpool, the battle, the orchestra) literally enact Norris's preoccupation with figuration, the ways exemplary modern forms, especially the city or the market, are the phenomenal traces, or hieroglyphs, of sublime forces revealed through them. On the other hand, we might read Norris's reliance on such figurative language and symbols as a defensive response to the sublime unrecordability of such forms, especially of the market during its fateful panic, when it defies, within the text, the hero's and the spectators' attempts to bring it under the control of language.

Norris's novel absorbs and relieves us, transfixing us (and also the protagonists) before two magnetic, arresting visual centers—the theater stage and the baffling trading floor—and then dispersing us outward again through metaphorical associations and narrative parallels. The striking immobility at the center of the two pits, literalized not only in the fixedness of eyes there but also in the paralysis of wheat and of crowds congested and panicked at various entrances and exits, is relieved by the mobility of the figurative associations that take us, for example, from the speculator's hand in the Board of Trade to the mesmerist's hand on the keyboard of the organ in Jadwin's home, or from one pit to the other. Such rhetorical displacements shift our attention from the sublime spectacle, move us outward, and provide a familiar language in which to contain, if not comprehend, it. Such a language helps us, and Norris, escape the bafflement of seeing more profound acts of metaphorization performed—for example, by the market itself. Norris's reliance on such insistent similes, symbols, and homologies, I am suggesting, is a defensive, perhaps inevitable, retreat from the kind of blinding revelation Norris so idealizes, a sign of the failure, not the power, of figuration to make sense of the sublime.

The theater offers Norris and his readers a related way of circumventing the hazards of the sublime. We witness the panic not from Jadwin's point of view—he has no point of view, broken as he is by the market's unapprehensible excess—but from Page's, Laura's sister. A secondary character in the novel until this point, she watches the entire panic uncomprehendingly from her theater chair in the spectators' gallery. She cannot "make anything of it at all," but, crucially, she finds it picturesque and "so exciting" (P 349). Page and Jadwin represent alternative ways of confronting the sublime. Jadwin tries to bring the market's sublime surfeit of signs under his imperial control; Page, in contrast, fetishizes the market's incomprehensibility. By witnessing the spectacle through her eyes and hearing her report afterward, we are drawn outward, not only from the trading floor to the gallery and then to Jadwin's house, where she gives her report, and not only outward from the central figure to a peripheral character, but also outward from the signifying machinery of the market to its phenomenal surface.

Our confusion and the dangers that may attend it are relieved, I am suggesting, by Page's blithe confusion. Her name is no accident, then, since she represents the only way to read the unreadable. We read her reading the panic, and we read her reading Jadwin's failure without comprehending it. Page thus stands in, finally, for the pages of Norris's book that must, in the end, fail to comprehend the panic in order to move us forward without our becoming mesmerized.

Chapter 4

Melodrama and the Moral Implications of Financial Panic

> Men do not make panics deliberately; they are
> their unconscious agents.
>
> Charles Albert Collman, *Our Mysterious Panics*

This chapter studies how Upton Sinclair and his Progressive contemporaries attempted to preserve and trace moral agency within modern economic collectivities—market crowds, financial networks, and large corporations—that obscured the source of widespread financial effects. Panics played a central and complicating role in this effort. Taking as my key text *The Moneychangers* (1908), Sinclair's fictional rendering of a banker plot behind the panic of 1907, I analyze financial conspiracy theories and melodrama as means of making moral accountability in the market visible and familiar. Departing from conventional accounts that concentrate on the villainous intentions of insiders, I focus on the ethical dynamics of complicity—the moral risk of outsiders becoming implicated in conspirators' designs. Despite its lurid melodrama, *The Moneychangers* takes up complex questions about the spread and scope of moral responsibility in a financial crisis. How far did accountability extend when designing insiders relied on the actions or resources of outsiders to carry out their plot? Were individuals morally accountable for outcomes they never wished for or predicted, even if their actions directly contributed to them? For Sinclair and his contemporaries, the fate of individuals' moral autonomy and the notion of republican responsibility hung on these questions, for if individuals could not resist becoming party to a financial conspiracy, or recognize that they were doing so, how could they act as virtuous citizens? By contributing to national financial catastrophe even when they most wished to prevent it, how could individuals act as responsible members of the public?

The Panic of 1907 and the Ends of Conspiracy

In early 1906, financial insiders, noting the scarcity of money in Wall Street, nervously wondered whether a major financial panic was about to erupt and wreak havoc on the nation's banks and businesses. The Federal Reserve System and its machinery for mitigating crises did not yet exist, and the current banking system seemed more likely to abet than assuage a shock. Newspaper editors were more sanguine, maintaining that a panic, should it strike, would pass quickly and affect only gamblers in Wall Street. The *Kansas City Journal* went further, arguing that a major panic could not occur, at least while basic economic conditions were sound. The fact that the money shortage had not yet triggered a panic indicated that "the United States is no longer dominated by Wall Street." If a panic came, its cause would have little to do with "New York brokers and speculators."[1]

Panic struck in the fall of 1907, shattering this confidence. Frightened by the sudden collapse of the Knickerbocker Trust, New York's third largest bank, depositors and borrowers formed huge lines at city banks to withdraw their money. New York's banks and, soon, financial institutions in other cities, unable to meet their liabilities, tottered on the brink of ruin. For two weeks, J. P. Morgan, seventy years old and nursing a cold, met one crisis after another, garnering massive loans from the U.S. Treasury and bullying the city's bankers to furnish funds —over $110 million, including the government money—to keep threatened banks afloat. Acting as a one-man central bank, Morgan saved the city of New York from bankruptcy and rescued the stock market, averting a major crash. He finally ended the bank runs and money drain when he sought President Theodore Roosevelt's permission to take over a rival steel company, the Tennessee, Coal, Iron and Railroad Corporation (TCI), claiming that the buyout, although potentially in violation of the Sherman Anti-Trust Act, was necessary to save one last dangerously extended brokerage firm and put an end to Wall Street's financial bleeding. In a decision that prompted two congressional investigations, the president agreed not to intervene, and the panic was over, although an ensuing depression racked banks and industries across the nation.[2]

Crowds outside Morgan's office at Wall and Broad streets during the panic
of 1907. The building to the right is the United States Subtreasury.
Everybody's, January 1908. Courtesy of Brown Brothers.

From start to finish, the crisis, "the worst panic that any city or country has ever known," as Morgan's partner described it to a congressional committee, perplexed and fascinated the public.[3] The incredible failure of the Knickerbocker Trust, occurring at the peak of apparent prosperity; a press announcement put out by Morgan's proxy that invited a run on another major trust, followed by Morgan's rescue of that trust; and especially the president's acquiescence to the solidification of Morgan's steel empire—all of these provoked controversy and begged for explanation. Newspapers and journals at home and overseas obliged, offering varied and contradictory explanations of the panic's cause. Some saw only remote economic conditions to blame. Some focused on the money drain caused by the exuberant, even reckless, capitalization of new industry at home, the shadow side of the recent prosperity. Some focused on the inadequacies of the U.S. banking system; some blamed the jittery public; some blamed Roosevelt's untimely imprecations against "the malefactors of great wealth"; and some blamed the trust companies themselves, repeating insinuations of malfeasance that circulated during the crisis.

The mainstream press lionized Morgan as a savior and patriot. Newspapers enthusiastically described his extraordinary closed-door conferences with the city's leading bankers, his tireless strategizing, and his decisiveness. Most writers acknowledged that the panic represented an extraordinary business opportunity for Morgan, a chance, above all, to pocket a coveted steel rival, yet many accepted the TCI takeover as a fair reward for his herculean efforts on behalf of the public. The press granted Morgan such latitude not only because he possessed the executive genius and personal forcefulness to end the crisis, but also, more importantly, because he presided over the flow of money and credit at a time when no other individual or agency, private or public, rivaled his influence over the nation's financial life. As a congressional investigation of Morgan's "money trust" discovered in 1912–13, Morgan and his banking proxies held 341 directorships in 112 corporations—including over forty banks, trust companies, and insurance companies—controlling over $22 billion in resources. Morgan himself controlled a third of the country's railroads and, at the height of his power, over 70 percent of the nation's steel industry.[4]

During the panic of 1907, depositors waited in line outside the Trust Company of America for as long as twenty-four hours. *Everybody's*, January 1908. Courtesy of Brown Brothers.

Chief among the investment bankers overseeing the financial consolidation of American industry at the turn of the century, Morgan constituted, according to Carl Hovey, an early biographer, "the dominant business force in the country and the strongest single financial power in the whole world."[5]

Only a handful of reformers and radicals dared publicly to suggest that Morgan actively abetted the panic for his own benefit. One of these was Robert La Follette, then a freshman senator from Wisconsin, who, in an extraordinary series of speeches to Congress in March 1908, charged that the panic was a political terror tool and a financial shakedown, a way for Morgan's cabal of bankers to squeeze small investors and gain control over the public's bank and insurance deposits. According to La Follette, the crisis was "carefully planned and skillfully staged" and worked out "beautifully."[6] In addition to sweeping $500 million of the public's money into Morgan's and Rockefeller's banks, the panic "settled old scores," chastened regulatory sentiment, and prepared the way for emergency currency legislation that would give Wall Street bankers unprecedented influence over the nation's money supply.[7]

La Follette detailed not only how the conspirators ended the panic once it served their purposes but also how they scripted this end as a financial melodrama. As a novelist might, he vividly sketched what he imagined to be the scene behind the scenes, that of the conspirators' plotting: "The panic must be given a fitting finale, a dramatic finish. . . . A carefully elaborated climax, with Morgan and the Standard Oilers as the central figures would invest them with a halo of self-sacrifice and public spirit almost sublime. The floor of the stock exchange was chosen as the scene for the closing act, October 24 the time."[8] To his astonished colleagues, the senator insisted that "this is history."[9]

Remarkably, La Follette took this last phrase as well as his melodramatic image of the conspirators' plotting from a novel, *The Magnet* (1908), by the financial reformer Alfred O. Crozier, who had earned brief notoriety for heckling prominent bankers at a National Civic Federation meeting.[10] According to Crozier, La Follette actually read excerpts from the novel on the floor of the Senate. A feverish anti-banker diatribe, *The Magnet* details the successful plot of J. Morley Sterling Jr., the most powerful banker in the world, to create a cataclysmic Wall Street panic and then win the grateful praise of the nation by publicly orchestrating its end. The panic, Sterling hopes, will frighten Congress into passing legislation that will place the nation's currency at the mercy of his private money trust. Sterling's mastery over financial markets is matched by his covert control of the press, and his power is so complete that, even before setting the panic in motion, he prepares the hourly press reports of the panic's unfolding, including accounts of his rescue heroics and explanations of the crisis that advance his own political designs. Dictating these reports to his secretary, Sterling muses, "A handsome and alluring program and schedule of predetermined events, isn't it? But I think we can make it all real history."[11]

Crozier and La Follette were not alone in believing they had un-masked a vicious conspiracy behind a major financial panic or in offering a melodramatic vision of Morgan's financial and political stagecraft. In *The Moneychangers*, the centerpiece of a trilogy about greed, waste, and exploitation in New York, Upton Sinclair also aimed to expose "how Wall Street manufactured the Panic of 1907."[12] His muckraking credentials had been sensationally established by *The Jungle* (1906), his best-selling exposé of labor and living conditions in Chicago's Packingtown. Now Sinclair claimed that he got the inside story of the panic conspiracy from a lawyer friend who had visited the president of the Knickerbocker Trust at the start of the panic, just hours before the distraught banker committed suicide. A "thinly veiled allegory, the meaning of which no one could possibly miss," as Sinclair later described it, *The Moneychangers* shows how Dan Water-man, the Morgan character, produces the panic not only for the eco-nomic and political reasons that La Follette and Crozier outlined but also, above all, for personal reasons: to humiliate Stanley Ryder, the president of the Gotham Trust Company, the allegorical stand-in for the Knickerbocker Trust.[13] Waterman is jealous of Ryder because Ryder wins the affection of a ravishing newcomer to New York, Lucy Dupree, who, early in the book, refuses Waterman's advances. Taking his lines from La Follette (who took them from Crozier), Sinclair observes how the panic is "just like a play" and how it works out "beautifully" for Waterman, who ends the performance as easily as he started it, garnering, on top of his other bounty, the thanks of the nation.[14]

Like Crozier's novel, *The Moneychangers* is a melodrama, populated by one-dimensional characters (most of them clearly modeled after principal figures in the panic) whose intentions and desires we know from the start, and propelled by scenes of tragic seduction, sexual violence, sensational revelation, weepy self-castigation, and, at the end, outraged fulminations against Wall Street hegemony. Sinclair's representation of Morgan follows Crozier's and obeys the sensational formulas laid down by generations of anti–Wall Street and antibanker novelists.[15] Waterman is "master of the banks; and no man can take a step in Wall Street without his knowing it if he wants to." He "can swing the market so as to break a man" and draw on the U.S. Treasury "as if it were one of his branch offices" (TM 26). Out of the public eye, Waterman is violent, treacherous, and unable to bridle his appetite for power, as he demonstrates by attempting to rape Lucy after she refuses to be his mistress.

Like Crozier, La Follette, and scores of earlier financial conspiracists, Sinclair deploys melodrama to show that concrete, familiar forms of human deliberation and moral agency—here, the evil machinations of financial barons—cause financial crises.[16] Sinclair departs from these conspiracists, however, by extending the net of causality and moral accountability to include small investors, independent bankers, depositors, and all the outsiders who, doing routine business with Wall Street, in some way end up abetting the conspirators' panic plot. Indeed, The Moneychangers merits attention because it focuses more on the outsiders at the edges of the panic conspiracy than on the bankers at its center. The novel surveys various ways these outsiders become party to the conspiracy, how they allow themselves to fall into the conspirators' clutches or become part of the conspirators' design. In short, Sinclair's novel studies these outsiders' implication, in several senses. It examines how they implicate themselves in the taut and nearly totalizing causal web administered by the conspiracy. Thus entangled, they see the necessary and awful implications of their actions. In this way, they morally implicate themselves in the conspiracy's crimes because, despite foreseeing the dire outcome of their behavior, they fail to disrupt the causal chain by dislodging themselves from it.

Rather than focusing on conspiracy as the primary cause of financial panic, then, Sinclair focuses on conspiracy as a mediating agent, a causal matrix that, once entered, binds outsiders' private actions—and their intentions, it turns out—to inescapable and vicious public consequences. Waterman's conspiracy is so vast and powerful that merely to act in Wall Street is to risk having one's actions, even actions seemingly unrelated to business, used by the conspiracy and exploited for evil ends.

To clarify the ethical dynamics of this mediation and exploitation, Sinclair aligns conspiracy with two other causal matrices that produce financial evil. First, he compares conspiracy to the collectivity comprised of investors, bankers, businessmen, and depositors who never smoked cigars together in Morgan's private library but whose combined actions clearly compounded, and perhaps created, the panic of 1907. While conspiracy, anchored in collusion and deliberation, seems the opposite of such fortuitous combination, Sinclair studies how both conspiracy and the normal interdependencies of the financial system involve causal nets that, once activated by financial panic, trap those who do business in Wall Street, forcing them to choose between their own welfare and that of the nation. Second, to illuminate the moral hazards of such implication, Sinclair compares conspiracy to large corporations, another collectivity that, for Sinclair and Progressives, produced injury and disaster and potentially—depending on the rigor of the ethicist judging the matter—cast moral responsibility over thousands, perhaps millions, of agents, including shareholders.

Normally we think of financial conspiracies as clarifying moral accountability since they specify the agents designing and executing some economic villainy. However, because he examines how individuals consent to their entrapment within conspirators' plots, Sinclair blurs the line between abettors and plotters, outsiders and insiders. The task of determining moral accountability is made even more difficult, The Moneychangers shows, because conspiracy, resembling the other forms of efficacious combination noted above, easily colonizes them. When corporations and markets are used by—that is, become part of—conspiracies, individuals within them may not know they are serving the conspirators' design. Those outside the cabal of scheming bankers may only discover their complicity too late.

In short, The Moneychangers attempts to discern and trace moral responsibility in collective economic arenas that make moral accountability, at least as it had been understood in the American republican tradition, hard to map. Sinclair aims not only to expose the cause of financial panics—at least the panic of 1907—but also to determine how widely individual moral responsibility for these crises extends. For Sinclair, moral accountability extends as far as the conspiracy's causal reach. Any causal involvement in villainy, at least any that can be construed as conscious and free (thus exempting wage labor), constitutes a moral wrong. Because his novel aims to make middle-class readers—especially the hundreds of thousands of small investors who helped finance the corporate restructuring of the U.S. economy between 1898 and 1904—conscious of their own potential implication, it establishes their own potential sinfulness.

Crucially, it also points to a way out of this moral entrapment by providing readers with what Thomas Haskell, drawing on the work of the philosopher Douglas Gasking, calls "operative responsibility"—that is, a confidence that they can actively avoid or alleviate evil.[17] By showing how the net of moral accountability reaches beyond plotting bankers, Sinclair suggests how panics might be prevented: by convincing all who are complicit that they can, and, indeed, must, break from, thus breaking down, the causal web presided over by Wall Street insiders. Readers must become aware of the dire consequences of their potential implication and just say no to Wall Street. In addition, morally awakened by the melodrama of the narrative, "the people" must combine into what Sinclair, a self-avowed political writer since converting to socialism in 1904, images as a counterform of conspiracy, an outraged, activist electorate. Individuals must implicate themselves within this alternative collective in order to avoid becoming complicit in their own and the nation's corruption and ruin.

Distributing Blame

Although *The Moneychangers* goes beyond typical financial conspiracy theories in casting blame for panics and responsibility for their remedy on outsiders as well as insiders, it insists, like all conspiracy theories, on the importance and efficacy of individuals' intentions. Seeing human plots and not ineluctable laws, structural pressures, divine caprice, public moods, or chance behind all economic events, financial conspiracy theories preserve the idea that individuals, acting in concert, have the power to control economic life. Because they insist that economic events, however complex, mysterious, or injurious, happen for a discernible reason, that the financial universe is more intimate, familiar, and organized than it seems, conspiracy theories perform their most obvious heuristic work when the scale and complexity of economic networks expand beyond most people's understanding, when economic effects—such as the jarring price fluctuations, mass layoffs, money shortages, and stock collapses that afflicted the United States at the turn of the century—seem no longer to have comprehensible causes or connections to each other.

Rejecting the bankers and economists who sought to "discover the more occult and fundamental causes" of financial crises in technical features of "modern economic life," conspiracist novelists such as Crozier and Sinclair insisted, at least in their fiction, that panics resulted from the moral machinations of colluding individuals.[18] Other fiction writers at the turn of the century also saw the handiwork of powerful individuals behind panics (and in this way preserved a clear and direct link between human deliberation and economic outcomes), but their writing, far from indicting these characters, figured their manipulation as benign, even endearing. To bring the financial conspiracists' moralism into focus, we might read their texts against the work of two of these writers, Edwin Lefèvre and Robert Barr.

Lefèvre, a Wall Street insider and respected financial journalist who advised Frank Norris on The Pit, wrote magazine fiction about the manners and mechanics of Wall Street.[19] Collected in Wall Street Stories (1901), these wry tales focus on chastening but ultimately charming transactions between Wall Street insiders and various innocents such as novice speculators, clerks, ministers, and old widows. In these stories, Wall Street insiders are experts and professionals, genteel technicians who alone know how to operate the modern machinery of finance, but who graciously share their wisdom with novices. If they are villainous, they are villainous only to other insiders, and they always honor the rules of the speculative game. When they are caught cheating, they are punished in the market, and they accept their loss or ruin as a normal hazard of the business.

Lefèvre's formally polished tales, authoritative but unsensational, struck reviewers as a "vein in fiction heretofore scarcely suspected."[20] Lefèvre popularized the genre, but Robert Barr paved the way with similar kinds of stories for McClure's in 1894. (Indeed, Barr may have shown popular magazines the commercial wisdom of publishing Wall Street fiction.) Barr's and Lefèvre's stories offered, above all, reassurance to the magazine's middle-class readers, whose savings, by 1900, were falling under the control of Wall Street bankers. Focusing on just a few characters operating in Wall Street, these stories humanize and miniaturize finance, representing it as a series of discrete, private transactions. Titans control the market, but they have no interest in despoiling the public. Whether they are after money or teaching someone a lesson, they alone are responsible for the market's volatility. The speculative campaigns of the titans are more like sporting events than warfare. Rules ensure some degree of order and predictability to the game, and these rules guarantee that blood does not spill outside the stock exchange. Once the titans get what they want, they stop their manipulation.

The clever, often ironic, resolutions to Barr's and Lefèvre's stories succeed in balancing financial and moral accounts: there is no remainder of desire or disorder. Rather than moralizing against Wall Street, its leaders, or its ethical standards, the tales emphasize how stock speculation, even panics, can be used for socially salutary ends. For Lefèvre, the brokerage houses and stock exchanges are sites of male intimacy and education, not vicious conspiracy. For Barr, they are sites where gender and domestic conflicts can be resolved. Through the market's agency, immoderate and uncivil individuals get their just deserts.

Barr's "A Deal on 'Change: A Tale of Revenge" offers a typical example of how these writers represented panic.[21] In the story, the daughter-in-law of Druce, the richest man in America, is snubbed by the daughters of his only rival in Wall Street, Sneed. Sneed's girls refuse to call on her because she was once poor. Druce likes his daughter-in-law very much, and when he learns about the snub, he vows to "arrange the whole business in five minutes" ("Deal" 438). He meets with Sneed in a corner of the stock exchange, where traders can see them in close conversation. Speculators panic, fearing that the two titans are planning some devastating market action. Druce, accustomed to speaking to businessmen only about financial matters, fumblingly tells Sneed about his daughter-in-law's embarrassment, and Sneed cordially promises to see that his daughters make the visit. The two men's handshake, misunderstood by the crowd of traders, completely unsettles the world's markets. Markets remain jittery several days later when Sneed reports to Druce that he has been unable to persuade his daughters to make the call. Believing Druce will be sympathetic, Sneed rationalizes nervously that "the women have their world, and we have ours"; he explains: "What would you think if Mrs. Ed were to come here and insist on your buying Wabash stock when you wanted to load up with Lake Shore? Look how absurd that would be. Very well, then; we have no more right to interfere with the women than they have a right to interfere with us" ("Deal" 440). Druce rejects this conventional appeal to separate spheres, grumbling that he would do anything his daughter-in-law asked, whether it made financial sense or not.

He then promptly ruins Sneed. Agreeing to "leave social questions alone" and stick to business, he invites Sneed to hand over his gilt-edged securities as part of some market campaign. Sneed, despite his suspicions, does this and even agrees to go with the titan aboard his yacht. While they are sailing, the market collapses again, and all of Sneed's stocks plummet. Without his securities and out of communication, Sneed is helpless to steady the market. On his return, he recognizes his ruin as Druce's handiwork and accepts it with equanimity. The climax of the story comes afterward when Druce sends Sneed a note: "I often wonder why these flurries come. . . . Perhaps they are . . . sent to teach humility to those who might else become purse-proud. . . . How foolish a thing is pride! And that reminds me that if your two daughters should happen to think as I do on the uncertainty of riches, I wish you would ask them to call" ("Deal" 442). He explains that he has wrapped up Sneed's securities and given them to his daughter-in-law to give to Sneed's girls as a present, should they call. He notes that if the Sneed girls do not visit, he will sell the securities and "found a college for the purpose of teaching manners to young women whose grandfather used to feed pigs for a living, as indeed my own grandfather did." In the punch line of the story, Druce writes, "Should the ladies happen to like each other, I think I can put you on to a deal next week that will make up for Friday. I like you, Sneed, but you have no head for business" ("Deal" 442).

Lefèvre's and Barr's droll tales share more than we might expect with the shrill conspiracy melodramas against which they were frequently contrasted. In both kinds of fiction, because market (and social) effects follow efficiently from the personal intentions of market titans, unrefracted by chance or the unpredictable behavior of market crowds, agency is easy to discern and moral accounting easy to perform. Both kinds of fiction preserve the moral coherence and clarity of the marketplace. What distinguishes the one sort of writing from the other is how each deploys this moral vision. In Barr's story, personal desires, not conventional market motives, prompt the titan to act in the market, but since these desires dissipate once they are fulfilled and because they serve to strengthen the community (by deflating the invidious personal pride produced by the market itself), they pose no threat either to the public or to the proper function of the stock exchange. In Sinclair's novel, too, personal desires—vengeance, sexual frustration, wounded masculine pride—drive the titan's market activity. However, these desires produce widespread disaster, threaten the republican premise and promise of the nation, and corrupt countless individuals who submit to the insider's extortion or bribes. Just as importantly, because such desires are organic expressions of the titan's vicious character, not chastening responses to cultural accidents such as the Sneed girls' snub, we know they will always haunt the market's performance.

Indeed, these desires make clear why crises are endemic to Wall Street: not because panics are necessary concomitants of capitalist accumulation or symptoms of an archaic banking system, but rather because Wall Street insiders, dominating the machinery of finance, will do anything to satisfy their craving for power and prestige. Although the unremitting turpitude and totalizing power of Dan Waterman are meant to scandalize Sinclair's audience, they also serve, crucially, to illuminate the risks, financial and moral, of doing business with Wall Street. This is clearly one reason for Sinclair's use of melodrama: melodrama places the moral risk of investment where it can be seen, assessed, and acted on by the public.

Financial conspiracy theories at the turn of the century aimed not only to expose the vicious aims and dangerous economic agency of titans like Druce or Waterman but also, more significantly, to make the uncanny agency of collectivities, both organized and unorganized, comprehensible in familiar terms. Conspiracy theories showed that moral responsibility within these vast collectivities could, in principle, be specified and tracked, a possibility acutely desired by Sinclair's contemporaries, conspiracists and nonconspiracists alike.

The emergence of huge industrial consolidations, the expanded scale and complexity of financial transactions, the unprecedented entanglement of business and banking, and the new connectedness among economic actors (such as the centralization of financial markets and the expansion of communications networks) at the end of the nineteenth century made the assessment of moral accountability in business more urgent and complicated than ever. The extraordinary density and scope of economic exchanges dramatically enlarged the causal web across which economic effects could be felt. Economic villainy now affected institutions and individuals over wider distances, geographic and temporal, than ever. The problem for business ethicists, as for conspiracists, was that most people could not see or recognize such criminality. Confronting alien forms of economic agency and interconnection, the public, as one sociologist of the time put it, "overlooks the subtle iniquities that pulse along those viewless filaments of interrelation that bind us together."[22]

By acknowledging the complexity of collusion, Sinclair followed the lead of his Progressive contemporaries who focused on the ethical accounting problems presented by massive corporations. Under the new corporate dispensation, according to Progressive reformers, directors delegated their offending work to beholden employees or absent intermediaries such as bankers or shareholders, cloaking their own accountability. The sociologist Edward Ross devoted an entire book to the "grading of sinners" under modern corporate conditions. For Ross, who later became a frequent correspondent with Sinclair, the villain now most in need of curbing was the corporate director, "the respectable, exemplary, trusted personage who, strategically placed at the focus of a spider-web of fiduciary relations, is able from his office-chair to pick a thousand pockets, poison a thousand sick, pollute a thousand minds, or imperil a thousand lives" (Sin 29–30). For Ross and other Progressive ethicists, this spiderweb of relations constituted the enabling condition of modern criminality.

Progressive reformers faced the novel moral accounting problem posed by big business and widening spheres of economic intimacy by insisting defensively on the efficacy and integrity of individual responsibility, wherever it lay. Because liberty was "always personal, never aggregate," as Woodrow Wilson declared, guilt was also personal.[23] The diffusion of modern business ownership complicated this moral quarantine, however. Although Ross insisted that corporate directors, consciously setting the policies of their companies, were to blame for corporations' corrupt and abusive practices, he acknowledged the potential implication raised by the vast, new infusion of middle-class wealth into Wall Street: millions of shareholders might be held morally responsible for the harmful or unfair actions of the corporations they partly owned. In a remarkable description, Ross characterized this uncanny, colonizing character of complicity under the new corporate regime as a form of conversion: "The device of capitalizing and marketing the last turn of the corporation screw has a diabolic power to convert the retired preacher or professor (who has exchanged his life's savings for aqueous securities at par) into an oppressor of Tennessee miners, or Georgia operatives, or Kansas farmers, as relentless as an absentee Highland laird or a spendthrift Russian nobleman" (Sin 111–12). In such a view, directors passed not only financial but also moral costs on to investors, transforming them into villains.

Sinclair took Ross's description of stockholders' villainization literally. To own stock was to share the guilt of the corporation and its directors, just as to do business with a conspiracy of bankers (whose proxies often served on corporate boards) was to make oneself accountable for the events they plotted. Shareholders' moral character had no effect on corporate practices, and for this very reason, to avoid implicating themselves, individuals had to refuse to buy shares.

The Moneychangers

The Moneychangers exposes how financial outsiders become party to conspirators' designs and assume moral responsibility for the catastrophic effects that ensue. The novel does this by contrasting how the two main characters, Lucy and the lawyer hero, Allan Montague, respond once they realize that they are implicated in Wall Street con-spiracies and recognize the extent and stakes of their implication. Astonishingly, Sinclair blames Lucy for the panic of 1907, melodra-matically revealing how "it was to her that it all came back" (TM 169). She is to blame because she allows herself to be seduced, thereby making herself morally liable for the chain of ruinous effects, includ-ing the national catastrophe, her seduction activates. Should we doubt the logic of such extensive liability, Sinclair has Lucy insist on her own moral culpability; she acknowledges that her seduction precipitated the panic and also, more damningly, that she knew from the start that some disaster would follow from her action. Indeed, "hateful in [her] own sight" (TM 187) for submitting sexually to Waterman at the end of the novel in a last-ditch effort to "undo" (TM 180) what she has done, Lucy flees New York and kills herself. By contrast, Sinclair figures Montague's enlistment in insiders' nefarious designs as a contractual arrangement from which he quickly, safely, and legitimately with-draws once he realizes that he has been deceived, that he has been denied the information that would have allowed him to assess (and refuse) the moral risk of implicating himself. Sinclair celebrates Mon-tague's prudent disengagement from the conspiracy and his subse-quent turn to muckraking politics, conspiracy's solvent and, for Sin-clair, its virtuous counterform.[24]

Sinclair indicts Lucy because she ignores the ethical risks that come with allowing her behavior and character to be taken up by collective dynamics beyond her control. Like so many women protagonists in American republican romances, Lucy allows herself to be seduced. Early in the novel, dismissing Montague's warnings, she blithely suc-cumbs to the blandishments of Stanley Ryder, the married president of the Gotham Trust Company, and appears as his escort in a parade. For Montague, through whose admonishing eyes we track Lucy's fall, her exposure to potential scandal reflects a choice, a risky one, for which she alone must take responsibility. He tells her, "If a woman chooses to set out on a publicity campaign, and run a press bureau, and make herself a public character, why, that's her privilege" (TM 41)—but a dangerous one. Lucy gives up the shelter of privacy and tosses the appearance of sexual propriety, the baseline condition of a woman's social success, into the public realm where her actions risk being swept up by resistless currents of social gossip and the self-interested designs of society matrons.

Lucy goes public in another, equally fateful way: she sells her family's stock to Wall Street insiders. In this way, Sinclair links her exposure to uncontainable rumor directly with her complicity in the financial conspiracy that plays a featured role in Waterman's panic design. Lucy comes to New York to dispose of Mississippi railroad stock left to her in her father's will. Montague learns that the stock's value will skyrocket if the railroad, which her father built, is extended to the doors of a thriving Mississippi steel plant, an apparent rival to Waterman's steel empire. Montague, who grew up on a neighboring Mississippi plantation and now has a modest law practice in Wall Street, agrees to help her find a buyer, but Lucy sells the stock behind his back to Ryder. Seeing immediately how the railroad might be exploited, Ryder forms a syndicate to plunder it, and he puts the shares on the open market, where the public buys them. When Montague accuses Lucy of allowing herself to be used by the banker, she resentfully maintains that "what I have done, I have done of my own free will" (TM 66)—Montague's allegation all along. By putting her property in the hands of a conspiracy, Lucy further compromises her social and moral standing, since Wall Street spies and gossips are everywhere and construe the sale as proof of her illicit intimacy with Ryder.

Lucy not only forfeits her property and reputation to the will and whim of collective agencies but also tacitly consents to the effects that follow from this forfeiture, including the panic. Going public, Lucy causes the financial disaster by inflaming Waterman's jealousy and ultimately his ruinous vengeance. Imagining that his unrivaled wealth and prestige will induce her to accept his sexual advances ("that if Ryder was a rich man, he was a ten-times-richer man" [TM 65]), Waterman invites her aboard his private yacht, where, after introducing himself, he assaults her. She resists, insisting she would not have come had she known his intentions, but her claim provokes his mockery, for he insinuates—and we are meant to see the force of his argument—that someone who publicly attaches herself and sells stock to

Stanley Ryder, a known womanizer, must "know the world" and entertain such arrangements (TM 49). By his logic, her boarding the yacht signifies her informed consent to a sexual transaction. More to the point, her balking signifies her reneging on her tacit agreement to such an exchange. Montague serendipitously arrives and rescues her, but Waterman vows to follow her and never to give her up, a threat he makes good when, months later, he casts the Gotham Trust into bankruptcy, initiating the panic and inducing Lucy to go to his house at night to bargain for Ryder's financial life.

Her choice to go to Waterman's house and fulfill the contract she apparently abrogated aboard his yacht signifies how seduction and extortion fall along the same slippery slope. We are meant to see that by going public Lucy risks having to consent to her own ruin or the ruin of the nation. Sinclair highlights her choice in order to remind us that she is morally accountable for her private actions and their dizzying public ramifications. Sinclair makes it clear that Lucy initiated of her "own free will" (TM 66) the causal chain leading to this seeming necessity and, equally important, that she knew her affair would set Waterman against Ryder and lead to some ruinous display of Waterman's power. She bears the blame for the panic not despite but rather because of the manifest villainy of the titan. Indeed, she abjectly confesses that "I have known all along that Waterman was following me. . . . I have felt his power in everything that has befallen us" (TM 179).

Sinclair equates Waterman's sexual extortion of Lucy with the titan's financial extortion of Wall Street bankers during the panic. He does so in order to emphasize the victims' culpability, however paradoxical that may seem. Both Lucy and the beholden bankers confess their powerlessness in the same phrases, and Montague makes the link overt, lamenting that "you can't punish them [Waterman and his proxies] for anything they do, whether it is monopolizing a necessity of life and starving thousands of people to death, or whether it is an attack upon a defenseless woman" (TM 53). It is precisely because they are powerless that the bankers, like Lucy, are morally accountable for the role Waterman compels them to play in his panic design.[25]

Should we doubt that individuals have themselves to blame for entering Wall Street and becoming implicated in its conspiracies, Sinclair has General Prentice, the president of a major trust company and one of Wall Street's few good men, melodramatically convict himself for being "made" to promise to join Waterman's conspiracy and ruin Ryder: "I am a puppet—I am a sham—I am a disgrace to myself and to the name I bear!" (TM 174). When Montague insists that Prentice can "refuse to play their game" and avoid becoming party to the disaster Waterman has planned, the general, using phrases similar to those Lucy speaks before she goes to Waterman's house, declares, "I have chosen my part" and "must play it through" (TM 175). Like her, he emphasizes that he has no right to excuse himself since he knows, and, indeed, knew all along, that he could have acted differently, preventing his own implication, if not the panic, by resigning from the trust when he realized that he had become an impotent figurehead without influence over the men who now controlled the bank (TM 175). Prentice sees now, as never before, his humiliating dependency and, inseparably, his despicable complicity.

The Moneychangers asks how seemingly virtuous individuals abet capitalism's corrupting and destructive effects. It answers by showing how individuals are either seduced or fooled into lending aid or money to villainous conspiracies. Either way, they are morally culpable since they shirked their moral obligation to research and predict the forms of private and public dependency that follow from their actions. Montague's example makes this obligation clear. In contrast to Lucy and the beholden bankers, Montague shows how individuals can ensure their moral virtue by investigating the moral risks attending their entanglement in collective agencies, especially corporations and financial networks.

For Montague, individuals can avoid implication and thus guilt by refusing to enter causal webs they see as morally risky or by withdrawing from them once their risk becomes evident. Those who do not withdraw accept the risk of entrapment or extortion and thus remain responsible for their own fate and the fate of others whom they may help cause to injure. Montague enforces this republican ethic of refusal—a libertarian ethic, in fact, of inertness, since almost any action in Wall Street is morally risky—over and over again in the novel.[26] Whenever he enters a collective arena in which he does not approve of the things he is made to do, he simply quits. After the climactic financial panic, unwilling to continue even a social acquaintance with one of the conspirators, Montague explains his fear of entanglement and moral taint: "I am simply trying to protect myself. I'm afraid of the grip of this world upon me. I have followed the careers of so many men [in Wall Street], one after another. They come into it, and it lays hold of them, and before they know it, they become corrupt" (TM 203).

His most significant refusal comes when he angrily withdraws from the stock market conspiracy that Ryder dupes him into joining (a conspiracy, Montague learns later, that serves, unbeknownst even to Ryder, a more powerful and embracing conspiracy governed by Waterman). Ryder asks him to represent the syndicate of developers who want to take over the underachieving railroad Lucy's father built; hoping Montague's reputation for honesty and his Mississippi ties will convince the principal stockholders to cede control of the company, he offers to make Montague president of the new corporation.[27] In the belief that the development of the railroad will help his home state, Montague agrees to represent the new corporation, but his rigorous conception of personal accountability requires him to know exactly what he represents and how far his accountability extends. The new directors, Montague learns, also control the Mississippi Steel Company, and when Montague begins to suspect that they are corrupt, that their public representations cloak their malevolent designs, he goes to Mississippi to see the steel company for himself.

He goes to see the "actual property" behind the corporate directors' representations and behind the "pieces of paper" he handles as their representative and as a stockholder in the railroad (TM 97). Wishing to "keep this reality in mind" and penetrate the veil of reification (TM 97), he wants to see everything he represents—and thus, to his mind, everything for which he is potentially responsible—by signing on as the new corporation's promoter. He wants to survey the causal mechanism into which he has lodged himself along with the original shareholders who counted on his good faith and full disclosure; he wants to make sure that he sees the moral hazards of his, and their, implication. He also realizes that his representation of the company shapes "the destinies of living people" (TM 97), including thousands of laborers. Such an investigation, we are supposed to see, is crucial under an industrial and corporate regime that obscures labor's fundamental connection to the goods people buy, the securities they trade, and the money they use.

His visit to the steel plant constitutes one of the melodramatic set pieces of *The Moneychangers*, and it marks the first step in Montague's conversion from corporate to civic representative, from dummy to spokesman, and from dupe to leader of a collective agency. The corporation turns out to be ruthlessly exploitative. Montague sees a laborer accidentally slip from a ladder and fall to his death into some whirling machinery. Investigating, Montague learns that such falls are an accepted feature of the industrial system, that "steel can't be made without accidents" (TM 99). Even chance is incorporated into the moneymaking design. The totalizing nature of the corporation's evil becomes all the more shocking to Montague when he flees Mississippi and goes straight to Newport, where he has been invited to join high society in its leisure. The journey from the realm of productive labor to the realm of idle consumption jars Montague, for the vacationers do not realize that their leisure and luxury depend on (and are integral to) a system of production that systematically exploits, injures, and kills workers. He sees complicity built within the very structure of their fetishes: "With every glance that he cast at the magnificence about him, he thought of the men who were toiling in the blinding heat of the blast-furnaces" (TM 101). Montague lists all the families in Newport whose wealth somehow derives from the production of steel and then envisions, as Sinclair's heroes so often do, the matrix of complicity in all its sublime, sentimental, and structural vastness: "His thoughts roamed on to the slaves of other mills, to the men and women and little children shut up to toil in shops and factories and mines for these people who flaunted their luxury about him" (TM 101–2).

Returning to New York, Montague soon learns that these moral bonds extend not only across the industrial system, actually undergirding it, but also throughout the realm of corporate finance. What connects producers and consumers also connects corporate representatives, including himself, and stockholders who finance the corporation and share its earnings. When he learns that the railroad's new directors have conspired to plunder the company and defraud investors, he realizes that he has allowed himself to become part of a conspiracy. Unwilling to be enlisted or to implicate others in systematic exploitation and larceny, Montague angrily resigns. He learns for himself what insiders have told him all along: in Wall Street one has to "pay or quit" (TM 94)—and he refuses to pay. Any moral cost is too much, but here it is fatal, given the scope and power of the conspiracy. Because all of Wall Street seems part of it, the likelihood of entanglement in wrongdoing appears certain, and because it controls even politicians, this wrongdoing threatens the very integrity of American democracy. Wall Street corruption means "the overthrow of Republican institutions" in the United States, and to Montague that would be the ultimate disaster: "I value this Republic more than I do any business I ever got into yet" (TM 94).

Although he quits the corporation, Montague soon realizes that disengaging himself, just saying no, is morally insufficient. He must take active steps to free others from the system's infectious hold. Montague's full conversion into a public activist, a muckraker, and a Progressive reformer comes after the second melodramatic set piece of the novel, when he finds himself literally tied to the most nefarious and encompassing conspiracy of all, Waterman's panic plot. Montague is with a reporter, Bates, whose assistant, Rodney, a former steeplejack, rappels down a rope from their hotel window in order to spy into the room below, where Waterman, in secret conference with the nation's top bankers, lays out the campaign to "bring down every bank in the city" and throw the nation into turmoil (TM 169). Helping anchor the rope, Montague learns that the financial crisis brewing in New York has been plotted from the start, that Waterman intends to ruin Ryder's trust, squeeze other independent banks, put Lucy in his power, and force the government to legitimize his takeover of the Mississippi Steel Company. Even worse, Waterman wants to win—that is, extort—the public's gratitude by staging a dramatic rescue once the panic has served its purpose.

We are meant to compare this climactic exposure scene, where

Montague literally works hand in hand with a muckraker and a manual laborer, to Montague's similarly privileged vantage over the worker's accident in the Mississippi factory. In both scenes, Montague not only sees the reality behind the financiers' misleading public representations but also the full implications of the financiers' vicious intentions, the direct connection between their designs—economic, political, and personal—and the vast public injury they produce. Both scenes demonstrate the conspirators' hegemony, their power to implicate others, to entangle helpless workers in their industrial machinery and to entrap the middle class in their equally implacable financial apparatus.

Montague's rope-work reverses this implication. Instead of helplessly watching the factory laborer fatally fall, Montague actively holds up Rodney, turning entanglement into a weapon against Waterman's "huge machine" (TM 179). Instead of accepting the worker's alienation and accident as a necessary component of the capitalist juggernaut, Montague turns chance into choice, running into Bates by accident and then enlisting himself in this espionage attempt. In short, Montague transforms both the steel worker's and his own prior implication in Waterman's conspiracy—for Montague now sees that it is actually Waterman who controls the Mississippi railroad syndicate—into a conscious plan to disable the banker plot and protect others from such a fall. Joining Bates's muckraking conspiracy, he decides to save the nation from allowing itself to be financially ruined and morally implicated by the panic.

Outraged by what he's just seen, Montague at last sheds his reticence and inertness. He seeks out Ryder and warns him of Waterman's plan to ruin him. More significantly, when the owners of Bates's paper, beholden to Waterman, refuse to publish Bates's exposé, Montague realizes he must go into politics and "teach the people" about Wall Street's corruption and conspiracy (TM 203). He becomes a "public character" (TM 41), the role he counseled Lucy to spurn. No longer afraid of having his words picked up by gossipers or financial schemers and used for purposes he disapproves of, Montague gives himself over to public representation, vowing to speak to and for the public. Montague will attempt to rescue the public from Waterman's clutches just as he rescued Lucy on board Waterman's yacht, but clearly he hopes the public, unlike Lucy, will heed his warnings, properly assess the dangers of doing business with Wall Street, and stay clear of corporate finance. This is the lesson of *The Moneychangers*: the people must not repeat Lucy's mistake, her willed helplessness, her seduction and entrapment. They must just say no and refuse the risk of implication.

Montague's momentous step up into the collective arena of politics marks the culmination of his moral awakening. We are meant to read it against Lucy's solitary fall to Waterman, of course, but also against Montague's earlier refusal to fall captive to two collective agencies: financial conspiracy and financial crowds.

First, Montague's turn to politics reverses his unwitting participation in the Northern Mississippi conspiracy. The book ends without telling us what political remedy, beyond "teaching" the people, will dissolve the investment bankers' stranglehold on the nation's economic, political, and moral life. (In the next volume of the trilogy, *The Machine*, Montague will continue his radicalization by falling in with socialists.) Nonetheless, we are supposed to see that in politics, unlike in the corporation, Montague can safely embrace the totalizing extensiveness of his representation and responsibility. Speaking to and for the people, he need not choose between the public's welfare and his own. Here his private scruples, public representations, and their transmission across the collective body remain aligned. Because representations are transparent and organic, not artificial and alienable, and because the lines connecting intention and effect, conscience and consequence, cannot be corrupted, his implication in this social body frees rather than paralyzes him.

Montague wants to stimulate the public to direct its own affairs and not cede control of the commonwealth to corrupt, private interests. He wants individuals to reclaim the civic space—popular government, but also public opinion—that they have forfeited to self-aggrandizing financial barons and their lobbyists. He wants to ensure that the republic, a public trust—like the Northern Mississippi, handed down from founding fathers, but embracing the whole nation, not just a region— will stay in the hands of the people whom it is supposed to serve.

Going into politics, Montague aims to promote not only a rival form of trust, a stakeholder democracy characterized by full transparency, equality, and inclusion, but also a rival, idealized form of conspiracy. Colluding openly, legally, and responsibly, such a conspiracy expands, rather than limits, the domain of civic and commercial freedom. Like Waterman, Montague wants to enlist whomever he can in this collective, to extend its material and moral boundaries endlessly. However, instead of misleading and strong-arming individuals, he teaches them, giving them the information they need to judge the prudence and purity of their engagements. Having seen Wall Street's corruption firsthand and having freed himself from its causal web, he wants to expose the potential risks of doing business there. Montague wants to amass a constituency not simply because there is strength in numbers—the might of 80 million voters dwarfs the political influence of the banker conspiracy—but also because the enemy, ubiquitous and assuming many forms, potentially implicates and endangers everyone. Only by implicating themselves in Montague's collective, by disengaging from Wall Street and acting together to dismantle its power, can individuals be sure they will not find themselves extorted by bankers or corporations.

This, above all, is his mission: through his teaching, Montague aims to widen the sphere of public accountability. He wants to outrage the people and show them they have the means and also the obligation to protect themselves and the republic from ruin and moral degradation. He offers them the choice that Waterman gives Lucy and the public at the climax of the panic: to align themselves with his interests or be destroyed. But his choice presents an obvious difference: by consenting to Montague's design to restore an unsellable and unsulliable republic, they retain their self-respect and moral purity. As more individuals become implicated in this counterconspiracy, the wider the sphere of freedom—the right of every individual to say no—extends. As more people serve the common good, the freer each person becomes.

Going into politics also marks Montague's attempt to forge a rival form of crowd. Unwilling to bind himself to any collective agency that produces evil or injurious outcomes, he refuses to join the panicky depositors amassing outside Ryder's trust. Montague knows the crisis is artificial, and he recognizes that by joining the crowd, he would intensify its violence, however incrementally. Refusing to join, he refuses to implicate himself in the panic's collective, runaway dynamics. Once begun, the panic indeed expands, implicating more and more individuals as abettors and victims. Moreover, it soon takes on an apparent life of its own. The runs on Ryder's trust produce runs on other banks; fear engulfs the city and then spreads across the country. Teetering banks in every state beg unsuccessfully for money from New York to safeguard their dwindling reserves, but the conspirators hold it all (TM 192).

The financial panic represents the most dramatic and disabling form of collective implication in *The Moneychangers*. We are meant to compare the clamoring depositors' behavior to Lucy's. Like her, they invited this dishonor and debt upon themselves; they deposited money with trusts they knew to be unregulated and reckless; and they knew that only a tiny fraction of depositors would be able to rescue their savings in a crisis. Now, by withdrawing their money, they threaten to bankrupt everyone else; their selfishness and cowardice lead directly to general ruin. And they realize all this—waiting in line, a friend of Montague's confesses it.

What is important, however, is that each panicky depositor can as easily quell the panic as compound it. As Montague argues, because the panic is purely a result of manipulation, unjustified by economic conditions, each depositor can help end it by following Montague's own example and refusing to join the crowd. Without bank runs, there can be no crisis. When his friend, bewildered by Montague's refusal to get in line, exclaims, "But, man, there'll be a run on [the trust]!" Montague makes the moral law and social logic clear: "There will, if everyone behaves like you" (TM 190). Such Kantian necessity ensures disaster if each acts as others do, but it also promises a remedy if each acts as everyone should. Each depositor must trust others not to rush the bank, and each depositor can induce others not to rush the bank by staying clear of the gathering crowd. In short, it is in each depositor's power to save himself, other depositors, and the nation from ruin.

In Montague's eyes, the public, by refusing to prevent the panic, invites its own moral entrapment and civic degradation. As he predicts, the bank run leads to a full-blown panic that only Waterman's money trust, controlling the credit supply, can end. The terms of such a rescue are extortionate, however. Unless the federal government consents to Waterman's private takeover of the Mississippi Steel Company, "thousands of firms [will] be ruined, [and] the business of the country [will] be paralyzed" (TM 195). The helpless nation, like Lucy, must submit to Waterman's cruel bargain. Worse, unaware that Waterman forced such a choice on them, the public will thank and celebrate him, heedless of the fact that he has further tightened his iron crown—his steel monopoly—around them.

Unlike Lucy, the depositors lining up outside Ryder's trust do not recognize that they are implicating themselves in a vicious plot. However, their unwitting implication, together with the fact that by rushing the bank they induce others to do the same, makes the panicky depositors the primary bearers or agents of the conspiracy's will. The conspiracy, like a possessing spirit, has colonized their desire and costumed its intention as their own. The material work of this hegemony becomes even clearer once the panic becomes self-sustaining, fueled entirely by the public's own frenzy (TM 192). The panic's designers, in effect, have turned its operation over to the people.

The panic sensationally exposes how "one man's peril was every man's, and none might stand alone" (TM 194). However, this frightening interdependency provides the public with a means of escape: individuals can join Montague's constituency. Following Montague, they can reverse the oppressive logic of bank runs and market panics; each individual, seeking his or her own safety, will protect rather than ruin others. As more investors and depositors refuse to finance the conspiracy (that is, as more of them refuse to purchase stocks in corrupt corporations or store their savings in reckless trusts), the more they will disable the conspiracy. In the panic, the people themselves fueled the panic and their own ruin. Joining Montague's reform army, the people will likewise shape their own destiny, but by freeing themselves from the conspiracy's design, they will preserve, not sacrifice, their own autonomy and civic virtue.

The *Moneychangers* shows what can happen to the nation when citizens forfeit their economic and moral independence by investing in Wall Street. Conversely, it shows what can happen to individuals when citizens, through their ignorance of Wall Street's villainy, fail to protect the republic from the corrupting pressure of large corporations and investment bankers. Preoccupied with informed consent, the novel brings to light the increasingly complicated links between the citizen's moral virtue and the health of the republic under an emergent corporate order where property ownership, rather than securing the citizen's moral and political autonomy, seemed to compromise it. If the novel seems labored and incoherent—Sinclair himself thought the book was weak, and some reviewers thought the novel so turgid that they begged him to quit writing fiction—it is because it laments the seeming inescapability of the new corporate economy while at the same time demanding a political morality consistent with an older market ideal. Put simply, Sinclair relies on a political and moral idiom of the 1890s to address moral challenges presented by the transformed political economy of the 1900s. Urging its readers to say no to Wall Street and the stock debauch consuming the nation, *The Moneychangers* insists on an increasingly outdated notion of republican virtue, an equation between moral independence, economic self-determination, and civic protection wedded to an obsolete economic dispensation.

The novel follows the polemical lines laid out by Populists, silverites, and Bryan Democrats during the depression of the 1890s. Like these financial antimonopolists (as the historian Gretchen Ritter calls them), Sinclair illuminates the public destructiveness and moral viciousness of economic combination, and he decries the corrupting effects of big business and bankers on representative government and citizens' moral life. Like these earlier writers (and Greenbackers before them), he focuses on financial panic as the doomsday weapon of bankers, the most dramatic and destructive consequence of Wall Street's control over the people's money. Like them, too, he sees the public interest as being dependent on the fairness and openness of the

markets in which "producers"—as well as self-employed professionals such as Montague—exchange the products of their labor. Only
dispersed markets ensure the economic freedom on which the moral
virtue and independence of each citizen, and thus the political health
of the republic, depend.[28]

To these antimonopolists, the stunning transition from competitive to corporate capitalism between 1898 and 1904, the accompanying
emergence of Wall Street as the linchpin of the new economy, and the
rise of the banker regime at the helm of hundreds of new mergers, all
appeared to undermine the moral autonomy of citizens. In buying
stock, former producers (along with a growing number of urban professionals) no longer managed the property they owned or controlled
the uses to which their property was put. The "personal virtues" that
came with "personal contact" with one's property could no longer be
counted on.[29] Shareholders often had "with deep mortification to co-
operate in the doing of things" they knew were "against the public
interest."[30] As Edward Ross put it, they were now "converted" into sinners: oppressors of laborers, corruptors of politicians, and instigators
of panics. By buying shares and depositing their surplus with trust and
insurance companies, citizens threatened not only their own moral
purity but also that of the republic because they financed a corporate
and financial regime whose lobbyists perverted democracy and whose
conspiracies undermined competition.

If the novel's elegy for civic virtue and small, competitive markets
fits squarely within the tradition of the antimonopolist jeremiad, the
novel's emphasis on revelation, renunciation, and reform fits squarely
within Progressivism's emphasis on publicity as an instrument of citizens' moral awakening and activism.[31] Picking up the moral gauntlet
thrown down by the muckrakers, the outraged citizen was expected, in
Richard Hofstadter's words, to "reclaim the power that he himself"—
or, Sinclair would add, she herself—"had abdicated" to money lords,
industrial conspiracies, and other powerful interests that defrauded
the public, bribed its representatives, and conspired to close markets
and frustrate Americans' entrepreneurial energies.[32] Citizens elected
legislators who passed the laws that governed corporate behavior.
Informed citizens, through the ballot, could actively bolster and barb

such laws. This is why Sinclair teams Montague with Bates and, indeed, makes Montague, a lawyer, take over Bates's role when the journalist is silenced during the panic. If the intrepid press is no longer free to expose corporate villainies, the politician must become a muckraker; if reforms take shape as new laws, then the lawyer must become a reformer, for who could better ensure the laws' trenchancy?[33]

We are never told just what Montague will teach the people, but we are led to believe that he will publicly expose everything he has discovered about Wall Street's plans to monopolize the nation's economic and political resources. Presumably, his revelations will produce several effects urged by Progressive reformers: they will scare "the people" from involving themselves with Wall Street (thus preventing artificial panics); incite people to demand reforms that will defang finance capital's menace and "*restore* our politics," as Woodrow Wilson put it, "to their full spiritual vigor *again*, and our national life . . . to its purity";[34] and, finally, place the moral burden of this restoration—or its failure—squarely on the shoulders of "the people."

Sinclair's melodramatic technique brings together the Progressive emphasis on corporate transparency and the antimonopolist emphasis on individuals' moral autonomy. *The Moneychangers*' melodramatism—its sensational exposures of public plots and private crimes as well as its stark delineations of virtue and vice—serves these projects, first, by exposing how the bankers' zone of extortion, like the panic's zone of destruction, spreads even into the most intimate aspects of citizens' lives. This is why we are shown the sexual assault, Lucy's decision to submit to Waterman late in the book, and her self-abasement afterward. Only such agonizing and intimate revelations of abuse and degradation can uncover the degree to which the new economic dispensation threatens Americans' most anxiously guarded personal freedoms. Sinclair's melodramatic exposures—the rape attempt, in particular—also show the inadequacy of contemporary polemics, such as Arthur Twining Hadley's *Standards of Public Morality*, in lamenting the discrepancy between businessmen's personal virtues, conspicuous in their home and philanthropic life, and their corrupt or harmful business activities, which much of the public considered routine and necessary. Low standards of business morality, Sinclair wants to make clear, cannot explain Waterman's violence toward Lucy. Indeed, no business imperative or exigency can justify it.

Above all, Sinclair's melodramatism, through its privileged glimpses of plottings, personal crimes, and confessions, allows us to see that deliberating—that is, morally accountable—agents are behind even the most complex, abstruse, and catastrophic economic events. Like other kinds of melodrama, financial melodrama exaggerates the clarity of moral accounting otherwise obscured or attenuated in the real world. Like financial conspiracism, it performs its most essential service when moral responsibility in the economic arena is no longer easy to trace, when moral crimes in business become "lost to view" (*Sin* 11–12), either because they have taken unfamiliar forms or because conventional means of assigning and describing personal accountability have become inadequate. *The Moneychangers'* focus on personal viciousness registers Sinclair's fear, shared by many of his contemporaries, that without the moral articulation and familiarization provided by melodrama, the public would fail to achieve the sentimental focus required to agitate against financial crimes, including panic-starting, that endangered the moral and material health of the nation. Without a clear and recognizable target on which to cast its outrage, the public could not be provoked to demand reform.

Ross's *Sin and Society* (1907), which Sinclair excerpted in his anthology *The Cry for Justice*, offers the most explicit account of the difficulties of recognizing criminality and animating moral outrage under modern business conditions. One problem for Ross, as I have noted, was that personal responsibility seemed maddeningly diffuse in the financial world. Observing how many agents within a corporation might be considered accountable for its crimes, Ross worried that public opinion "is impotent so long as it allows itself to be kept guessing which shell the pea is under. . . . How easily the general wrath is lost in this maze! Public indignation meets a cuirass of divided responsibility that scatters a shock which would have stretched iniquity prone" (*Sin* 125). Melodrama refocused this disciplining shock.

A more striking problem was that economic wrongdoing, especially corruption and fraud (but also legal forms of extortion and exploitation), did not resemble older, familiar kinds of villainy. The modern criminal, sitting in his office, failed to stir the same loathing as the highway robber or rapist. "Unlike the old-time villain," Ross observed, "the latter-day malefactor does not wear a slouch hat and a comforter, breathe forth curses and an odor of gin, go about his nefarious work with clenched teeth and an evil scowl. In the supreme moment his lineaments are not distorted with rage, or lust, or malevolence. One misses the dramatic setting, the time-honored insignia of turpitude" (Sin 10). Financial melodrama satisfied, or at least served, this nostalgia for moral drama and gestural transparency. It allowed its audience to see conventional evidence of vice and viciousness, such as Waterman's glaring into Lucy's eyes "like some terrible wild beast" (TM 49). In short, to be effective, reform required melodrama's familiar dramaturgy: "villainy must be staged with blue lights and slow music" to be identified, scorned, and countered (Sin 32).

For Ross, not only villainy but victimization, too, had to become more theatrical and obvious. The public "needs a victim to harrow up its feelings" (Sin 32), and yet it was not always clear in modern finance who the victims of modern sin were. It took "imagination to see that savings-bank wrecker, loan shark, and investment swindler, in taking livelihoods take lives" (Sin 41). Clearly this is one reason Sinclair pairs Waterman's assault of Lucy and his attack on defenseless banks and companies (and ultimately the public): Sinclair wants to make the second attack familiar in terms of the first, to activate his audience's older, attenuated sentimental response system. Like Thomas Lawson, whose lachrymose fiction was paired with Sinclair's by critics—and, indeed, like sentimental novelists before the Civil War who focused on financial panic's effects on middle-class homes—Sinclair aims both to personalize and generalize financial suffering. Melodrama not only gave traditional legibility to modern sin, then, but also, making this sin's effects concrete and pathetic, conjured forth the traditional judgments and sympathies that encouraged punishment, motivated reform, and, ideally, constrained criminality.

Incorporation and, more broadly, reification deadened the shock and sensationalism of modern criminality. Sinclair uses melodrama to clear away the fogginess of modern business guilt and show that insiders know the effects of their actions and see these effects as destructive and exploitative. Only if individuals know they are morally culpable can the full force of moral scorn and scandal be legitimately cast upon them. Only if agents produce the effects they intend can business morality have any disciplinary force and, as Sinclair labors to prove, the republic be preserved. If individuals were allowed to cloak their criminality in the collective agencies through which they operate, their moral accountability, like an escaped gas, might simply dissipate or pass beyond detection. The accounting structure would fail its office where it was most needed.

Seen this way, melodrama performs its ethical office most obviously in the confession scenes of *The Moneychangers*, when General Prentice and, especially, Lucy, breaking down in tears, admit to Montague that they knew all along what the massive consequences of their failure to dis-implicate themselves from Wall Street's conspiracies would be. They stand in, clearly, for the reader who, reading this exposé, can no longer claim to be unaware of the hazards of doing business in Wall Street. Bearing witness against themselves, they take over the moralist's function.

Sinclair's insistence that there are no unconscious agents in Wall Street, however, is perhaps clearest when the claim seems most in doubt, when the individuals most responsible for Wall Street's crimes appear not to recognize their own guilt. Late in the book Montague finds himself invited to the home of Jim Hegan, Waterman's partner and one of the notoriously corrupt "wreckers" of the Street. Studying Hegan, Montague is "possessed by a sudden desire to penetrate beneath [his] reserve; to spring at the man and surprise him with some sudden question; to get at the reality of him, to know him as he [is]" (TM 136). Sinclair pairs the lawyer's desire to see the "reality" of Hegan's character with Montague's earlier impulse to visit the "actual property" of the steel company in Mississippi. Awed and outraged by the causal net binding stock dividends and consumer pleasures to labor exploitation in the mills, Montague insists on the mapability of the moral net binding capitalists, shareholders, and consumers. Montague wants desperately to confirm—and he ends up desperately asserting—that Hegan is conscious, at some level, of his moral culpability, that his public charm and confidence mask some hidden shame and misery. Montague asks: "And how was he to himself? When he was alone with his own conscience? Surely there must come doubt and wonder, unhappiness and loneliness! Surely, then, the lives that he had wrecked must come back to plague him!" (TM 137). The effectiveness of republican reform requires this sentimental necessity. Readers must both demonize and identify with the guilty capitalist.

Historical Fiction

There is a final reason why The Moneychangers is so melo-dramatic. Like stage and screen melodramas in the early 1900s, Sinclair's novel invites us to see how it creates its own sensational effects.[35] It does so in order to train readers to see the public narrative of the panic of 1907 as a created production, a plot and a fiction—in fact, a melodrama like The Moneychangers. To make this clear, I want to focus on what reviewers, and Sinclair himself, considered to be the narrative crux of the novel, the extraordinary scene when Montague and Bates suspend Rodney outside the window of the conference room where Waterman and his bankers are plotting the panic. The scene offers a classic example of the conspiracist sublime. Stunned and terrified "as if he had found himself suddenly confronted by a bottomless abyss" (TM 167), Montague grasps in an instant the totalizing reach of Waterman's conspiracy; he sees the vast causal net that links Waterman to Lucy, Ryder, the Northern Mississippi, the Mississippi Steel Company, the recent financial storms, and the imminent national catastrophe. Overhearing the fateful conference, Montague realizes that he is witnessing "the making of history" (TM 170). We are supposed to understand the phrase literally. Waterman makes history, first, by manufacturing the panic, dictating its effects, and, as Montague learns later, orchestrating its ending. Waterman makes history a second way by controlling the press and thus scripting and spinning the panic's public representation, its emplotment as a historical event. The panic, Montague realizes, is a publicity stunt that works "just like a play" (TM 187).

The seeming incredibility of Waterman's panic plot is matched, curiously, by the seeming incredibility of Sinclair's plot contrivance,

Rodney's muscular high jinks. In no other scene does Sinclair dramatize Montague's discovery of Wall Street's villainy in such a sensational, literally over-the-top way. Up to this point, Montague has educated himself about Wall Street by listening patiently to the chatter and confessions of financial veterans. We might explain the incongruous theatrics of the rope scene as a vestige from Sinclair's days as a dime novelist, a generic atavism he confessed to being unable to repress, but I want to suggest that its melodramatism is strategic. Sinclair, who pointed to the scene with Rodney when he noted in his prospectus that "this will make a very effective story for picture [movie] purposes," wanted his readers to recognize the scene as an artifact, an invention, a novelistic device.[36] More exactly, we are supposed to recognize an equation between the conspiratorial plotting Montague witnesses and Sinclair's own narrative plotting, his ability to enlist all the characters, events, narratives, and details that appear in The Moneychangers, even this far-fetched action scene, into a single overarching design.

As scholars of conspiracy frequently note, conspiracist narratives often take on features of the conspiracies they claim to unveil, especially the urge toward totalization, where the conspiracists' proofs, no less than the conspiracy's designs, "fit together beautifully" (as Montague puts it), if incredibly (TM 186). The homology between conspiracist narratives and conspirators' plots becomes particularly pronounced in conspiracist fiction, where the narrative design, the causal chain pulling the narrative forward, is intentional or plotted. Unlike most conspiracists, however, Sinclair deliberately focuses our attention on the homology. He does this to make us entertain the possibility that the public record of the panic of 1907 and Morgan's actions, the narrative of events during and after the panic fed to the public by the bourgeois press, is produced "just like a play" no less than the novel we are reading. It is not enough for Montague, within the diegesis, to see and say this; readers must be made to see how, by reading the novel, they are embracing the very premise of conspiracism: that the various events they experience are part of a single plot. Only in this way can they be made to accept the possibility that a banker conspiracy really exists in Wall Street, controlling money, markets, and the media.

The novel thus performs its major work, provoking suspicion of Wall Street and its propaganda, not by privileging the truth and reliability of its own account, as we might expect from a muckraker and journalist, but rather by privileging its artifactuality. Clearly, Sinclair wants us to believe the allegations that leaven and anchor the novel, but he also, through the obvious fictionality of the key exposure scene, wants us to accept the possible fabricatedness of the "public history" his own plot retells and counters (TM 193). In short, if we can accept the incredibility of the rappelling scene in the panic novel we are reading, then we must accept the possibility, also seemingly incredible, that the panic of 1907 is part of a conspiracy's design and that the story about the panic crafted by the mainstream press is also part of this design. Montague clearly stands for the reader, then, when he realizes, in the rappelling scene, that every fact he has accepted about the Steel Trust, the most embracing and covert conspiracy of all, has been fed to him by the conspiracy's agents.

Of course, even the most realistic novels showcase their artifice, and fiction writers rarely (if ever) expect readers, even the most sympathetic ones, to forget that they are reading a scripted, plotted narrative. The Moneychangers is extraordinary, though, because most contemporary readers, at least most reviewers, focused on its exaggerated factualism, its extreme lack of invention. The Nation noted that "only some hermit, some inconceivable recluse, who did not read the papers at all would find anything fresh in Mr. Sinclair's anecdotes" and charged that Sinclair had merely cast "a veil of fiction" over data scavenged from journals.[37] The Bookman likewise complained that Sinclair had simply pasted together the novel from his "fund of scandalous stories and newspaper clippings."[38] Even positive reviews, few as they were, saw the novel as something other than a novel. Celebrating Sinclair's bold revelations, Benjamin Flower, the reformist editor of the Arena, insisted that The Moneychangers was "history rather than fiction."[39] I am arguing, against these readers, not only that Sinclair exaggerates the fictionality of his novel through this crucial exposure scene, but also, more significantly, that he does so in order to show how the newspapers, directed by Morgan, "make" history in the same way he makes his novel. If he culls pieces of The Moneychangers from newspapers, as he readily acknowledges in The Brass Check (1919), his study of capitalist bias in American journalism, he does so to illuminate how newspaper stories can be made to serve larger plots, whether thinly veiled, as in his novel, or completely veiled, as in the panic of 1907.

Sinclair's attempt to highlight the fictionality of the historical record by exaggerating the artificiality of his own historical fiction seems particularly noteworthy because he took his most sensational and self-consciously novelistic scenes from Robert La Follette's congressional speeches in which the senator used melodrama to highlight how history—real and alleged events as well as the press's account of them—functioned as fiction. Given a few months before Sinclair wrote The Moneychangers, La Follette's speeches laid out the senator's sensational allegations of a banker conspiracy behind the panic of 1907. Commenting on his own argument, a narrative account that links the panic to Wall Street's unsuccessful attempt to seduce the public in 1906 and Wall Street's subsequent anger and humiliation—a narrative Sinclair rewrites as the rape plot—La Follette declared, "This is history, Mr. President." However, as I noted at the start of this chapter, far from defining this "history" against melodrama or fiction, as we might expect for someone attempting to set the historical record straight, the senator averred that history, at least the history of the panic's origins, was in fact a stage plot, a melodrama, one in which a financial titan heroically rescues a helpless country bankrupted and prostrated by a panic. Actually, La Follette went even further than this, showing how the plot's behind-the-scenes production also constituted a melodrama. He painted for his colleagues the same drama Sinclair sensationalizes in The Moneychangers, a scene of Morgan and his bankers in covert conference, working out the dramaturgy of the panic, the "stage setting," the "scene for the closing act," the "dramatic finish."[40]

Like Sinclair, then, La Follette uses his own thrilling picture to prove that mainstream accounts of the panic, offering their own "thrilling picture" of the bankers' heroics, are not only fabricated and false, but also, of more importance, part of a larger plot to hoodwink the public. La Follette's speech, not being part of a novel, does not invite attention to its own artifice as Sinclair's exposure scene does, but La Follette and Sinclair confound "history" and melodrama to emphasize the same basic point: fed such thrilling fictions by the mainstream media, especially in the heat of a panic, the public cannot "determine how much is real, how much is sham."[41] Unable to distinguish between melodrama's historical plots and history's melodramatic plots, the public, like Montague visiting the steel mills, must trace these fictions to their vicious source.

What source, though? As I have noted, La Follette took his speech, at least this melodramatic tableau and his line about history, from *The Magnet*, Alfred Crozier's historical novel, a melodrama. Recall that in Crozier's novel the arch villain, Sterling, even before he activates the panic, dictates to his secretary the press reports that will describe and interpret the ensuing catastrophe for the public. (Sterling muses, "A handsome and alluring program and schedule of predetermined events, isn't it? But I think we can make it all real history.")[42] What makes the titan's ability to convert his "alluring program" into "real history" so interesting is not the seeming incredibility of marshaling crises at will and micromanaging the economic destiny of the nation. After all, J. P. Morgan, the model for Sterling, did just this in 1907, at least according to the conspiracy theories I have been discussing. What makes the pre-scripting of the panic's "real history" interesting, instead, is the fact that Crozier claimed he wrote his melodrama—"a new work of . . . startling disclosures, documentary proof of the great Wall Street and bank conspiracy"—in 1906, *before* the panic.[43]

The panic, plotted in advance by Morgan, the alleged melodramatist, was plotted even earlier by a novelist, another melodramatist. Crozier's prophecy brings Sinclair's melodramatic intentions into clearer relief. If a novelist could "make history," emplotting the plotting of the panic, its production and reception, in advance, then why could not financial titans who actually controlled the nation's banks, industries, and newspapers? They had the might and the motive: not just to consolidate their financial and political hegemony but also, reformers widely alleged, to counter the stinging portraits painted by muckrakers, reformers, and fiction writers. In this sense, Crozier's melodrama not only prophesied the panic but also caused it. Morgan put on his "play" to dramatize Crozier's fiction's falseness.

The Moneychangers melodramatically exposes and enacts the plotted-ness of panics and their history. Positioned within the narrative machinery of Sinclair's plot, readers learn, along with Montague, that they are caught within a causal matrix, a net that spans the economy, linking stockholders and steel workers, consumers and capitalists. It is an economic matrix, clearly, but, more important for Sinclair, it is also a moral matrix across which guilt flows efficiently, making investors, once warned, liable for insiders' villainous behavior. Readers must see the conspiracy and its villainy, but what matters more is that readers must recognize the reach of this villainy, the extent of the "huge machine," and its implications for them all (TM 179).

Chapter 5

The Financier and the Ends of Accounting

"Ye'd made a good bookkeeper."
Theodore Dreiser, "The Mighty Rourke"

The Financier (1912) constitutes the first volume of Theodore Dreiser's massive trilogy about Frank Cowperwood, a charismatic and amoral financial titan modeled after Charles Yerkes, a notorious municipal railroad tycoon who died in 1905. Recounting Cowperwood's first thirty-six years, from 1837 to 1873, *The Financier* traces his education as a youth, the development of his uncanny gift for brokerage and finance, his quick rise in the world of Philadelphia city finance, his conviction and imprisonment for embezzling city funds, and his financial redemption soon after his release. Two financial panics play crucial roles in the novel. The first, a consequence of the catastrophic Chicago Fire in 1871, occurs almost three hundred pages—just over a third of the way—into the narrative. It threatens to bankrupt Cowperwood and leads directly to his unauthorized cashing of a city check, the moral and legal legitimacy of which is interrogated throughout the remainder of the book. The second panic, triggered by the collapse of Philadelphia's leading investment house in 1873, concludes the novel. Free from the financial entanglements that made him so vulnerable two years before, Cowperwood exploits this panic and dramatically recoups the fortune he lost in 1871.

Dreiser focuses on financial panic to study the limits of all accounting schemes, financial, ethical, legal, and narrative. Dreiser uses panic to show that a naturalist universe—a fluxional world where, as he puts it in a later philosophical essay, "nothing is fixed" and everything is "unbalanced, paradoxical and contradictory"—must defy any attempt to encompass the future within a plot or design.[1] In the novel, Cowperwood's ambitious pyramiding of bank loans serves as the primary example of such an attempt. Like any debtor, he is hostage to the future, obligated to pay off his debts when they are due or demanded.

However, by buying new stock with his loans and paying his debts with each speculative windfall, lodging each debt within a larger project, the end of which he envisions clearly, Cowperwood labors to gain advantage over the future and its contingency. The first financial panic mocks this work. A chance catastrophe, the panic offers a clear lesson Dreiser adapted from Herbert Spencer: any vision that pretends to contain everything within its margins and to see the future completely, as if from a vantage above and outside of history and its contingency— a vantage, put simply, that imagines it can account for everything—is doomed.

The panic and the fateful treasury debt that it leaves the financier unable to pay offer a second and equally important lesson: in this naturalist universe, plotting inevitably activates the counterplotting of others. To be in debt makes one hostage not only to an unpredictable future but also to the designs of all the self-serving individuals who inhabit the jungle of city finance and politics. For Dreiser, this entanglement does not expand the field of individuals' moral accountability as it does for Upton Sinclair, who insists in The Moneychangers that individuals are morally liable for all the harmful effects of their behavior in Wall Street since they know, or should know, that their actions will be exploited by villainous conspiracies. Nor, for Dreiser, does this entanglement serve as a pragmatist injunction to disavow fatalism and embrace the ethical obligations opened up by an acceptance of the contingency of human interdependence. This distinguishes Dreiser from William Dean Howells, who, in The Rise of Silas Lapham (1885), also focuses on the impossibility of closing financial and moral accounts in a world typified by the unpredictability of the stock market. As Brook Thomas argues, Howells studies various forms of debt, obligation, and accounting to "make visible the realistic possibilities for human action that otherwise might seem determined by transcendental forces such as The Market or Fate." For Thomas, the aim of Howells's narrative is to "transfer to readers the task of responsibly judging what constitutes responsible action" in a world where chains of human actions and reactions cannot be predicted with certainty.[2] Dreiser disavows such an aim. In Dreiser's view, the financial underworld is completely amoral. Individuals there do not assess the ethical ramifications of their actions; rather, tested by panic and debt, they are driven by an innate will to plot and seek advantage.

By building the novel around Cowperwood's covert and criminal use of public debt, his private borrowing of city loan certificates, Dreiser highlights the tension between forms of obligation, or debt, that serve the private schemes of individuals such as Cowperwood and forms of public or civic obligation that obstruct these schemes. For Dreiser, the first kind of obligation, to settle one's financial accounts with an eye toward advancing one's own interests, is a natural or "chemic" imperative that individuals like Cowperwood fearlessly obey, and it is dependent on forms of accounting, financial and amoral, that are inexplicable to the general public. The second kind of obligation, to obey public laws, juridical or religious, is artificial and contemptible, an expression of "those shibboleths of the weak and inexperienced mentally."[3] The first half of the novel, focusing on Cowperwood's financial accounting, and the second half, focusing on his legal accountability, bring the two forms of obligation, self-interested owing and self-sacrificing ought, together and bring their opposition into relief. The Financier focuses on these forms of obligation to illuminate the conflict between natural and conventional forms of accounting. More strikingly, it uses them to document the natural and sociological forces that determine the limits or margins of accountability, the line that distinguishes what can and cannot be brought to book, what falls within and without the edges, literally and figuratively, of various kinds of accounts: financial ledgers, the Philadelphia Public Ledger (the city newspaper), the reports of Pinkerton detectives, law books, the Bible, and The Financier itself.

The novel's meticulous detailing of what can and cannot be brought to financial, legal, and moral account has a direct—and, I claim, intentional—bearing on the novel's literary argument about genre. In studying the limits of what can be brought to account, Dreiser exposes the limits of conventional biographical and fictional accounting. Indeed, one of The Financier's primary aims is to show how conventional biographies and biographical fiction cannot adequately describe, let alone explain, Cowperwood or his status as an agent of nature. Put simply, these conventional literary genres cannot adequately convey the sociology that accounts for the financier's demise or the metaphysics that accounts for his "inevitability."[4] *The Financier* highlights their failure and self-consciously inaugurates, in their place, a new genre, what we might call, borrowing today's familiar televisual term, the nature special.

Dreiser indicated the main aim of the nature special and its difference from biography when he explained to a reviewer that *The Financier* studies a "condition," not "a man."[5] It examines the social activity and psychological attitude encouraged by particular historical circumstances and their predominating ethics. Dreiser is less interested in Cowperwood (or Yerkes) as an exceptional individual than as a symptom or representative of such an activity and attitude. He set the plot of the novel in the economic boom after the Civil War because these years, like periods in ancient Rome or Machiavelli's Italy, according to Dreiser, featured singular examples of "mental action spurred by desire, ambition, vanity, without any of the moderating influences which we are prone to admire—sympathy, tenderness and fair play."[6] Philadelphia, the nation's financial center after the Civil War, provided an ideal setting to study the "natural action" of men, such as Yerkes, who were unrestrained by "convention, theory, prejudice and belief of any kind."[7]

The Financier's main interest is not finance, per se, but rather the sociological truths and natural laws that financial life, under such no-holds-barred conditions, obeys. *The Financier* studies what Dreiser imagines to be men in nature, or, more precisely, men as nature, driven by their instinct for self-preservation and satisfaction, relentlessly scheming for advantage over each other, making alliances of convenience, and preying on others the moment their vulnerabilities become exposed. *The Financier* follows the growth of a natural creature (Philip Gerber calls him *Genus Financierus Americanus*), documents the training of his instincts as a opportunist and plotter, and, beginning with the financial panic following the Chicago Fire, focuses on a dramatic, prolonged test of his survival skills.[8] In short, *The Financier* documents the operation of nature and its laws as they reveal themselves in the title character's fights with other men and his attempt to impose stability on an unpredictable universe.

More exactly, and more centrally for my argument, The Financier documents how nature and its laws express themselves through artificial forms of and attempts at accounting. Accounting provides the medium and idiom in which Cowperwood's fight for survival is carried out. This focus marks The Financier's difference from Dreiser's earlier published novels, Sister Carrie (1900) and Jennie Gerhardt (1911), which also study natural desires in conflict with conventional morality.[9] This focus explains why Dreiser constructs the novel around the financial panic and the legal case against Cowperwood, why he not only likens them to each other but also leads us inexorably from one to the other. In the same way that financial accounting serves as the instrument through which Cowperwood acts out his will to power, legal accountability (combined with narrative accounting, in surveillance reports and news stories) serves as the instrument through which his enemies attack him after the panic. I want to argue, in fact, that Dreiser's nature special narrates the fate not of the financier, exactly, but of accounting itself.

Critics commonly note that in Dreiser's fiction individuals act as agents of impersonal forces and imperatives. In The Financier this force or imperative assumes the form of the will-to-account, or, what amounts to the same thing, the will-to-make-accountable. Cowperwood and his antagonists achieve importance primarily as bearers of this will, as instruments through which accounting attempts to colonize more and more spaces, material (in Cowperwood's hands), moral (in his nemesis, Butler's, hands), and disciplinary (in the court's hands). Accounting, for Dreiser, resembles Spirit for Hegel or Capital for Marx. The Financier follows this apotheosized abstraction—Accounting, or Accountability—as it manifests itself through the social activity of men, most obviously under crisis conditions that encourage the full play of individuals' natural instincts.[10]

Reading The Financier as a tale of "accounting" rather than as a tale of desire answers two questions students and scholars routinely ask about The Financier: why Dreiser gives such sustained attention to technical aspects of Cowperwood's financial operations and the legal process, and why the narrative repeats itself so much, sometimes including four or five accounts of the same event in a single chapter.

Dreiser's editors at Harper's, struggling to streamline his massive manuscript, also wondered about this. They observed that such intricate and repeated accounts made "rather involved, difficult reading" and emphasized that "it is the main point of the situation that the reader wants to grasp."[11] For Dreiser, however, the presence of these seemingly extraneous accounts may be the main point of the novel. In the universe of *The Financier*, accounting precedes human subjects, constituting them, shaping their ambitions, providing both the instrument and the language in which individuals, acting out the mandates of nature, understand and carry out their plots. The wearying expository accounts, seen in this way, do not so much interrupt the novel's plot and plotters as frame or embed them. Accounting, in a very real sense, is the main character, certainly the main subject, of the novel. The accretion of so much detailed explication, like the pairing of the panic and the trial, illuminates the fate of accounting, its success and failure, its expansion and delimitation.

Panic and Prospect

For Dreiser, the world of finance typifies the world of nature and reveals its sociological laws. In the stock exchange, "men came down to the basic facts of life—the necessity of self care and protection. . . . Force governed this world—hard, cold force and quickness of brain. . . . To get what you could and hold it fast . . . that was the thing to do" (TF 102–3). Conventional morality holds no sway here; each man looks out for his own interests. The law of survival of the fittest, under which, according to Spencer, "personal ends must be pursued with little regard to the evils entailed on unsuccessful competitors," determines the fortunes of stock operators.[12] However, as Cowperwood's early success demonstrates, individuals, to advance their own interests, must depend on and do business with each other. They must plot at least a segment of their future together by binding themselves to contracts, loan schedules, and other financial obligations. For Dreiser, debt serves as the most obvious sign and instrument of this interdependence. In flush times, debt binds lenders and borrowers productively, advancing each's interests. In financial panics, such as the one that triggers the action of the novel, however, debt transforms cooperation into desperate competition. Financial panic serves as an exemplary naturalist moment, a trial or test intensifying and revealing the stakes of Darwinian struggle. The weak, the cowardly, and the shortsighted, unable to compete for scarce credit to pay off their debts, go bankrupt. Panic institutes a "hard logic, sad, [and] cruel," that licenses creditors' ruthlessness and activates their predatory instincts (TF 92).

More exactly, panic initiates their plotting. The strong do not impulsively attack the weak but rather strategize how best to capitalize on their vulnerabilities. Before the panic, constructing his seemingly hazard-proof accounting structure, Cowperwood imagines that he can circumvent or protect himself against such plots. However, during the panic and, indeed, directly because of it, his every action triggers plotting by others, and their plots continually trigger new plots and counterplots as everyone calculates how best to exploit Cowperwood's shortfall. Every effort of his to balance his financial accounts must account for these counterdesigns. Crucially, however, Cowperwood's efforts fail because the counterdesigns initiate forms of accounting— new financial bookkeeping, retribution, surveillance, ethical investigations, legal adjudication, and penal discipline—that circumscribe his strategic options.

Two forms of accounting, what I will call "prospect" and "payback," echoing Dreiser's own language, propel these schemes and counterschemes. "Prospect," by which I mean both a temporal outlook and a spatial or mental overview, describes Cowperwood's confidence, shattered by the panic, that he has accounted for everything related to his future. It also describes the efforts by Butler after the exposure of the defalcation and the affair to bring the financier and his financial manipulations within the "purview" (TF 672) of the law, the limits of which become the focus of the trial. The second form of accounting that drives the novel, "payback," describes the attempt by everyone who has borrowed money or speculated on margin to meet their financial obligations to brokers, banks, and, in Cowperwood's case, the city treasury, after the fire. It describes, similarly, the effort by Cowperwood and the city officials to eliminate the unexpected and incriminating shortfall in the city treasury exposed by the panic. Crucially, payback also refers to Butler's attempts to exact vengeance on the financier for taking his daughter ("ye had to steal my daughter from me in the bargain" [TF 615]), a settling of accounts that we are clearly meant to pair with the paying of debts, as Dreiser's use of financial language makes clear. Butler seeks to "pay" (TF 745) Cowperwood back in "return" (TF 440) for his theft, to make things "even" with him (TF 744), to take back what is "belongin'" to him (TF 368). (In his philosophical essay "Equation Inevitable," Dreiser equates "vengeance," "repayment," and "strik[ing] a balance.")[13]

Operating against these two kinds of accounting activity is another kind of determinism that drives *The Financier*'s plot—and plotters—forward: *contagion*, the epidemic agency characterized by the Chicago Fire, the financial panic incited by the fire, and the resistless spread of news, rumors, and other narrative accounts prompting and prompted by the panic. *The Financier* studies how these countervailing determinisms, one that seeks to contain accounts and one that serves to spread them, fuel and foil each other. Contagion, taking the form of fire, panic, and publicity, generates the urgency to settle accounts (to pay off financial debts, to pay back enemies); conversely, the urgency to settle accounts produces the very forms of contagion (publicity and more debt) that inevitably disable and undermine any full accounting. Dreiser buoys his narrative on this dialectic to show that accounts are never closed or closable: there is always some remainder, something "extra"—an "outstanding obligation" (TF 293), an "extra" news account (TF 292), increased brokers' margins, an irrepressible desire, some act of nature—that not only endures but also incites more acts of accounting. Indeed, the clash between closing accounts and opening new ones underwrites *The Financier*'s basic thesis that nature and the individuals through whom it operates cannot be fully accounted for.

For Dreiser, the financial panic caused by the Chicago Fire serves as the central exhibit of this clash of determinisms. In it, we see how Cowperwood's efforts to gain prospect, to bring space (the expanding city) and time (the expanding future) within the margins of his accounting, is frustrated by the epidemic effects activated by the Chicago Fire. Put simply, Cowperwood fails because he imagines that he can account for everything. Hired to help the city pay back its debts (significantly, to float one debt to pay off another), he has free access to the city's funds, which he is allowed to borrow and invest on his own account so long as he "render[s] an accounting" (TF 191) or strikes a "balance" (TF 572)—that is, returns the principal—at the end of every month. He puts this money to work with exquisite efficiency, buying up undeveloped railroad lines, issuing new stock in these lines, and using the profit as margin for more speculations, more hypothecations, and more purchases. It is all "a mere matter of bookkeeping" (TF 191), of shifting around the massive accounts, hundreds of thousands of dollars each, and "transfer[ring] the balances" (TF 279) that he carries "on his books" (TF 275). At the peak of his power—that is, just before the panic—Cowperwood has "surrounded and entangled himself in a splendid, glittering network of connections, like a spider in a spangled net, every thread of which he [knows] . . . and he [is] watching all the details" (TF 275). Dependent on such vast, intricate, and fragile credit arrangements, this accounting structure collapses when banks ask him for more collateral or margin to safeguard their loans in the aftermath of the fire. When the stock market crashes, he cashes a $60,000 city check without authorization, and, not long thereafter, denied access to the treasury's mother lode, he is forced to close his doors.

Cowperwood fails, clearly, because he is trapped by his entanglements. He cannot pay the higher brokerage margins generated by the panic. More significantly, he fails because he tries to bring everything within a totalizing vision. Dreiser signals the importance of this vision —and also anticipates its failure—in a crucial image that connects Cowperwood's watchfulness over his accounts, his supervision of his expanding railroad operations, and a prophecy of his career prospects: "By the summer of 1871, when Cowperwood was nearly thirty-four years of age, he had a banking business estimated at nearly two million dollars . . . and prospects which looked forward along a straight line to wealth which might rival that of any American if he continued" (TF 275). The panic exposes and enforces the limits of such prospect(s). Despite his apparent vantage over his massive web of accounts, despite the close monitoring of the margin accounts on his books, Cowperwood fails to consider the margins *of* his account books; he fails to see what cannot be accounted for, what lies outside accountability: the "unforeseen, incalculable" financial panic that follows the Chicago Fire (TF 275).

Panic puts an end to Cowperwood's prospects because, for Dreiser, the universe, governed by inscrutable and impersonal forces, subject to chance and flux, must frustrate any attempt to bring the future into line, to plot it, to see it prospectively. ("Nature seeks, if She seeks anything, motion, although apparently in no straight line," wrote Dreiser elsewhere.)[14] Nature defies any attempt to contain it within a single vision or to hold it hostage it to a single design. Nature marks the limits of such a design by spreading its effects uncontainably. Raging "unchecked," the Chicago Fire spreads its ruinous financial effects across the nation, from city merchants to their insurers to bankers out East and ultimately to all the businessmen and investors in Philadelphia whose loans the bankers call (TF 293). Panic shatters Cowperwood's prospects because it radiates beyond his, or anyone's, ability to control. Indeed, the chain of indebtedness that links all of these actors, triggering the stock stampede in Philadelphia, mocks the "endless chain" of Cowperwood's borrowing and leveraging, terminating it and turning it against him (TF 198).

The panic makes sensationally obvious how every attempt to pay back one debt generates another debt, culminating in Cowperwood's fateful decision, for which he is ultimately sent to prison, to pay on one debt (the $500,000) by taking out another (the $60,000). The panic shows, just as importantly, how the contagion of indebtedness produces a contagion of narrative accounting, how news reports, rumors, and stories spread like debt and because of it. The epidemic radiation of fire ruins him, specifically, because it activates an uncontainable proliferation of narrative lines that ultimately rupture and replace the "straight line to wealth" encompassed within Cowperwood's prospect(s). These narrative lines play a crucial thematic and narrative role in *The Financier*, and they serve, much like Cowperwood's "extra" financial lines, to model the narrative machinery of *The Financier* itself.

The first instance of such narrative contagion comes as an immedi-

ate consequence of the fire and occurs, significantly, just as Cowperwood surveys a prospective rail extension, the very line, we are led to
believe, that will ensure his "straight line to wealth." Out with his
bankers, the financier hears a newsboy shout, "Ho! Extra! Extra! Chicago burning down! Extra! Extra!" (TF 292). Radiating outward from
the city center, the "extra" account spreads the financial panic, mock-
ing Cowperwood's prospect(s) by achieving what he fatally cannot: it
brings the unaccountable disaster to account. It incorporates what is
outside accounting—what is "extra"—within its textual margins and
capitalizes on it. Dreiser signals why Cowperwood will fail—and fore-
shadows the importance of accounting's margins throughout the remainder of the novel—by training our eyes on the margins of the news
account. Under the banner "ALL CHICAGO BURNING" (TF 293), he
presents the thirty-five word headline as an inverted pyramid, the only
such typographical gimmick in the novel:

FIRE RAGES UNCHECKED IN COMMERCIAL SECTION SINCE YESTERDAY
EVENING. BANKS, COMMERCIAL HOUSES, PUBLIC BUILDINGS
IN RUINS. DIRECT TELEGRAPHIC COMMUNICATION
SUSPENDED SINCE THREE O'CLOCK TO-
DAY. NO END TO PROGRESS
OF DISASTER IN SIGHT.

The placement of the break between the last two lines is richly sugges-
tive, for it encourages us literally to see how the prospect of endless
progress becomes, once our eyes account for the margin, the prospect
of endless disaster. The inverted pyramid shape is likewise crucial
since it anticipates—even as the panic-producing headline activates—
the upending of Cowperwood's own "pyramiding" scheme (TF 190).[15]
Reporting the "unchecked" spread of fire, the proliferation of narrative lines, like the spread of credit and railroad lines that underwrite
the financier's progress, points to disaster. Broadcasting alarm, these
lines disseminate the panic and ensure that debts cannot be paid in
full, that accounts remain open.

The spread of narrative accounts, like the spread of indebtedness,
produces more attempts at accounting. We see this when Cowperwood, having no other way to balance financial accounts with the city,

goes to Butler to confess his predicament and ask for more money. His decision to give a verbal report of the treasury shortfall backfires, since, exposing Cowperwood to the accounting (literally, the financial auditing) of city insiders, it sets in motion the financial, personal, and juridical payback schemes, led by Butler, that doom him. Significantly, Cowperwood's confession is punctuated by the newsboy's cries of "Extra! Extra!" (TF 304). We are meant to see that efforts to balance accounts, to contain potential scandal and exposure, lead inexorably to new(s) accounting that proliferate beyond his, or anyone's, capacity to contain. To signal this proliferation, Dreiser employs a narrative strategy he relies on throughout the novel: he repeats himself. He has Butler retell Cowperwood's account of the treasury shortfall three times within a single chapter.

This series of narrative accounts triggers the predatory instinct in every city insider who discovers Cowperwood's vulnerability. Like every predatory act in The Financier, the insiders' attack takes the form of an effort to bring to account. Akin to Cowperwood's effort to square financial accounts, however, this bringing-to-account is frustrated by the epidemic spread of narrative reports, particularly in the newspaper. The city insiders realize that if Cowperwood fails and the treasurer is left "short in his accounts" (TF 319), their own illicit borrowing of city money might be exposed, and the publicity attending the missing $500,000 might cost them the upcoming election. They understand that public discredit, like debt, proliferates contagiously, that "nothing is . . . so indiscriminate as public clamor" (TF 411). Unable to get rid of the massive treasury deficit, they search for a way to deflect accountability from themselves. Tipped off by Butler, they decide to use Cowperwood's $60,000 bank draft to scapegoat the financier. They decide, that is, to make him accountable. They do this literally by bringing him to book, compelling him—a master bookkeeper, someone who even as a boy knew "how to keep books" (TF 44)—to turn over his account books to their accountants. They want to determine the scope of his record keeping, to make visible what he's kept on and off his books, to determine, in short, what and where the margins of his accounting are.

Such a reckoning spreads rather than squares accounts, however.

To highlight this, Dreiser plays on the shared vocabulary of finance and rumor: he has an auditor also be a teller. Albert Stires, one of the city accountants now poring over Cowperwood's books, was the bank teller who delivered the fateful $60,000 check to the financier; he is the one who alerts Cowperwood to a rumor he has heard concerning the insiders' plot to make the financier pay for his (out)side accounts. Dreiser signals the thematic importance of accounting's interminability by tracing how the rumor spreads through the city's back rooms, one account's auditor becoming its next teller. In a striking instance, Stires tells Cowperwood what someone named Robert Wotherspoon had told him about what "Harmon had said to Strobik and Borchardt that Mollenhauer had said to Butler, in some conference which had been reported to Harmon" (TF 454). The contagiousness of rumor endangers the insiders' scheme and provokes more accounting. News editors, catching wind of the stories that are on the loose, sniff a scandal, and the city insiders realize they must spin the inevitable exposure. When it becomes clear that a "public storm might break loose at any hour" (TF 457), the insiders craft a public account of Cowperwood's malfeasance, emphasizing that he acted alone, without authorization, and, since much of his borrowing went unrecorded, outside any accounting ("It would appear that he has been held to no responsibility in these matters" [TF 463]). Pressed by Butler, they go further and set Cowperwood up to be tried, to be "made" (TF 368) criminally liable for his off-the-books financial dealings. They expand the scope of their accounting, transforming what had been the "trivial and uncertain matter" of the $60,000 into the centerpiece of their media campaign (TF 457). Their campaign works. Cowperwood is "written down as 'failed' on a score of ledgers in Philadelphia" (TF 379) and, more disastrously for him, exposed to a public "storm" of ill will when the citizens' watchdog group, the Citizens' Municipal Reform Association, broadcasts his activities in the *Public Ledger*, the same paper that mapped the spread of the fire and whose "extra" account fanned the panic.

The machinations of the city insiders are important to *The Financier* not only because they focus our attention on the construction of the margins of accountability—the determination of what accounts are on and off Cowperwood's books, what accounts fall within or without the city's supervision, and how public blame is shifted from inside to "outside the party lines" (TF 465)—but also because they introduce the connection between private accounting and public accountability that constitutes the thematic crux of the novel. They initiate the bringing-to-account—the auditing, surveilling, and disciplining of the financier —that gathers momentum, depth, and breadth as it is taken over by the court and the prison system through the rest of the novel. The machinations of the insiders are important, above all, because they end in Cowperwood's being written down in public accounts. Exposure in the *Public Ledger* marks the irreversibility of his subjection to others' bookkeeping. With his scheming exposed to the uncomprehending, moralistic public, the account of his illicit operations spreads beyond his or anyone's ability to stop. In this sense, the proliferation of the news report, the widening of the "fatal, poisonous field of press discussion" (as Dreiser calls it in *The Titan*), continues, even culminates, the work of the panic.[16]

Cowperwood is not the only one whose attempt to square accounts and limit the radiation of scandal backfires. Butler, for example, wants nothing more than to keep his daughter's affair secret, and he seeks to bring Cowperwood within the clutches of the law as much to end the affair and prevent its potential exposure as to avenge Cowperwood's theft. Dreiser dwells for several pages on this potential exposure when he has Butler hire Pinkerton detectives to spy on Cowperwood and confirm the affair. (Like Cowperwood, Aileen uses private bookkeeping to cover her illicit activity: "a private circulating library" provides the "loophole" through which her activity outside the home has escaped her father's notice [TF 364].) Alive to the "danger of publicity" (TF 504), Butler fears that the detective's report will somehow circulate, spreading the scandal it is meant to contain. Indeed, at the end of the novel, despite the Pinkertons' professional discretion, Butler's effort to preempt rumor becomes the subject of rumor—just as the city insiders' effort to deflect their own accountability onto Cowperwood backfires when it becomes the focus of a subsequent exposé in the *Public Ledger*. In fact, the rumor that eventually circulates about the affair focuses not on Aileen but on Butler's own accounting, for the rumor starts as a way to explain the mystery of Cowperwood's harsh punishment; Butler's son hears someone report that his father "got even" (TF 744) with the financier by sending him to prison. Neither this gossip nor the accounting it aims to account for stops, however, for when one of Butler's sons asks him about it, Butler says "I'm not through with him yet . . . He's had somethin' to pay him for his dirty trick, and he'll have more" (TF 745). Only a page after this, Butler's other son is alerted to the same rumor being passed around his athletic club. He confronts the talebearer, and, to pay him back for what he's heard (and also to challenge him to repeat it), the son strikes the gossiper. Instead of quelling the scandal, the incident only "make[s] more talk" (TF 750).

The spread of news and scandal is important because its contagion, like that of fire and panic, exposes the limits of the various schemes to close accounts in The Financier. The dissemination of the newspaper is crucial because it also represents the most powerful expression of conventional moral and civic bookkeeping outside the margins of which Cowperwood, as a self-satisfying agent of nature, operates. The name of the Public Ledger, along with its fateful association with the Citizens' Municipal Reform Association—an association prompted by Butler's belief that "he was serving God when he did his best to punish Cowperwood and save Aileen" (TF 498)—makes the newspaper's status as moral and civic auditor plain. Like the city insiders who scrutinize Cowperwood's accounts and the Pinkertons who report on Cowperwood's affair, the newspaper attempts to bring what was previously unaccountable or outside accounts to view and to judgment. It aims, inexorably, to account for everything, for the Citizens' Municipal Reform Association is committed to following the treasury scandal "closely to the end" (TF 459)—a commitment, should we need to be reminded, that mocks Cowperwood's failed prospect over the arc of his career. In this sense, the publication of the Public Ledger reenacts the panic, which also exposed, through a similarly epidemic agency, the failure of individuals to meet their public (financial) obligations—and, in Cowperwood's case, exposed his betrayal of a "public trust" (TF 464), the public debt itself.

In "Ideals, Morals, and the Daily Newspaper," Dreiser observed that mainstream newspapers performed the work formerly done by preachers and reformers; papers were "guardians of all phases of virtue, honesty, and the like, to say nothing of those shibboleths of the would-be intellectually dominant, 'justice' and 'truth.'"[17] Advocating "moral self-control, public and private," for "the good of the other man," the newspaper expressed the obstructing ethics and civic ideals of the "little man."[18] In The Financier, the Citizens' Municipal Reform Association, publishing its investigations, represents this ethical counterforce. It embodies what Dreiser, drawing on Spencer, understood to be a metaphysical counterbalance to the natural activity of Cowperwood and the municipal underworld. For Dreiser, physical and social life is simply a balancing act, an "eternal battle" between opposing metaphysical tendencies that, whatever their specific character, keep the universe from resting at any extreme.[19] His point, elaborated throughout his essays in Hey Rub-a-Dub-Dub (1920), is not that the universe achieves a static balance, but rather the opposite: that the natural universe, the world of human society and striving, and the realm of ethics are each always in the process of balancing. The Financier clearly traces the battle between the moral vigilance represented by the Citizens' Municipal Reform Association and the amoral license represented by Cowperwood, but Dreiser figures this battle as a clash between abstractions, the accountable and the unaccountable, between the compulsion to achieve balance—he explicitly calls it "repayment" in "Equation Inevitable"—and the compulsion toward imbalance.[20] As he makes clear in another essay, the kind of moral and civic obligations rejected by Cowperwood represent nothing but "balances struck between man and man," a form of bookkeeping that keeps the stickling public from seeing the unaccountable world "beyond" their makeshift morality: the realm of nature that knows nothing of debts.[21]

In "Equation Inevitable," the essay critics most often cite in connection with The Financier, Dreiser summarizes the bottom line of his metaphysics of accounting: "Only a balance is maintained."[22] Here, "balance" has the same meaning as it does in financial bookkeeping: it describes what remains to be balanced, what must still be paid for a transaction to be settled or an account closed. It signals a state of suspension or disequilibrium, not stasis. This (im)balance, exposed by the financial panic, drives the narrative of The Financier. It constitutes the sustaining force that Walter Benjamin, describing novelistic suspense, compares to the "draft" in a fireplace which "stimulates the flame . . . and enlivens its play," a vacuum that maintains its drawing power even as (and because) it is continually filled.[23] Benjamin's image is useful here in that a "draft" resulting from a fire creates The Financier's only suspense: whether Cowperwood will balance his accounts and avoid having to "suspend" his operations (TF 423). What pulls the novel's drama forward is the financial vacuum produced by the Chicago Fire, the massive drafting on banks that creates the financial panic and leads to Cowperwood's fateful $60,000 "overdraft" (TF 574). More exactly, what draws the novel onward is the spread of narrative accounts that follows from these drafts. When Butler, learning of his daughter's affair with the financier, demands that Cowperwood return what he owes ("I'll have to have what's belongin' to me today"), Cowperwood realizes that "the least phrase might set the fires blazing" (TF 368). The rest of the novel both maps and constitutes the spread of this blaze.

A map of spreading fire in The Financier actually provides a model for the novel's own narrative determinism. After he confesses his financial predicament to Butler (who subsequently transmits the financier's account to various city officials, as I have noted), Cowperwood scans a story in the Public Ledger about the Chicago Fire and its probable financial ramifications. The account features a map of Chicago that marks the boundaries of the burned-out region. Dreiser dwells on Cowperwood's fascination with the map, his fear that this report will unleash a panic and require him to find "large sums of money to meet various loans" (TF 336). Indeed, Dreiser seems to link the map image and the panic, for only a page after it appears the stock collapse begins. In the 1927 revision of the novel, the version in print today, Dreiser reprises the image when a state senator, fearing newspaper scrutiny of the treasury deficit, tells the city insiders that "we ought to map out our program very carefully," suggesting that they prosecute the city treasurer "on our own account" and, to this end, manipulate the emerging press accounts of the shortfall.[24] This figurative map, like the earlier actual one, leads directly to a fateful reckoning: Butler, seeing his chance, sets his payback scheme in motion by suggesting that they can scapegoat Cowperwood, citing as cause the financier's unpaid $60,000 draft on the city account. Both maps represent *The Financier's* own balancing act, its dialectic of contagion and containment. These maps spread as well as specify accountability; they circulate as well as circumscribe narrative accounts; they incite payback as well as illuminate its inevitable, unaccountable failure.

A third and final map image makes this even clearer. It appears at the very end of the novel, at the start of the second panic, news of which "was spreading like wild-fire" (TF 771), despite the law's efforts to contain it ("a policeman arrested a boy for calling out the failure of Jay Cooke & Co."). Dreiser notes that Cowperwood had "once, not unlike the Chicago Fire map, . . . seen a grand prospectus and map" of Jay Cooke's intended railroad empire (TF 770). This prospectus now represents the limits, not the expansion, of prospect, for Cooke's "vision of empire" (TF 764), overextended, collapses suddenly, triggering the panic. "The project was so vast that it could not well be encompassed by one man" (TF 765). The map signals Cooke's catastrophic failure to settle accounts (and the epidemic of public indebtedness that this failure precipitates), but it also highlights Butler's ultimate failure to make Cowperwood accountable, for Cowperwood, pardoned and freed from prison, exploits the spreading panic and becomes a millionaire.

Purview

Dreiser structures *The Financier* around two events, the financial panic and Cowperwood's court case. Both focus on Cowperwood's unpaid debt to the public, his failed obligations, financial and ethical. In both events we see how others, prompted by Butler's secret vengeance, try to make the financier publicly accountable: to make him pay, financially and personally, for his illicit borrowing, and, more important, to make him and his "extra" accounts—his side deals, his rail extensions, his unrecorded speculations, his extramarital affair, and, finally, his unpaid treasury balance—subject to increasingly conventional and constricting forms of public discipline. In the panic he is subjected to the auditing of city accountants and the muckraking of the Citizens' Municipal Reform Association, two forms of bookkeeping that find expression in the *Public Ledger*. In the court case, he is subjected to the written law and its accounting. The trial exposes and explains the financier's manipulation of the public debt, but what matters even more is that, in the name of the court's "obligation" to the public (as Dreiser puts it in his 1927 revision of the novel), it renders its judgment on him.[25] Butler's private campaign to make Cowperwood publicly accountable, to make him pay his debt to the public (and to Butler himself), and to bring him under the law's discipline, culminates when Cowperwood is convicted by a jury and sentenced to prison, where his every action is brought under the panoptical gaze and accounting of the law. This accounting is literalized when Cowperwood is led naked into a "record and measurement room," where his body's measurements—"arms, legs, chest, waist, hips . . . the color of his eyes, his hair, his mustaches"—are written down in an overseer's "record-book" (TF 686).

Such a plotline—the accountant made accountable, the railroad baron "railroaded" (TF 507) into prison, the visionary brought under prison surveillance, the bookkeeper reduced to figures in a prison ledger—might seem to suggest that accounting can be brought to a close. However, the last part of *The Financier* makes plain that Cowperwood, as an agent of nature, cannot be accounted for. He cannot be explained, reckoned with, or convinced of the legitimacy and relevance of public morality and obligation, not even by the seemingly totalizing public discipline of the state, the most thorough of all public bookkeepers.

Dreiser uses the court case, just as he used the financial panic, to study the limits of accountability and, more exactly, the forces determining these limits. Just as the financial panic exposes the limits of what Cowperwood can bring to account or bring within his financial "prospects" (TF 275), the financier's court case exposes the limits of what the law can bring to book, what it can bring within its "purview" (TF 672). The court case focuses on these limits by interrogating not simply whether Cowperwood's overdraft of the $60,000 during the panic constitutes a loan or a theft, and not simply whether Cowperwood should be considered a legally accountable agent (that is, whether he acts on his own or acts for the city, and whether by following city custom he acts inside or outside the law), but also whether a decision against him makes every debtor in a panic a potential felon. As an appellate judge argues, a guilty verdict "extends the crime of constructive larceny to such limits that any business man who engages in extensive and perfectly legitimate stock transactions, may, before he knows it, by a sudden panic in the market or a fire . . . become a felon" (TF 633). At issue in the court case, in other words, is not only the extent of Cowperwood's accountability but also the extensiveness of legal accountability itself: how far can or should the law apply in a world where unaccountable nature makes certain obligations unfulfillable. For the dissenting judge, a guilty verdict, extending wherever indebtedness extends, makes the spread of legal accountability coterminous with the spread of panic itself.

For Dreiser, the law comes against its own limits when it has to bring unaccountable events—disasters that strike unexpectedly and spread uncontrollably, impelled by fire, panic, or the desire for financial survival—into its own accounting, when it has to decide, that is, the degree to which unaccountable events cause individuals to fail to obey the law, thus exonerating them. A financial panic occasions such an interrogation because in a panic, through no discernible fault of their own, trapped in a falling market, individual investors and businessmen find themselves suddenly short in their accounts, either because banks and brokers demand more margin, or because there is suddenly no cash available to pay off the debts they already have. In a panic, good-faith obligations (such as debts and contracts) cannot be met, and, for this reason, unpaid loans cannot be distinguished from thefts except by determining beyond a reasonable doubt whether a borrower knew he would be unable to pay back a loan when he took it out. Panic, however, being unforeseeable and, even after its onset, unpredictable, makes this determination of criminal intent impossible. In short, nature, obeying its own inscrutable laws, sets limits to the application of "all written law" (TF 549).

At least this is what Cowperwood's lawyer, Steger, argues. He in-

sists that "only the most unheralded and the unkindest thrust of fortune . . .—a fire and its consequent panic" have brought his client
"within the purview of the law" (TF 672). He makes this final, futile
plea at Cowperwood's sentencing, where the judge determines the
scope of the law's discipline by deciding the appropriate length of
punishment for each criminal. The sentencing makes clear how and
why Dreiser pairs the financial panic and the legal case. The sentencing, like the panic, imposes a form of payback whose terms Cowperwood cannot control. By enforcing this debt, the sentencing judge,
like Cowperwood's creditors in the panic, puts the financier's future
under obligation by deciding exactly what Cowperwood must do, and
for what duration, before he is free to plot his destiny for himself.

Dreiser pairs the sentencing judge and the financier's creditors in
order to bring the contrast between their kinds of law enforcement into
relief. For Dreiser, they express two sociological extremes, the antagonism and intersection of which *The Financier* aims, through its examination of the construction of the financier's accounting and accountability, to trace. At one extreme stands the world of finance during a panic.
This, as I have noted, embodies the world of nature tooth and claw,
where economic animals—"tigers facing each other in a financial
jungle" (TF 354)—fight each other for suddenly scarce resources, and
where the strong (that is, lenders) assert their strength over the weak
(that is, borrowers) in order to advance their own schemes and consolidate their own advantage. Uncontrollable agencies—the contagion of
fire, indebtedness, and panic—activate this naturalist drama. Cowperwood's creditors exploit these agencies and enforce the natural law of
the survival of the fittest. At the other sociological extreme stands the
court, where a jury, moved instinctively by a desire for consensus,
enforces the "wabbling" law of convention (TF 661), and where a
judge, acting out his ostensible obligation to protect the public and enforce civic morality, determines what Cowperwood owes for his crime.

The sentencing focuses our attention on the limits—the reach as
well as the futility—of the law's efforts at accounting by pairing Cowperwood with a petty thief who, like Cowperwood, fails to be disciplined even as he is punished. The thief, a slow, slouching African
American named Ackerman, seems oblivious to the entire point of his

sentencing and, for that matter, the law. He fails to grasp that taking what does not belong to him constitutes a crime, and he exasperates the judge, who attempts to make him obey the law by suspending his sentence, holding it over his head in perpetuity. Like Ackerman, Cowperwood does not recognize his own culpability. Also like Ackerman, Cowperwood is put under a potentially endless obligation, for Butler privately vows to spend his last dollar ensuring the financier's downfall (TF 376), and he insists, even after Cowperwood goes to jail, that he has not "got even" (TF 744) with the financier yet, that Cowperwood has "had somethin' to pay him for his dirty trick, and he'll have more" (TF 745). However, endless payback schemes, as the dismantling of Cowperwood's own accounting structure shows during the panic, cannot succeed: Cowperwood is sentenced to four years in prison, but he never serves his full term. The governor, urged by Cowperwood's lawyer, pardons him after thirteen months, once Butler dies and there is no longer any political obligation to make the financier continue to pay.

In short, Butler and the written law never close accounts with the financier. Cowperwood never pays Butler the money he owes, never returns Aileen, never pays the full price for his crime, and, most important for Dreiser, never acknowledges the moral and civic pedagogy that is supposed to attend the law's discipline. "I have had my lesson," he notes to himself at the end of the book, but the lesson simply confirms how the law cannot contain him: "They caught me once, but they will not catch me again" (TF 775). Moreover, his punishment does not change him. In the frenzy of the second panic, he is "perfectly calm, deadly cold, the same Cowperwood who had pegged solemnly at his ten chairs each day in prison" (TF 771). Nor does his punishment diminish the relentless drive for profit that made him vulnerable to the law in the first place. Indeed, as I have noted, it enables him to recoup his losses and begin again, for he is able to exploit the second panic precisely because the court and his creditors, in the desire to make him pay, have shorn him of his entangling accounts, allowing him to operate freely in a falling market.

Cowperwood's case exposes the limits of accountability not only because Cowperwood, obeying the laws of financial survival and self-advancement, resists having to pay his public and personal debt in full, but also because the conventional law masks and enables the kind of illicit scheming it is meant to punish. From the start, we are meant to see that the prosecuting lawyers and judges are driven by the same relentless plotting that compels Cowperwood. They are all what Dreiser elsewhere calls "tools" of nature.[26] Like Cowperwood, they advance their careers by incurring and paying off debts. "Owing to [their] political connections and obligations" (TF 630), they meet the demands of the city insiders who seek Cowperwood's conviction. In short, self-interest, constituted through such illicit and ubiquitous forms of payback, motivates the law's attempt at accounting.

Indeed, self-interest thrives *because* of this accounting. Dreiser demonstrates this most clearly when the sheriff at the county jail accepts a bribe from Cowperwood's lawyer, who hopes to keep the financier out of jail for a few more days. The jailer takes the money while offering to show the lawyer a "line of law-books" in his prison office (TF 640). We are supposed to see that conventional forms of public accounting—the jail and the written law—cannot contain even the law's overseer. Conventional forms of legal and moral bookkeeping can never bring men like him and Cowperwood, or their desire for profit, to account except in this winking, parodic way. The very books that cover, or discuss, the financier's crime, also cover, or mask, the law's circumvention, and they do this at the very moment and in the very place the financier seems most captive to the law's accounting. The law, in sum, literally contains, even as it fails to quarantine, its own subversion. Nature, expressing itself in the desire for such illicit deal making and extra accounting, thrives within and on the regime that ostensibly aims to obstruct it.

The Margins of Accounting

The Financier focuses not only on the margins of Cowperwood's financial accounts and legal and moral accountability but also—as suggested by the importance of books, bookkeeping, and the margins of written accounts within the story line—on the margins of its own narrative account, its own literal and figurative borders. Two extraordinary features of Dreiser's account shed light on this narrative self-consciousness. The first is the novel's ending, a formally idiosyncratic wrapping-up that enacts as well as reflects on the impossibility of closing narrative accounts. The second is the expository density of Dreiser's original manuscript (a density still recognizable in the aggressively reduced 1927 edition), its surfeit of technical explication and philosophical rumination that, gumming up the novel's narrative machinery, frustrated his editors at Harper's, who labored to distinguish the essential from the extraneous features of Dreiser's accounting—that is, what belonged inside and outside the margins of the book.

We might see both features of The Financier, the absence of a conventional ending and the cumbersome detail, as authorial failures, signs of graphomania, an inability to reign in a sprawling account, a miserly incapacity to discard any research finding, or simply an unmanageable prolixity. Reviewers and critics have found Dreiser guilty of all of these faults, and Dreiser himself, by welcoming H. L. Mencken's offer to pare down the manuscript, seemed to confess his own helplessness.[27] I want to suggest, however, that the limits of the novel's accounting, the margins determining the narrative's length and mass, represent strategic choices by Dreiser. They are not simply textual symptoms of his decision to cleave the Cowperwood manuscript at a convenient place and tie up the first volume as best he could to ensure that it would be marketable as a discrete—that is, finished—work. Rather, in keeping with the novel's repeated attention to forms and failures of accounting, they directly serve his argument about the limits of genre.

The Financier overtly invokes the formulas of biography and biographical fiction in order to mark how it moves beyond them. For its first 275 pages, up to the outbreak of the financial panic, The Financier adheres closely to the narrative formulas of financial biography—very closely, in fact, for portions of Cowperwood's boyhood are plagiarized, as Philip Gerber has shown, from a 1907 biography of Jay Cooke, the famous Philadelphia financier.[28] With the onset of the panic, however, the narrative suddenly abandons these conventions, most notably by narrowing its temporal scope, devoting its remaining five hundred pages to Cowperwood's accounting failure and its aftermath. The financier's failure is crucial for Dreiser because it exposes the inevitable failure of human schemes to square accounts and serves as a model for all the things that resist accountability throughout the remainder of the novel, most notably the financier himself. It exposes the formal and ethical inadequacy of conventional biographical and fictional plots. It does this by exposing the limitations of conventional endings to which these plots invariably tend and without which these plots remain morally inconclusive.

Dreiser shows how conventional biography and fiction, because of the contrivance of their teleology and closure, turn their protagonists' lives into moral fables, narrative molds too rigid, formally and ethically, to contain "life as it is, the facts as they exist."[29] Unlike these genres, the nature special, the experimental genre *The Financier* initiates exactly at the moment Cowperwood finds himself unable to balance his accounts, acknowledges the irreducible openness of the universe, the interminability of human plotting and counterplotting, and the impossibility of bringing any of these plots to a successful close. The nature special acknowledges the permanence of imbalance, or, put differently, the remainder of a balance at the end of all accounting.

The ending of *The Financier* illustrates this. Dreiser abandons the obligation felt by most biographers and fiction writers to construct an ending that frames the protagonist's life as a moral drama. Frederic Cooper explained this obligation in his review of *The Financier*. Most finance novels, he observed, followed a predictable formula: the hero rises, achieves success through "spectacular strokes of fortune," and falls as a result of some fatal mistake that "sends the whole carefully built structure tumbling, card-like, to the ground."[30] At the end, the hero, chastened by bankruptcy or dishonor, learns a moral lesson. The narrative "foreordains" such an ending; every part of its design points toward it, even if, as is often the case, the reader only sees this in retrospect, after he or she, upon reading the ending, steps back and gains interpretive prospect over the plot, seeing it as a closed whole. *The Financier*'s plot follows the rough outline of this formula and this "theory of endings" (as Cooper titled his review), but Cowperwood, as I have mentioned, draws no moral lesson from the trajectory of his career except, as Cooper himself notes, never to fall within the clutches of the law again.

Mencken, who viewed the "formal plot" as "that curse of fiction," celebrated Dreiser's rejection of moral lessons, his refusal to point his plot toward any overtly moral end.[31] In a review of The Titan, which he described approvingly as "a novel without the slightest hint of a moral," he complained that "the makers of best-sellers, if they could imagine [Cowperwood] at all, would seek to account for him, explain him, turn him into a moral (i.e., romantic) equation."[32] Mencken knew that Dreiser rejected such a moral equation as philosophically naïve. As Dreiser put it, "Life seems to prove but one thing to me, and that is that the various statements concerning right, truth, justice, mercy are palaver merely, an earnest and necessitous attempt, perhaps, at balance and equation where all things are so very much unbalanced, paradoxical and contradictory."[33] Despite the "religionists" and "moralists" and their metaphysics of duty, debt, and obligation, Dreiser believed that "there is scarcely a so-called 'sane,' right, merciful, true, just, solution to anything."[34] Endings did not confer coherence or moral order on the narratives—literary, biological, or philosophical—that led up to them. Life and lives could not be stabilized as an equation or balance, and the narratives that writers employed to convey them should not pretend otherwise.

The Financier rejects the formal—that is, moral—expectations not only of biographical fiction but also of biography. Dreiser's ambitions regarding genre become clearest, perhaps, when we consider The Financier in relation to a biographical essay on Yerkes that Dreiser consulted when conducting his research. The essay—"What Availeth It?"—was written by Edwin Lefèvre, a respected financial journalist and popular author of finance fiction whose Wall Street stories and novels exemplified—indeed, served as the template for—the formally balanced and morally predictable plots anatomized by Frederic Cooper and decried by Mencken. As I noted in chapter 4, the clever, often ironic, resolutions of Lefèvre's stories always succeed in balancing financial and moral accounts: immoderate and uncivil individuals always get their just deserts in the stock exchange. In the Yerkes article, Lefèvre insists that both human and fictional plots achieve their meaning only in retrospect, when seen as closed wholes or complete arcs, from a vantage beyond their ending: "The Great American Novel can be nothing but pages taken from the lives of Americans Who Do Things. Only in death is the moral of their tale plain. You read 'Finis' and then you begin to think. The glitter tarnishes; the jingle of the dollar ceases; envy is stilled. What remains?"[35] Lefèvre wrote this brief biography, he explains, to illuminate the "lesson"—actually two lessons—taught by the death of the famous financier. One lesson is that "there must be, always in the builder, *the sense of Death*" ("WAI" 836). Individuals must always aim to gain prospect over their own lives, to imagine reviewing their careers as if from the grave, and, inspired by such a perspective, fulfill their "duty . . . to leave the world the better for [their] having lived" ("WAI" 836). Their end—their aim and their death—is to serve this public obligation. The other lesson is that nature will pay back those who fail to pay their public debts—those, like Yerkes, who *"had taken and had not given"* ("WAI" 847). Nature holds borrowers accountable. For Lefèvre, this is why, when Yerkes died, the executors of his estate, instead of carrying out his will, sold his house and famous art collection at auction. In death, Yerkes was forced to pay his debts.[36]

The Financier, although it deals only with Cowperwood's early career, rejects such a zero-sum balancing. The novel exposes the limits of this balancing not only in its thematic preoccupation with unpaid debts (financial, moral, political, and penal) and forms of contagion (such as fire, indebtedness, publicity, and panic) that radiate outward, defying any attempt to circumscribe them, but also in the way the narrative concludes, or, rather, fails to reach a conclusion. In other words, Dreiser interrogates the margins of accountability not only within the story but also at, or, more precisely, as, the literal margins of his textual account. In the same way that the lawyers in Cowperwood's court case debate where his (or anyone's) accountability ends, Dreiser highlights the problem of where conventional narrative accounts end, what their limits are, what they can and, more important, cannot account for.

He does this by giving *The Financier* three provisional endings. Only the first of these is actually part of the story. It sums up how Cowperwood takes advantage of the panic of 1873 and recoups the fortune he lost during the panic two years before. At first glance, this abrupt ending, occupying just fifteen pages, appears to constitute the novel's attempt to square accounts. Cowperwood, forced because of debt to forfeit his property, his financial books, and his freedom, seems here to wipe the slate clean. Moreover, this balancing act evidently serves financial justice, for success seems the natural reward for his brilliance, the focus of the first third of the novel. Such an ending—the hero triumphing, regaining what he lost—might be regarded as a satisfyingly conventional way to complete the novel. Despite initial appearances, however, the ending does not square accounts. Indeed, by having Cowperwood win back his money through a financial catastrophe, it clearly mocks the idea, axiomatic to "the Christian and other metaphysical idealists," that "disaster" signifies "repayment" or retribution for "things done in opposition to [their] code."[37] It also recapitulates one of the ongoing themes of the novel: that every effort to close accounts, to make something accountable, to bring something within the margins of an account book, whether a financial ledger, a Bible, or a law book, not only fails but also produces more accounting, more balancing acts. Thus the story ends with Cowperwood plotting his future by scrutinizing financial clearing house books that tally credits and debts.

Accounts never close in The Financier. This comes, perhaps, as a surprise, since the novel, as I have discussed, beginning with the first financial panic, traces Cowperwood's subjection to increasingly panoptic and paralyzing forms of accounting, culminating in his conviction and imprisonment. According to this narrative logic, the financier's solitary confinement in prison should mark the end of the book. It does not, of course. Dreiser moves us straight from an image of the prison gates locking behind Cowperwood as he exits the prison to an announcement that "the banking house of Jay Cooke . . . closed its doors"; he moves us, that is, from the failure of the court's payback scheme to the "wide-spread ruin and disaster" of the panic of 1873 (TF 761). In short, one failure at payback (that is, Butler's vengeance and the law's punishment) leads sequentially and causally to another, more massive, one (that is, the catastrophic indebtedness that ruins borrowers in the panic). The law's accounting does not chasten or bankrupt Cowperwood; instead, it allows him to exploit others' debts and accounting failures. What remains is not any kind of moral lesson or ethical dividend, as Lefèvre would have it. Cowperwood, looking over his past, vows only to remain unaccountable. Indeed, defying the formulas of biography and biographical fiction, the past does not matter at all. The shape or plot of Cowperwood's life conveys no significance since he is simply acting out nature's mandate to move forward, profit, prey, and be preyed on by other natural creatures—to survive in a universe constantly threatening to undermine his prospects. Poring over bank balance sheets, he simply moves on.

The ending amounts to this: nature is not accountable. It cannot be conveyed by or contained within conventional accounts that, in their ending, offer moral (or any other) prospect over the lives they have narrated. Nature has no end: no aim, no conclusion. But even this conclusion does not close the novel, for Dreiser appends two additional endings that, instead of capping off the narrative, justify its open-endedness.

The first of these extra or outside accounts is a short study of the black grouper, a fish whose power to camouflage itself exemplifies, for Dreiser, the values privileged by nature: not virtue, obligation, or fairness, but "subtlety, chicanery, trickery" (TF 779). Dreiser presents this self-contained nature special, "Concerning Mycteroperca Bonaci," as a meditation on ends. He justifies the presence of the essay, for example, by noting its "considerable value as an afterthought" (TF 778). An afterthought is a remainder, something extraneous and yet accretive, building on what precedes it, indebted to it, marking its limits while also advancing them. We are meant to compare this afterthought with what is supposed to remain after Cowperwood's prison experience, the moral reflection, the disciplinary payoff, that, according to conventional moral bookkeeping, is supposed to steer him in the future. (The passage about the "lesson" Cowperwood takes from his experience comes shortly before this essay on the grouper.) However, both afterthoughts show only the irrelevance of such bookkeeping, for "Concerning Mycteroperca Bonaci" mocks the notion of providence or an "overruling, intelligent, constructive" intention that shapes the ends of men and nature (TF 779). In "Secrecy—Its Value," an expanded version of the grouper essay, Dreiser dismisses the "morality which is constantly seeking to befog or misinterpret" the universe.[38] He insists that "life" cannot be accounted for since one can never be sure how complete one's accounting ever is. Because "Nature reveals Her secrets to no man," the project of bringing her to book "is all a process of inclusion, and hence exclusion." For this reason, her bookkeepers must constantly interrogate the margins of their accounts and ask, "How little included? And how much excluded?"[39] These are precisely the questions, I am suggesting, that The Financier's endings, marking the ends and limits of its own accounting, raise.

"Even the longest of novels must have an end," noted a reviewer of The Financier, but the novel casts suspicion on this claim, since not even the "afterthought" about nature's ends brings an end to the text.[40] After he completed a draft of the novel, as Donald Pizer notes, Dreiser appended a second postscript, "The Magic Crystal," which, rather than capping off the narrative that precedes it, previews the remainder of the Cowperwood saga.[41] This brief prospectus signals a new beginning. The act of closing accounts opens new ones—a textual necessity (and perhaps also a commercial one) when one ends the first volume of a trilogy, but also a formal enactment of one of The Financier's central ethical and narrative claims. One who had been "a mystic or a soothsayer," Dreiser writes, might have seen in "the mystic bowl" (TF 779) a future of wealth and power for Cowperwood and "a whole world reading with wonder, at times, of a given name" (TF 780). Dreiser insists, though, that this prophecy must fail, for the fortune-teller's instruments will not reveal the full story of the financier's future. They will conjure forth all the signs of success the reader of a conventional success story might expect, all the signs a reader of The Financier, too, might expect, given the upward and onward trajectory of Cowperwood's career after exiting prison; however, such signs, Dreiser emphasizes, will obscure the more fundamental incompleteness of a life that will end in "sorrow, sorrow, sorrow" (TF 780).

Dreiser concludes the novel by asking, "What wise man might not read from such a beginning, such an end?" (TF 780). At first glance the question seems to suggest, against everything I have been arguing, that prospect is possible, that accounts can be given in full, that plots can be mapped out in advance, and, above all, that Cowperwood pays for his sins, that he is made accountable after all. However, nothing in this coda indicates that Cowperwood deserves such sorrow. The future vision simply documents his future unhappiness, interpreting it as a natural concomitant of success, not a punishment for any choice Cowperwood makes. Indeed, like the point of the epigraph from Richard III that opens the novel—"I came into the world feet first and was born with teeth. The nurse did prophesy that I should snarl and bite"—the point of the last line is that Cowperwood has no choice but to live life the way he does.[42] He does not choose his vocation or his fitness as an agent of nature; he simply fulfills it. He never becomes anything other than what he already was. This is why no ending can confer meaning or shape on the story of his life: his life, like that of an animal studied in nature, has no plot, no formal design, since it simply expresses nature's compulsions. It has no end, no purpose that its ending might reveal.

My final claim is more speculative. I want to suggest that Dreiser calls attention to the limitations of conventional biographical and fictional accounting not only in the way he ends (or fails to end) the novel but also in the way he forestalls this ending by encumbering the narrative with "the sheer mass of detail" that reviewers, even those who celebrated the novel, found exasperatingly redundant and wearisome.[43] "You wonder, for page after page, if there is any actual end to get to," wrote one reviewer, a question many students, slugging through the comparatively zippy 1927 edition, echo today.[44] Mencken asked, "Why give the speeches of the lawyers in full? Why describe so minutely the other prisoners sentenced with Cowperwood? . . . All of these things are well described, but they have nothing to do with the story."[45] As James Hutchisson details, Ripley Hitchcock, Dreiser's editor, cut out epigraphs, lengthy descriptions of financial operations, sections of turgid philosophizing, a whole chapter mingling quotations from artists and Dreiser's glossings, and other passages seemingly extraneous to the novel's "main point."[46]

Dreiser consented to these changes and made cuts of his own, agreeing that the manuscript was too long. Close to the publication date, he even wrote Mencken, "If you think of any whole chapters that could be taken out bodily, wire me."[47] However, despite the editorial pressure to reduce the manuscript, Dreiser may have bloated and encumbered his narrative on purpose. The massiveness of the text is not due, at least not primarily, to Dreiser's "oafish clumsiness," or to his ambition to paint a panoramic canvas of America and its exceptional energies, or to his effort to "give order and direction to an extraordinary complex muddle of events," both civic and personal, spanning several decades.[48] Rather, he wrote "with a hand that is unrestrained by any sense of the eternal fitness of things" (as one reviewer chided) because things, not being eternally fit, could not be comprehended within the conventional conveyances of biographical or fictional form.[49] Contrary to Hitchcock's assessment, the apparent digressiveness—the seeming marginality of the sections that focus on financial and legal accounting and the philosophical passages that explain this accounting—directly serves Dreiser's argument about the limits of conventional accounts.[50] Mencken, despite his enduring qualms about Dreiser's "rambling, formless, chaotic" style and his private conviction that Dreiser had "got drunk upon his own story and ran amuck," seems to have recognized this, for he acknowledged and, indeed, admired, how in The Financier "the irrelevant, in the long run, becomes, in a dim and vasty way, relevant."[51] What seems marginal is actually central; what seems outside the main account is actually inside it.

Within the diegesis, the novel focuses on the limits of conventional financial, legal, and ethical accountability. These limits are exposed by extra accounts—Cowperwood's illicit side deals, the news accounts that spread panic, the brokers' margins created by the panic, the unpaid balances that sustain the narrative action. Dreiser's own extra accounts, expanding the novel, do the same thing. By including so much seemingly extraneous exposition, Dreiser aims to provide a more capacious and flexible vehicle for describing nature's unaccountability, its resistance to being brought to book. If Dreiser seems driven by an urge always to add more, to explain more, to stop and comment on his narrative, to go on endlessly, it is because in nature accounts never close.

Epilogue

Panic fiction offers an extraordinary lens—or, more exactly, prism—through which to read how modern understandings of economic crisis, crowds, and markets emerged. Through it, we can see how Americans of the late 1800s and early 1900s struggled to conceptualize financial modernity—a modernity Americans saw as cause and corollary of other forms of social transformation—and test their conceptualizations in narrative form. In addition, we can see how turn-of-the-century writers fixated on financial markets, especially markets in crisis, to confront the boundaries of novels' political, economic, and aesthetic capabilities.

My chapters have explored a number of ways in which fiction during this period shaped financial markets, constructing their social meanings and leveraging their material effects. I want to conclude my study by looking at the converse relation: how financial markets shaped fiction, serving not simply as the subject and setting of a popular subgenre of novels but also as an engine and condition of fiction writing itself.

Reflecting on the sensational manipulations, booms, and crashes that unbalanced Wall Street between 1900 and 1904, the banker Henry Clews concluded that "there is no more interesting or exciting serial story than the stock ticker tells, from day to day, . . . or one that often excites more joy or sorrow, or carries with it more weal or woe, prosperity or ruin."[1] Novelists located the market's narrative appeal in the unpredictable spiking and plunging of prices, and they drew their suspense from the market's ups and downs, hanging their plotlines on the reward or ruin potentially befalling their protagonists. In their novels and critical writings, writers often reflected on the enabling condition of this suspense, tracing it to the peculiar operation, formalized within financial markets, by which otherwise unremarkable goods become objects of speculation. Henry K. Webster's panic novel *The Banker and the Bear* (1900) offers one of the clearest articulations of this operation. Training our attention on the moment when goods are imbued with narrative life, Webster's narrator notes: "The hog is an uninteresting beast. . . . There is no individuality about him; no interesting variation from the normal to attract our studious attention. But when, by a swift and highly ingenious metamorphosis, he ceases to be a Hog, and becomes Provisions, he assumes a national importance; his fluctuations become fascinating, romantic. . . . He builds fortunes for some men, and others are brought to irretrievable ruin from yielding to his alluring seductions."[2] Webster is describing the moment when market objects become awakened, as it were, into narratability.

Webster's depiction of the birth, phenomenologically speaking, of the commodity differs markedly from the Marxian account that, until recently, has dominated cultural and literary studies of "the marketplace." Rather than lamenting nature's fall into the realm of exchange, a fall that leaches objects of their sensuous reality and drains the commodity-dominated world of human significance, Webster documents how, in becoming transformed into exchange value, speculative goods open up rich and historically fateful imaginative and emotional possibilities. Disencumbered of their materiality, goods become prices and as such—indeed, only as such—become capable of inspiring fantasies and fears about the shape of the future. As exchange value, they provoke observers to wonder where the market will go and what will happen to the personal, social, and national fortunes balancing on it. In short, speculative goods, becoming "fascinating" and "romantic," take on not simply economic but also aesthetic value. They exert a hold on individuals' imagination and emotions, triggering chains of real-world effects (such as bull markets, bankruptcies, and civic catastrophes) and consequently inciting projections of the many plotlines the future might follow.

In calling attention to the aesthetic (and other forms of cultural) energy made available by the phenomenological gap between Hogs and Provisions or objects and commodities, I mean to highlight something besides the semiotic status of financial signifiers, the central concern of many critical accounts of the relation between fiction and "the market." These accounts look closely at stock certificates, futures receipts, and paper money, asking whether such scriptural forms of

value are true or false, realistic or symbolic, close or distant representations of the "real" things that they ostensibly signify (tangible as-
sets, actual commodities, labor time, and the like). I wish to focus on
these scripts less as signs than as stories, less on the credit that readers invest in these representations than on the cultural, economic, and
aesthetic effects set in motion—the future imagined and brought into
being—by this investment.

Speculative markets do more than generate imaginative narratives.
They certify the narrative imagination as a driving force in national
economic and cultural life, for market fluctuations and their historical
effects are both pretexts for and products of speculative narratives. The
"fascinating" and "romantic" projections described by Webster are
what shape the confidence and calculations of the aggregation of individuals who constitute and control the market. Markets are moved by
narratives that appeal to the imagination and emotions of market
readers—narratives that excite, allure, and alarm or, in the extraordinary case of Thomas Lawson, discussed in chapter 2, elicit mass outrage and tearful sympathy.

Critics of financial speculation have always been astounded by the
power of published stories, whether true or false, invented or fac-
tual, to move markets. Throughout the nineteenth century, American observers warned against the power of promotional pamphlets
and books, including those identified as fiction, to capture investors'
imaginations and stimulate price bubbles—or, in the case of western
land promotions, "paper cities"—that collapsed disastrously the moment new story lines about diminishing returns or actual conditions
displaced, in the minds of investors, the glowing narratives that set the
boom in motion. My point here is not to rehash what market reporters
take for granted, that stock and commodity markets are extraordinarily sensitive to exciting rumors and reports, but rather to suggest
that we see the market as a realm shot through with narrative, an arena
constituted and continually reshaped by the imaginative projections of
a vast collection of market readers and writers. It is an arena materially
constructed out of and driven by storytelling, since speculations are at
bottom stories about the future, attempts to bring the future into

narrative line. I want to suggest, more exactly, that fiction writers at the turn of the century saw the market in this way and acted on the aesthetic and political commitments this vision entailed.

The sociologists Karin Knorr Cetina and Urs Bruegger clarify the notion of the market as a matrix of always-unfolding narrativizations in their study of the computer screens that amass and organize market data for traders at a Swiss investment bank. For Knorr Cetina and Bruegger, the market is the product of countless acts of interpretation and speculation by market participants, all competing with each other to render scattered, incomplete, and often contradictory bits of displayed data (such as prices paid and trades made) into profitable narrative shapes—claims and hunches that outline where prices will go and why. An aggregation of "processes and projections," the market is not a discrete entity signified by and thus separate from the screens.[3] Rather, the market is convened by these displays and constituted through myriad acts of reading and projection, the collective search for story lines. Crucially, the market can never be apprehended in its completeness. Pushed and pulled by events and the anticipations of other market participants, the market is always mutating, recomposing and redefining itself. It is "open, question-generating, and complex" ("Market" 149). Incapable of encompassing all the data relevant to a fluid and future-directed market, the representations on the display "never quite catch up with the object" ("Market" 155).

For Knorr Cetina and Bruegger, this incompleteness is significant for psychosocial reasons: it incites in traders a set of desires, professional and personal, which, because they are wedded to an urge for interpretive mastery, maintain their intensity precisely by remaining unfulfillable. For my purposes, the idea of the market as a narrative object sustained (and, indeed, constituted) by such a lack is important because it highlights how financial markets, and panics in particular, served as engines and conditions of fiction writing at the turn of the century in the United States. Like the traders and analysts in the sociologists' study, and like their own protagonists and narrators trying to make sense of the snowballing dynamics of the crowded marketplace, American novelists sought to gain cognitive and narrative control over price movements, to convert them into stories that promised aesthetic, if not financial, value. Their efforts were both frustrated and fueled by the market's chaotic significations and unknowable ramifications—frustrated, because the market threw the future open to question; and fueled, because this contingency furnished the uncertainty that gave literary plots their suspense. Writers like Frank Norris eroticized and sensationalized the market's narrative pull, its always-just-out-of-reach payoff of transparency and control. Theodore Dreiser went further and built into the very form of his fiction the market's "capacity to unfold indefinitely" (as Knorr Cetina and Bruegger put it ["Market" 149]). Dreiser serves as a fitting culmination to my study because he offers an unblinking analysis of the market's power to continually incite and undermine narrative. In fact, for Dreiser, it is the market's power to to draw forth new narrative accounts by deranging old ones—like a spreading fire that constantly sucks in air to fill the vacuum it creates—that makes evident the need for a new, open-ended, endlessly unfolding literary form. In Dreiser's aesthetic, the "incompleteness" of the market, exemplifying the unknowability of the future in a social universe where individuals relentlessly compete and collude, constitutes the source and symbol of literary possibility.

The example of Dreiser highlights what I take to be the dynamics of arrangement and derangement that animate panic fiction as a whole around the turn of the century. Novelists sought to bring particular markets (such as the Chicago Board of Trade and the Boston copper market) under the dominion of literary plot and formal necessity, but they also sought to bring financial markets in general to narrative order. They aimed, that is, to explain and define organized markets' social meanings and to read the future of the cultural structures teetering on them—the political traditions, social relations, and ethical models generated and jarred by the markets' "fascinating, romantic" fluctuations. Financial panics foiled and fueled the drive to construct coherent narratives. By throwing social meanings and cultural structures into disarray, panics intensified novelists' desire to stabilize markets' protean meanings within familiar narrative forms, to bring markets' spreading effects into aesthetic line, and to make the future they unloosed knowable and controllable. Like reporters or politicians during a disaster, novelists rushed to fill the interpretive void, competing with each other to frame the confusion according to their own ideological and aesthetic designs.

Witnessing the sweeping economic and cultural transformations set in motion, at least in part, by financial catastrophe, novelists understood that the market and its meanings would exceed their narrative grasp. Like market traders and analysts, they saw that the market and the future it spun forth were incomplete, always coming into being and continually reshaped by events, emotions, and the narrative imaginings of writers and readers. But they also understood that the market's incompleteness, if marking the limits of their enterprise, signaled its necessity as well, for if the market was constituted by storytellers, then so was the world that the market engendered. Their literary attempts to figure and fix the market might be provisional, but they were also, novelists knew, productive: in telling the market's story, novelists were making and remaking the world.

Notes

Introduction

1 Alan Trachtenberg, Walter Benn Michaels, Howard Horwitz, Wai Chee Dimock, Martha Banta, David Leverenz, Cecilia Tichi, Brook Thomas, Clare Eby, and other literary critics have produced important studies of the literary, cultural, and intellectual ramifications of the corporate and financial transformation of the United States around the turn of the twentieth century. My study departs from theirs by focusing on panic, a topic that has only recently begun to receive sustained attention by literary scholars. This newer panic scholarship, concentrating on antebellum literature, includes Fichtelberg, *Critical Fictions*; Anthony, "Banking on Emotion"; Anthony, " 'Gone Distracted' "; and Templin, "Panic Fiction." See also Charvat, *The Profession of Authorship in America*, 49–67.

2 Fichtelberg, *Critical Fictions*.

3 Wharton, *The House of Mirth*, 119.

4 Wood, *The Political Economy of Natural Law*, 204.

5 Lawson, *Friday, the Thirteenth*, 77.

6 Steeples and Whitten, *Democracy in Desperation*, 137. The term "economic fiction" broadly encompasses literature focusing on industry, business, finance, markets, money, speculation, trade, and other commercial institutions and practices. For surveys of this fiction in the nineteenth century and the early twentieth, see Rose, "A Bibliographical Survey of Economic and Political Writings"; and Taylor, *The Economic Novel in America*.

7 Flower, "The Battle of Privilege against Democratic Government," 485.

8 Clews, *Fifty Years in Wall Street*, 755.

9 Moody, *The Long Road Home*, 95.

10 Moody, *The Art of Wall Street Investing*, 135.

11 Surveying the disaster after the panic of 1907, the veteran journalist William Allen White noted that he had never seen the nation so prostrated: "Factories that had been booming turned glassy-eyed windows to us. Inland towns in the Ohio Valley and Pennsylvania showed us crowds of idle workers on the streets as we whirled along. Cloth signs on store buildings in the little cities and villages advertised bankrupt sales. The banks were closed. Towns were issuing script in lieu of cash. Commerce and industry stopped dead-still" (*The Autobiography of William Allen White*, 195). Useful historical surveys and cultural studies of financial panics in the United States before 1913

include Sobel, *Panic on Wall Street*; Rezneck, *Business Depressions and Financial Panics*; Steeples and Whitten, *Democracy in Desperation*; Wicker, *Banking Panics of the Gilded Age*; Collman, *Our Mysterious Panics*; and Fabian, "Speculation on Distress."

12 "The market" encompasses a range of historically specifiable social practices, structures, and values that are shaped not only by institutional regulations (e.g., laws, policies) but also by cultural attitudes and meanings, including those crafted and circulated by novelists. In making this point, I mean to convey a more textured conception of "the market" than we often find in literary studies, in which the term has become so generalized that it may function as a synonym for any buying and selling; any rationalizing and self-interested social behavior; any structure of exchange that makes desire or risk productive; or capitalism itself. On the mistaken tendency to absolutize the concept of "the market" and disaggregate it from other historically specific intellectual, political, and sociological processes, see Barber, "All Economies Are 'Embedded' "; Haskell and Teichgraeber, introduction to *The Culture of the Market*; and Zelizer, "Beyond the Polemics on the Market."

13 This catalog comes from the first annual report of the United States commissioner of labor in 1886, quoted in Rezneck, *Business Depressions and Financial Panics*, 156.

14 Horace White, "Commercial Crises," 525.

15 Burton, *Financial Crises*, 1. Earlier generations of observers, drawing on the vocabulary of medicine, theology, and what we now call psychology, tended to lump panics, crises, depressions, and other commercial dislocations together, often throwing up their hands when they attempted to parse panic's protean characteristics. At the turn of the twentieth century, those who studied panics through the lens of economic and political science met this bedeviling refractoriness by distinguishing panics from crises and depressions. With diverse, often conflicting, principles in mind, they defined panics—now restricted to market crashes and bank runs—as short lived, violent, and mental. Rather than analyzing panics, they described *panic*, a state of heightened emotion as well as a psychological condition and a form of irrational behavior that might be soothed by encouraging news or some other form of popular mind-cure. Cast out of the field of legitimate economic investigation, panic, so defined, was left to the emerging science of crowd psychology, which saw financial markets as laboratories where the dangerous imitativeness of mobs could be studied with uncanny regularity. In contrast, economic crises and depressions were seen as prolonged, periodic, and, according to some schools of thought, inevitable under modern forms of industrial capitalism.

16 Lippmann, *Drift and Mastery*, 78. On the rise of industrial trusts, see Lamo-reaux, *The Great Merger Movement in American Business*; Trachtenberg, *The Incorporation of America*; Sklar, *The Corporate Reconstruction of American Capitalism*; Cochran and Miller, *A Social History of Industrial America*; and Chandler, *The Visible Hand*.

17 Horace White, "Commercial Crises," 524.

18 The Pujo Committee, quoted in Brandeis, *Other People's Money*, 49. On corporate capitalism as a defensive response to social as well as economic crises, see Livingston, *Origins of the Federal Reserve System*, 26–48, 54–55, 59–62; Livingston, "The Social Analysis of Economic History and Theory," 83–84; Sklar, *The Corporate Reconstruction of American Capitalism*; and Parrini and Sklar, "New Thinking about the Market." On the corporate leaders' self-image as servants of economic progress, cultural and class stability, and civilization, see Perkins, "The Modern Corporation," 155–70; Livingston, *Origins of the Federal Reserve System*; and Sklar, *The Corporate Reconstruction of American Capitalism*, 245, 252.

19 Quoted in Livingston, *Origins of the Federal Reserve System*, 140. On the relationship between the merger movement and the stock market, see Sobel, *The Big Board*, 147–205; Navin and Sears, "The Rise of a Market for Industrial Securities"; Livingston, *Origins of the Federal Reserve System*, 129–58; and Dewing, *Corporate Promotions and Reorganizations*.

20 Cochran and Miller, *A Social History of Industrial America*, 192.

21 Brandeis, *Other People's Money*, 63.

22 Untermyer, "Is There a Money Trust?" 9.

23 U.S. Congress, House Subcommittee of the Committee on Banking and Currency, *Money Trust Investigation*, 4.

24 Crozier, *The Magnet*, 471.

25 Review of Edwin Lefèvre's *The Golden Flood*, *Everybody's*, July 1905, 141.

26 Quoted in Bensel, *The Political Economy of American Industrialization*, 448. On the popular conspiracy literature produced by the silver movement, see Hofstadter, *The Age of Reform*, 70–81; and Davis, *The Fear of Conspiracy*, 149–204.

27 According to S. E. V. Emery's popular *Seven Financial Conspiracies Which Have Enslaved the American People* (1894), Wall Street money lords, able to "inflate or depress the business of the country at pleasure," produced the financial panic of 1873 as well as the rising tide of "murder, insanity, suicide, divorce, drunkenness and all forms of immorality and crime" that followed in its wake (quoted in Hofstadter, *The Age of Reform*, 75, 76). Gordon Clark's *Shylock: As Banker, Bondholder, Corruptionist, Conspirator* (1894) outlined similar allegations involving the panic of 1893. James Goode's novel *The Modern*

Banker (1896), like a number of other antigold texts, presented facsimiled documents to prove that the American Bankers Association deliberately caused the hard times.

28 On this antimonopolist tradition, see Ritter, *Goldbugs and Greenbacks*; Nancy Cohen, *The Reconstruction of American Liberalism*; Goodwyn, *Democratic Promise*; Hicks, *The Populist Revolt*; and Hofstadter, *The Age of Reform*.

29 Clark, *Shylock*, 121–22.

30 Reeve, *The Cost of Competition*, 548.

31 Payne, *Mr. Salt*, 65–66.

32 *Appeal to Reason*, 14 December 1907, 1.

33 *Appeal to Reason*, 28 December 1907, 1.

34 *Appeal to Reason*, 23 November 1907, 4.

35 Kammen, *Mystic Chords of Memory*, 7.

36 Lippmann, *Drift and Mastery*, 80–81.

37 Wilson, "The Lawyer and the Community," 608.

38 Lippmann, *Drift and Mastery*, 81, 101.

39 Wallace, *Mickey Mouse History*, 9.

40 Emerson Hough's best seller *The Mississippi Bubble* (1902), another panic novel overtly preoccupied with financial modernity, pushes the capitalist legacy back even further. Set in the early 1700s, it focuses on John Law, the brilliant monetary theorist who promoted a French investment scheme in Mississippi land. The novel repeatedly reminds us that the modern American banking system is heir to Law's financial designs and the imperial success of American commerce heir to his foresight and optimism. Like Isham, Hough reconstructs the past not merely as prologue but also as parallel to the present, backdating the corporate transformation and rewriting it as Law's turn from the "aimless struggles and unregulated avarice" of the Old World to the organic harmony of the New (*The Mississippi Bubble*, 211). The book associates this economic maturation with the racial whitening of the land, the "red West" bowing to a greater power and ultimately welcoming European economic incursion (*The Mississippi Bubble*, 177). The financial panic and Parisian mob violence that climax the novel certify that the Old World is unfit for this kind of saving enterprise and ambition.

41 Payne, *Mr. Salt*, 70.

42 Livingston, *Pragmatism and the Political Economy of Cultural Revolution*, 25.

43 Lefèvre, "Panic Days in Wall Street," 500. Lefèvre lingers over scenes of market reading throughout his fiction.

44 Selden, *Psychology of the Stock Market*, 109. Sociological studies of reading's role in financial markets include Preda, "Financial Knowledge, Documents, and the Structures of Financial Activities"; Knorr Cetina and Bruegger, "The

Market as an Object of Attachment"; and Snow and Parker, "The Media and the Market." On the broadcast media's effect on the stock market today, see Kurtz, *The Fortune Tellers*; and Shiller, *Irrational Exuberance*, 71–95.

45 On public forms of reading, see Henkin, *City Reading*, and Hendler, *Public Sentiments*. Accounts of reading's central role in the development of American markets include Parsons, *The Power of the Financial Press*, 1–47; Forsyth, *The Business Press in America*; Cole, *The Historical Development of Economic and Business Literature*; and Demaree, *The American Agricultural Press*. For accounts, more specifically, of reading's importance for the development of U.S. securities markets in the late nineteenth century, see Sobel, *The Big Board*, 174–205; Chandler, *Henry Varnum Poor*; and Grant, "Free Markets, Free Press."

46 Lawrence, "How Truth Saved the Day," 144. Mass reading could also quell a crisis. Discussing the reporting of the panic of 1907, Lawrence characterizes the financial press as a heroic, saving force, a sobering influence on a public needlessly frenzied by financial rumors.

47 Veblen, *The Theory of Business Enterprise*, 149.

48 Ibid.

49 Frederick Upham Adams, *The Kidnapped Millionaires*, 96.

50 Lefèvre, "Pike's Peak or Bust," 156. Political economists, struggling to explain the mysterious wavelike swings that characterized modern business and investment activity, had acknowledged the profound economic effects of collective commercial "moods" and expectations since at least the middle of the nineteenth century. In the 1870s, many economic analysts turned to the "sciences of the mind" to understand business and price cycles (John Mills, "On Credit Cycles and the Origin of Panics," 13). They identified specific mental states associated with cyclical phases and explained how economic actors' mental attitudes, through competitive emulation and other psychological mechanisms, infected and intensified each other. Few observers considered economic crises to be purely psychological phenomena, since mass confidence and fear, however irrational or misguided, triggered and were triggered by real economic activity; nonetheless, in 1900, Edward Jones, an economics professor, summarized what many economic analysts had come to take for granted: "Political economy is in an important sense applied psychology" (*Economic Crises*, 180). On economists' attention to psychology in the late nineteenth century, particularly to the psychological dynamics of commercial confidence, see Barnett, *Business-Cycle Theory in the United States*, 10–22; Jones, *Economic Crises*, 180–218; and Kammer, "Expectations." On American social psychology's connection to economic development and thought in the decades around the turn of the century, see

Livingston, *Pragmatism and the Political Economy of Cultural Revolution*, 158–224; and Sklansky, *The Soul's Economy*, 137–223. On American attempts to understand the psychology of speculators and gamblers in the nineteenth century, see Fabian, *Card Sharps and Bucket Shops*, 59–107. On the intersection of the sciences of the market and the mind in England in the late nineteenth century, see Schabas, "Victorian Economics and the Science of Mind"; and Maas, "Mechanical Reasoning." On the economist Stanley Jevons's interest in psychic phenomena, see Bazard, "Homo Œconomicus Mesmerized."

51 Ross, "The Mob Mind," 397.

52 Patrick, "The Psychology of Crazes," 286. On the evolution of the concept of "sympathy" from Hume and Smith to imitation theorists and crowd psychologists at the turn of the twentieth century, see Park, "The Public and the Crowd," 28–62. On the origins and development of crowd psychology, see van Ginneken, *Crowds, Psychology, and Politics*; McClelland, *The Crowd and the Mob*; Moscovici, *The Age of the Crowd*; Barrows, *Distorting Mirrors*; and Robert Nye, *The Origins of Crowd Psychology*. Analyses of the crowd's representations in American literature include Esteve, *The Aesthetics and Politics of the Crowd in American Literature*; and Nicolaus Mills, *The Crowd in American Literature*.

53 "Mr. Dooley," the voice of the popular humorist Finley Peter Dunne, made the problem clear when, listing all the participants in the panic of 1907, he threw up his hands and declared, "I blame no wan, an' I blame ivry wan" (*Mr. Dooley Says*, 66).

54 Ross, *Sin and Society*, 10.

55 Lippmann dismissed the widespread conspiracism as "the feverish fantasy of illiterate thousands" (*Drift and Mastery*, 23). On the contradictory deployments of the term "conspiracy" by enemies and supporters of industrial incorporation at the turn of the twentieth century, see Clymer, *America's Culture of Terrorism*; Wegner, *Imaginary Communities*, 119–46; and Sklar, *The Corporate Reconstruction of American Capitalism*, 106, 125, 196.

56 Sinclair's *The Industrial Republic* (1907), published a year before *The Money-changers*, offers this picture of the totalizing spread of the system's moral poison: "There is not to-day in the land a place where a man can take a dollar and invest it, and get back a copper cent that is not tainted with corruption, polluted by violence, treason, and crime, and stained with the blood and tears of uncounted thousands of agonised [sic] women and children" (166).

57 In addition to the conceptual and critical linkages I explore, these authors share a number of biographical connections. Isham, for example, supported Dreiser in a public censorship suit over *The Genius*; Sinclair and Dreiser each wrote Lawson asking to visit him, and both read and commented

on Lawson's muckraking in their works (see, below, chap. 2, n. 92); Norris famously promoted the manuscript of Dreiser's first novel, *Sister Carrie*, at Doubleday in 1900; and Sinclair and Dreiser each plagiarized anecdotes or phrases from Edwin Lefèvre, a respected financial journalist and fiction writer whom Norris consulted when writing *The Pit*.

Chapter One

1 Herron, *From Revolution to Revolution*, 4, 5.

2 Ibid., 5.

3 Isham is remembered today for writing plays and novels that were turned into popular Hollywood films, including *Nothing but the Truth*, starring Bob Hope, and, most recently, *Liar, Liar*, starring Jim Carrey. Better known during his career as a playwright than a novelist, Isham has escaped the attention of literary scholars. He wrote a number of moderately successful historical romances, appeared in several published author round-table discussions, and supported Theodore Dreiser in a public censorship suit. Before turning to fiction in 1902, he worked as an editorial writer for a Detroit newspaper. He died in 1922. The Universal Film Manufacturing Company made *Black Friday* into a film in 1916 and again in 1920.

4 Painter, *Standing at Armageddon*, 18. For a comprehensive account of Americans' views of the Commune, see Katz, *From Appomattox to Montmartre*. See also Painter, *Standing at Armageddon*, xi, 17–24, 343; and H. C. Richardson, *The Death of Reconstruction*, 85–89, 97, 185.

5 Painter, *Standing at Armageddon*, 24.

6 Isham, *Black Friday*, 100, 101; subsequent citations of this text appear parenthetically as BF.

7 Cooper, "The Web of Life and Some Recent Books," 366; "Black Friday," 329.

8 Reising, *Loose Ends*, 12. Lukács discusses the "apologetic bourgeois" pathologization of economic crises and revolutions and offers an influential account of the ideological pressures shaping late nineteenth-century novels' formal logic and narrative style in "Narrate or Describe?" (122–23).

9 Sobel, *The Big Board*, 75.

10 For accounts of the gold panic, see Ackerman, *The Gold Ring*; Sobel, *Panic on Wall Street*, 135–50; Henry Adams, "The New York Gold Conspiracy"; and Fowler, *Twenty Years of Inside Life in Wall Street*, 508–26.

11 Lloyd, "The Political Economy of Seventy-three Million Dollars," 77.

12 Quoted in Barrett, *The Greenbacks and Resumption of Specie Payments*, 93.

13 Ackerman, *The Gold Ring*, 227.

14 Isham's defense of federal intervention reprises arguments brought forward in 1869 and again at the turn of the century. Until the nation's economy
could be brought to rest on a gold foundation, many saw the U.S. Treasury's
intervention in financial markets as necessary, despite the obvious danger of
granting the secretary of the treasury, a political appointee, such "enormous
and uncertain powers over business interests" (Barrett, *The Greenbacks and
Resumption of Specie Payments*, 94). Even proponents of laissez-faire in business granted this exception in finance, since the fate of the general economy
depended on the stability of the money market. Leslie Shaw, the secretary of
the treasury when Isham wrote the novel, saw federal interference in the
money market as a moral and public obligation. According to Shaw, the
government had a duty "to protect people against financial panics just as it
protected them from yellow fever" (Studenski, *Financial History of the United
States*, 251). For an overview of the Treasury's gold operations and their
relation to the nation's political economy after the Civil War, see Bensel,
Yankee Leviathan, 238–302.

15 Writers frequently linked the gold ring and the Confederacy. One called the
gold clique "General Lee's left wing in Wall Street" (Oberholtzer, *Jay Cooke*,
141.) Isham's pairing of the gold panic and the Paris Commune develops
this association further, since the Parisian uprising was a civil war. Indeed,
as Philip Katz argues in *From Appomattox to Montmartre*, Americans' understandings of the Commune were profoundly shaped by their views about the
U.S. Civil War and Reconstruction. The Commune was a screen against
which postbellum Americans projected their anxieties about central government, class conflict, and social disorder.

16 The couple's reunion registers the reunification of the nation during the
tentative and troubled rapprochement after Reconstruction: Strong, like the
Radical North, acknowledges he was too skeptical and severe toward her;
Elinor, like the South after years of bridling, realizes her waywardness was
misguided. The legacy of the repudiated Confederate bonds, symbols of
states' rights and secession, is likewise reversed: Strong generously buys the
bonds from Elinor's father, confident that they will find some value in the
resurgent national economy. Should we doubt the redemptive promise of
Strong's national economic vision, we are shown former slaves, now waiting tables in Wall Street, grinning at Strong, having bought shares in one of
his railroads (BF 124). Like Grant, Strong has used his nation-building
power to help assimilate former slaves into the new economic order, converting bonds of tyranny into railroad bonds.

17 Elinor's coronation of her husband not only naturalizes his prerogative but
also redeems the masculine agency he forfeits in Paris when, in a turning

point of the romance plot, he bases his decision not to pursue her on the outcome of a chess match he observes—he leaves France once he sees that "the white king was mated" (BF 396). His coronation reverses that loss of will; it reanimates the king and transforms its capitulation into a popular embrace.

18 Moses, "Lydia Thompson and the 'British Blondes,'" 88.

19 Felski, *The Gender of Modernity*, 4. A British finance novel set in America, *The Earth for a Dollar* (1897), also links financial predators, market panics, bewitching New Women, and socialism. In the novel, seductive female socialists form a corporation, boom its stock, and, inducing other women to speculate, create a fictitious stock bubble. Robert Barr's 1894 short story in *McClure's*, "The Revolt of the ——: A Page from the Domestic History of the Twentieth Century," focusing on a woman speculator who preys on her husband in the stock market, overtly equates market manipulation and the transgression of gender norms, as does William Cadwalader Hudson's novel *J. P. Dunbar: A Story of Wall Street* (1906).

20 "The Coming Woman," 4.

21 Woodhull's sister served as Commodore Vanderbilt's mistress and psychic counselor, channeling financial advice and other messages for him from the spirit world. With his help, the sisters made enough money to establish the world's first brokerage house run by women (at a time when women were fighting for the right to open bank accounts), a professional turn that incurred the savage and sensational judgment of Wall Street men in 1870.

22 See Katz, *From Appomattox to Montmartre*, 139, 164; and Bernstein, "The Impact of the Paris Commune in the United States," 64–65.

23 "The Wall-Street Panic," 216. Beginning with its opening issue in 1868, the *Revolution* linked the government's gold policies, revolution in France, and women's rights—including the right to repudiate financial debts and marriage contracts. See, for example, "To Our Servants at Washington from the People at Home," 8 January 1868, 11–12; and "Plutocracy," 27 October 1869, 221.

24 Quoted in Katz, *From Appomattox to Montmartre*, 139.

25 "Women of Montmartre," 620.

26 Quoted in Katz, *From Appomattox to Montmartre*, 139. On the enduring image of the pétroleuse, see Gullickson, *Unruly Women of Paris*; and Katz, *From Appomattox to Montmartre*, 138–39.

27 Gullickson, *Unruly Women of Paris*, 109–119.

28 See, for example, G. A. Henty, *Two Sieges of Paris; or, A Girl of the Commune* (1895). Katz provides a comprehensive bibliography of American novels and plays about the Paris Commune in *From Appomattox to Montmartre*, 201–6.

29 Burrows and Wallace, *Gotham*, 1003.

30 Quoted in H. C. Richardson, *The Death of Reconstruction*, 87.

31 On this identification of women and revolutionary mobs, see Huyssen, *After the Great Divide*, 52; and Dijkstra, *Evil Sisters*, 23–26, 36, 40, 261–82.

32 Felski, *The Gender of Modernity*, 149.

33 Most Americans at the time saw the economic crisis, in which over 2.5 million workers, just under a fifth of the nonagricultural work force, lost their jobs, as an outcome of the massive panic of 1893. To most financial conservatives, the panic was primarily the result of the U.S. Treasury's inability to protect the stability of the currency. Doubting that the federal government could maintain gold payments, foreigners and Americans drained the Treasury's gold reserve below its legal minimum. To those who opposed a silver or bimetal standard, the draining of the reserve threatened to destroy the credit of the country. Not since Black Friday had the stability of the currency and, it was argued, the financial future of the nation faced such a threat. For an overview of the financial panic and economic crisis of the nineties, see Steeples and Whitten, *Democracy in Desperation*; and Sobel, *Panic on Wall Street*, 230–72. On the relation between the currency battle and class alignments, see Livingston, *Origins of the Federal Reserve System*; Bensel, *The Political Economy of American Industrialization*; Palmer, "Man over Money"; Ritter, *Goldbugs and Greenbacks*; and Goodwyn, *Democratic Promise*.

34 Kleppner, *Continuity and Change*, 108. Relevant accounts of the silver movement's seemingly revolutionary threat include Edwards, *Angels in the Machinery*, 122; and Tracy, "Menacing Socialism in the Western States." Silver agitation coincided with industrial warfare. In 1894, the gloomiest year of the economic crisis, almost 700,000 workers took part in 1,400 disputes, the most famous of which ended when troops, specially deputized for the occasion, clashed with Pullman railroad strikers near the Chicago World's Fair. In actuality, silver forces meshed uneasily with industrial labor, which largely supported the Republicans and the gold standard in 1896.

35 Quoted in Katz, *From Appomattox to Montmartre*, 190. Bryan's enemies made such comparisons even in 1900, during his second run for the presidency; see, for example, "Anti-imperialists Differ," *New York Times*, 10 July 1900, 3.

36 Quoted in Edwards, *Angels in the Machinery*, 120.

37 Quoted in Studenski, *Financial History of the United States*, 234.

38 Livingston, *Origins of the Federal Reserve System*, 59. Isham's equation of Gould and the Paris revolutionaries exploits a rhetoric of anarchy routinely used to describe the reckless competition embodied by Gould and displaced by industrial consolidation at the turn of the century. For an example of this rhetoric, see Vandervelde, *Collectivism and Industrial Evolution*, 55–58.

39 Quoted in Livingston, *Origins of the Federal Reserve System*, 61. On the arguments put forward to justify the corporate transformation, see Sklar, *The Corporate Reconstruction of American Capitalism*; Wiebe, *Businessmen and Reform*; and Kolko, *The Triumph of Conservatism*.

40 Livingston, *Origins of the Federal Reserve System*, 71. On certain bankers' faith just before the panic of 1907 that the corporate makeover had put an end to financial crises, see Noyes, "A Year after the Panic of 1907," 186.

41 Livingston, *Origins of the Federal Reserve System*, 56. On the apotheosis of the corporate titan, see Johnson, "The Crisis and Panic of 1907," 462–63. For representations of corporate leaders as public trustees, see Perkins, "The Modern Corporation"; and Sklar, *The Corporate Reconstruction of American Capitalism*, 245, 252. The economist Arthur T. Hadley singled out Jay Gould as the antithesis of the corporate trustee and (thus) a potential precipitant of socialist revolution in "Jay Gould and Socialism," 686–93.

42 The gold standard was signed into law in 1900, but it was useless as a means of stabilizing prices and preventing economic crises unless it was accompanied by a banking system, tied to the Treasury, that could ensure a stable money supply. Almost everyone agreed that some sort of central banking authority was needed, but what relation this authority would have to the federal government was the subject of energetic debate. To many, giving Treasury officials such monumental authority over money and securities markets was potentially catastrophic, since secretaries of the treasury could be unwise, capricious, and beholden. This is the warning offered by Emerson Hough's account of the disastrous government banking experiment in his best-selling panic novel, *The Mississippi Bubble* (1902). Many others saw federal interference as a moral and public duty. By partnering Strong and Grant, *Black Friday* celebrates the collusion between the new industrial regime and the federal government's financial authority.

43 Quoted in Hofstadter, *The Age of Reform*, 64.

44 Donnelly, *Caesar's Column*, 118.

45 Hofstadter, *The Age of Reform*, 75. On the conspiracy literature produced by the silver movement, see ibid., 70–81; and Davis, *The Fear of Conspiracy*, 149–204.

46 Goode, *The Modern Banker*, 148. Rose's "A Bibliographic Survey of Economic and Political Writings" offers a catalog, not always reliable, of other contemporary financial novels preoccupied with the money question.

47 Quoted in Sobel, *Panic on Wall Street*, 257. For a typical argument distancing industrial corporations from speculative enterprises, see Dill, "Industrials as Investments for Small Capital."

48 Quoted in Rideout, "Introduction," xi.

49 Bellamy, *The Way Out*, iv. In 1886, half a million workers participated in 1,400 strikes. Thousands of workers along Jay Gould's southwestern railroad lines, embittered by Gould's combativeness, rioted and clashed with armed marshals. On the widespread feeling that a working-class revolt was at hand in 1886–87 and again in the mid-nineties, see Painter, *Standing at Armageddon*, x, 58, 62, 65–66, 70, 95, 99; Brecher, *Strike!* 25–100; and Keller, *Affairs of State*, 489–90.

50 Quoted in Avrich, *The Haymarket Tragedy*, 148.

51 Painter, *Appointment at Armageddon*, 47.

52 On the Haymarket explosion and its significance for Americans, see Carl Smith, *Urban Disorder and the Shape of Belief*, 101–74; and Clymer, *America's Culture of Terrorism*, 33–68.

53 Painter, *Appointment at Armageddon*, 48.

54 Quoted in *Public Opinion*, 15 May 1886, 83.

55 *Red Ruin*, 10. A number of turn-of-the-century American novels take up the Haymarket violence explicitly, including Robert Herrick's *Memoirs of an American Citizen* (1905) and Frank Harris's *The Bomb* (1908).

56 All of these links are explicit in the newspaper editorials quoted in *Public Opinion*, 15 May 1886, 83.

57 McLean, *The Rise and Fall of Anarchy in America*, 33.

58 Ibid., 34, 33.

59 Avrich, *The Haymarket Tragedy*, 143–44, 145–49. Since 1871, American anarchists and militant socialists had invoked the Paris Commune as the crowning achievement of the revolutionary movement. In Chicago in 1879, as many as forty thousand workers gathered to commemorate the Commune, and calls for an American Commune energized anarchist rallies through the turn of the century.

60 Burrows and Wallace, *Gotham*, 1097. Most's anarchist primer, *Revolutionary War Science* (1885), which "sold like lager at picnics and meetings around town," outlined, among other things, how to dynamite balls "where monopolists are assembled" (ibid).

61 McLean, *The Rise and Fall of Anarchy in America*, 49. Henry Demarest Lloyd directly links Gould and the Paris Commune in "The Political Economy of Seventy-three Million Dollars," 80 (see this chapter's first epigraph). In *Mr. Salt* (1903), the novelist Will Payne has investors condemn a powerful bear speculator: "The man's an anarchist! an enemy of society! He ought to be hung up to a lamp post!" (24); later in the novel, anarchists attempt to assassinate him.

62 Hayden White, "The Historical Text as Literary Artifact," 44.

63 Most observers in the Gilded Age and the Progressive Era did not view labor

and capital as inherently or irreconcilably antagonistic. When capital and labor did clash, observers frequently blamed third parties, usually ruthless monopolists and speculators like Jay Gould. See, for example, Casson, "The Trade-Unionist and the Monopolist," 597. Likewise, many saw socialism and capitalism, especially with the emergence of massive trusts, as allied or, at least, overlapping phases of economic development, or saw socialism as an emergent tendency within capitalism. See Livingston's insistence on this point in *Pragmatism, Feminism, and Democracy*, 106–7, 160–63; also see Kolko, *The Triumph of Conservatism*, 16–17; and Sklansky, *The Soul's Economy*, 105–36.

64 Goldman, *Living My Life*, 309.

65 Newton, "Anarchism," 1.

66 Goldman, *Living My Life*, 304, 325.

67 Ibid., 304.

68 See, for example, H. K. Johnson, *The Woman and the Republic*, 30–33, 94–102, 206–9, 290, 314–19. On the actual and alleged intersection of gender and economic insurgencies in the decades around the turn of the century, see Edwards, *Angels in the Machinery*; Buhle, *Women and American Socialism*; and Tax, *The Rising of the Women*. Livingston's *Pragmatism, Feminism, and Democracy* offers a forceful counterargument that aligns the rise of feminism with (and within) the emergence of corporate capitalism.

69 Buhle, *Women and American Socialism*, 252. For additional accounts of the link between free love and anarchism, see Marsh, *Anarchist Women*; and Hutchins Hapgood, *An Anarchist Woman*.

70 Goldman, *Living My Life*, 216.

71 I have taken the term "nexus event" from Hellekson, *The Alternate History*. On the ideological ramifications of returning to the past in order to rewrite it, see Gallagher, "Undoing." Other relevant studies of alternate histories include Wegner, *Imaginary Communities*; and Jameson, "Progress or Utopia."

72 On these influences, see Watson, *The Novels of Jack London*, 99–100, 109–12. Wegner usefully qualifies the link between *The Iron Heel* and *Caesar's Column* in *Imaginary Communities*, 116–46.

73 Quoted in H. K. Johnson, *The Woman and the Republic*, 207.

Chapter Two

1 The most thorough discussion of Lawson among studies of the muckrakers is Filler, *Crusaders for American Liberalism*, 171–97. See also Filler, *Appointment at Armageddon*, 335–40; Weinberg and Weinberg, *The Muckrakers*, 261–96; Regier, *The Era of the Muckrakers*, 126–31; and Brasch, *Forerunners of Revolution*, 75–78. The most illuminating accounts of Lawson by his muckraking

peers are Sullivan, *Our Times*, 88–91; and Russell, *Bare Hands and Stone Walls*, 131–34.

2 The most useful sources for biographical information about Lawson are Fayant, "The Real Lawson" (1907, 1908); Fales, *The Life of Lawson*; McCall, *The Copper King's Daughter*; Walth, *Fire at Eden's Gate*, 13–33, 36–39; Mann, *Fads and Fancies*, 192–95; and Lawson, "The Remedy," 779–80.

3 Russell, *Bare Hands and Stone Walls*, 132.

4 Sullivan, *Our Times*, 90. Clarence Barron, otherwise disposed to brand Lawson a liar and a cheat, admitted in his private notes that *Frenzied Finance*'s allegations against Standard Oil and its financial officers were basically true (Josephson, *The Robber Barons*, 399n).

5 Lawson, *Friday, the Thirteenth*, appendix, n.p.; subsequent citations appear parenthetically as *Friday*.

6 Norman Hapgood, "The Epidemic of Exposure," 23.

7 Fayant, "The Real Lawson," 663, 664; subsequent citations appear parenthetically as "TRL."

8 See Donohoe, "The Truth about Frenzied Finance," 273. It is hard to overstate how sensational a figure Lawson himself was. Between 1904 and 1908 he was the subject of an admiring novel, *The Deluge* (1905), by David Graham Phillips; the focus of two book-length magazine series by Donohoe and Fayant; the target of a vicious four-hundred-page denunciation by a rival stock promoter and editor, C. F. King; and the focus of additional book-length attacks by Fales and Webb. Several contemporaries, including one of Lawson's harshest critics, Clarence W. Barron, founder of the financial magazine *Barron's*, devoted entire chapters of their memoirs to him (see Barron, *More They Told Barron*, 79–92; and Thayer, *Astir*, 249–70). Lawson also inspired jokes, poems, send-ups, at least one play, and countless cartoons. Lawson sought publicity in everything he did. In the 1880s and 1890s, before his turn to reform work, he made headlines around Boston for a variety of commercial stunts and for aggressively spending his way into the gathering places of Boston society. Often cited as one of the five or six richest men in the nation, he made national news when he paid $30,000 to name a carnation after his wife. He figured conspicuously in several political scandals, and he ran for mayor of Boston and senator from Massachusetts and was even named as a potential presidential candidate. Convicted of false advertising late in his life and bankrupted by his stock plunges, he died in 1925, long after he had retired from the public's gaze.

9 On Lawson's market operations and financial career, see Lawson, *Frenzied Finance*; Fayant, "The Real Lawson"; Donohoe, "The Truth about Frenzied Finance"; Barron, *More They Told Barron*, 79–92; Barron, *The Record of the*

Boston News Bureau; King, The Light of Four Candles; and Lawson, "Mr. Lawson's Advertised Stock Operations," 98–104. Relevant secondary sources include Holbrook, The Age of the Moguls, 168–80; Josephson, The Robber Barons, 384–85, 396–98; Josephson, The Money Lords, 24–27; and Neill, The Inside Story of the Stock Exchange, 157–59.

10 On Lawson's publicity machine, see Donohoe, "The Truth about Frenzied Finance," 149–52. Even before the Amalgamated imbroglio, Lawson was the nation's most notorious publicist, garnering a reputation as a "financial guerrilla," a press agent who would use any means to destroy the stock value of rival companies (Fayant, "The Real Lawson," 720). Lawson gained equal notoriety conducting spectacular promotional campaigns for which he produced circulars, booklets, posters, maps, newspaper articles, biographies, and interviews. He created a city from scratch this way in 1890, luring merchants and residents to a mining site in Kentucky that was destined, he claimed, to rival Pittsburgh, even printing advertising for the venture on butchers' wrapping paper—until no metal was found and the place disappeared from the map a few years later.

11 "Copper Stock Speculation."

12 Amalgamated accepted subscriptions for $412 million of stock, more than five times its advertised capitalization of $75 million. Lawson claimed that late bids and bids unaccompanied by checks raised the figure to over a billion dollars but that only $132 million of the subscriptions could be counted as legitimate. The massive oversubscription resulted in investors' receiving only a fifth as much stock as they had subscribed for, less than half of the amount of stock they were due. In the end, according to Lawson, the public paid two-thirds of the purchase price of the new corporation while Standard Oil kept two-thirds of the property.

13 For other accounts of the copper mania and the Amalgamated fiasco, see Howe, Confessions of a Monopolist, 66, 69, 99; The Tale of Coppers; and Donohoe, "The Truth about Frenzied Finance," 487–91, 505–7, 521–24, 545–46. The manipulation of Amalgamated stock and its wildly gyrating prices over the next decade became a running joke in the financial press and Congress.

14 Barron, The Record of the Boston News Bureau, 21. See also Barron's "The Dream-Menagerie," ibid., 8–9. Poems parodying Lawson can also be found in "Frenzied Poetry"; Masson, Mary's Little Lamb, n.p.; Fales, The Life of Lawson, 40–41; and Biggers, "The Frenzied Outcast."

15 King, The Light of Four Candles, 45.

16 "Storm Dies Out."

17 Lawson, "Mr. Lawson's Advertised Stock Operations," 99.

18 Fayant, "Sidelights on Lawson," 3.

19 King, *The Light of Four Candles*, 90.
20 Russell, *Bare Hands and Stone Walls*, 131.
21 See, for example, ibid., 133.
22 Lawson, *Frenzied Finance*, 540; subsequent citations appear parenthetically as FF.
23 "The 'Lawson Panic,' with Lawson Left Out," 832.
24 Fayant, "Sidelights on Lawson," 3. The fullest accounts of the Lawson panic can be found in Donohoe, "The Truth about Frenzied Finance," 70–74, 152; and Fayant, "The Real Lawson," 821–22, 868.
25 The Greene affair ended when the two men, after drinking champagne in Lawson's office, appeared arm in arm before a waiting crowd. On the bizarre drama, see Sonnichson, *Colonel Greene and the Copper Skyrocket*, 137–48; and Thayer, *Astir*, 261–62.
26 Givens, "Wall Street's Estimate of Mr. Lawson," 1112.
27 "Storm Dies Out."
28 "Stock Market Stirred by Lawson Manoeuvres."
29 "Lawson as a Prophet."
30 "The 'Lawson Panic,' with Lawson Left Out," 833. Lawson's motives, as always, provoked feverish public debate. The evidence advanced by his critics suggests that Lawson swindled the public for his own profit, by one account taking in over a million dollars (Donohoe, "The Truth about Frenzied Finance," 74, 152). James Keene, the notorious manipulator who succeeded Lawson as the chief marketer of Amalgamated stock, wryly noted to Barron, "This market has been made by a man who bought all the stock in a panic of his own creation. Lying is an art and you will yet be erecting a monument to Lawson" (Barron, *More They Told Barron*, 92).
31 "Lawson's Frenzied Finance Answered."
32 Givens, "Wall Street's Estimate of Mr. Lawson," 1112.
33 Ibid., 1113–14.
34 "Rest for the Weary."
35 "Lawson to Policy Holders."
36 Quoted in Leary, *Mark Twain's Correspondence*, 590 n. 1.
37 Osborn, "Frenzied Finance and Its Author," 307.
38 *Life* smirked, "It is not safe nowadays to leave out overnight any sort of panic, fiscal disturbance, lapse of concord, calumny, conspiracy, or convulsion that is not plainly marked with the owner's name. Lawson claims to have committed or inspired all such things that turn up" ("The Boston Claimant").
39 Lawson, "Why I Gave up the Fight," 288.
40 "A Reply to Mr. Lawson."

41 Lawson, "Why I Gave up the Fight," 288.

42 "Mysterious Instruments," 497.

43 Adler and Adler, "The Market as Collective Behavior," 86.

44 Clews, *Fifty Years in Wall Street*, 203–4. Edwin Lefèvre, himself a financial journalist, fiction writer, and stock operator, denies the collusion of the press in "The American Newspaper."

45 On the rise of these tipster reports, see Sobel, *The Big Board*, 179–80. With Lawson likely in mind, the pioneering financial analyst John Moody noted that these tipsters could "ruin the country in one hour and save it in the next" (*The Art of Wall Street Investing*, 149).

46 Accounts of the relation between large corporations and the press at the turn of the century include Baker, "Railroads on Trial"; Morse, "An Awakening in Wall Street"; Marchand, *Creating the Corporate Soul*, 7–47; Ewen, *PR!* 73–101; Miraldi, *Muckraking and Objectivity*, 64–65; and Schiller, *Objectivity and the News*, 179–97.

47 Quoted in Thornton, "Muckraking Journalists and Their Readers," 35.

48 Irwin, *The Making of a Reporter*, 150. Although we commonly identify the first decade of the twentieth century as the Muckraking Era, civic-minded literature exposing political and economic corruption achieved popularity in waves throughout the nineteenth century.

49 Tarbell, *All in the Day's Work*, 242.

50 Ibid., 281.

51 "Editorial Announcement," 575.

52 Praising the *American*'s new staff of writers, an Omaha newspaper observed, "Their muck-raking has been of the convincing rather than the frenzied variety and they have reputations for literary honesty to be maintained. It is an attractive aggregation of talent, with the David Graham Phillips and Thomas Lawson element conspicuously absent" (quoted in Dorman, " 'Deliver Me from This Muck-Rake,' " 123–24).

53 "The Literature of Exposure," 17.

54 Lawson, "The Remedy," 472L.

55 Quoted in "In the Mirror of the Present," 624.

56 Norman Hapgood, "The Epidemic of Exposure," 23.

57 Roosevelt, Speech, 19.

58 Ibid. That Roosevelt was targeting Lawson is clear from Roosevelt's letter to William Taft (15 March 1906) written just a few days before the speech, in Morison, *The Letters of Theodore Roosevelt*, 183–84. Lawson responded to the president's speech in "The Muck-Raker." For Roosevelt's colorful assessment of Lawson's danger and duplicity, see his letter to John Allison, 18 November 1905, in Morison, *The Letters of Theodore Roosevelt*, 80–81.

59 Roosevelt, Speech, 19.

60 Quoted in Beltz, "Preachers of Social Discontent," 235, 188.

61 "In the Mirror of the Present," 625.

62 Baker, *American Chronicle*, 184.

63 Quoted in Dorman, " 'Deliver Me from This Muck-Rake,' " 125.

64 Roosevelt, Speech, 19.

65 Quoted in Miraldi, *Muckraking and Objectivity*, 75.

66 Sedgwick, "The Man with the Muck Rake," 111.

67 Quoted in Reaves, "How Radical Were the Muckrakers?" 767.

68 Ibid., 766. On socialists' ultimate disillusionment with Lawson, see "The Doctrine of the Destroyers and the Remedy of the Redeemers" and "Fair Finance."

69 Lawson, "A Prediction Roll-Call," 73.

70 Fales, *The Life of Lawson*, 9.

71 "Inferno of Packingtown Revealed," 651.

72 Flower, "David Graham Phillips," 256.

73 Ibid., 252. Sam McClure urged his investigative journalists to mimic novelists; he told Lincoln Steffens that the "ideal method" of exposé writing "is that pursued by Alexander Dumas in his great D'Artagnan romances, [where] once in every so often the narrative comes to a powerful climax" (quoted in Leonard, *The Power of the Press*, 182).

74 "Editorial Announcement," 575.

75 "The Artist Who Preaches," 635.

76 Donohoe, "The Truth about Frenzied Finance," 521.

77 Norman Hapgood, "How Much of a Liar is Lawson?" 25.

78 "Lawson's Frenzied Finance Answered," 9.

79 Kemp, "The Value of the Exposé," 164.

80 Givens, "Wall Street's Estimate of Mr. Lawson," 1111.

81 "Who Writes 'Frenzied Finance'?"

82 Fayant, "Sidelights on Lawson," 4.

83 "A Test of Friendship," 144.

84 Lawson, "To My Readers," 718.

85 Donohoe, "The Truth about Frenzied Finance," 149.

86 Put simply, the literature of exposure was considered dangerous because it resembled fiction. Mark Sullivan made this point explicit by defining respectable muckraking as the antithesis of fiction: "The literature of exposure during the early years . . . was on a basis that was the exact opposite of fiction; it had a definite technic of its own, of which the essential detail was austere, restrained, underemphasized statement of bald fact. It was not fiction" (Sullivan, *Our Times*, 93). Sullivan was distinguishing muckraking

not from accounts that were false or invented—fictive in the more restrictive, technical sense—but rather from narratives that were thrilling and agitating, narratives that had a novelistic appeal, both in the sense of being interesting and also demanding certain emotions and actions from the reader. Ida Tarbell, who first tried to write her monumental history of Standard Oil as a novel, offered a similar assessment, judging that muckraking was fine when it was "informed, candid, restrained," but pernicious "whenever it was sensational, that is, carried on simply for the sake of telling an exciting story and stirring up resentment." The disparaging distinction she made between a "good story" and a "serious study" (quoted in Beltz, "Preachers of Social Discontent," 21) presented certain problems for reform writers, since even the most conscientious investigative reporters wanted to tell a story that would captivate their readers—indeed, most muckrakers were also novelists or had ambitions to become novelists—and reform fiction writers were obliged to tell a good story, regardless of their other intentions. Relevant discussions of the relation between muckraking journalism and fiction, or between reporting and storytelling at the turn of the century, include Tichi, *Exposés and Excess*, 62–104; Miraldi, *Muckraking and Objectivity*; Connery, "A Third Way to Tell a Story," 3–20; Schudson, *Discovering the News*, 88–120; Leonard, *The Power of the Press*, 209–213; Francke, "An Argument in Defense of Sensationalism," 70–73; and Francke "Sensationalism and the Development of 19th-Century Reporting," 80–85.

87 Glazener, *Reading for Realism*, 101.

88 Sinclair, *The Metropolis*, 255. Frederick Upham Adams's novel *The Kidnapped Millionaires* (1901), a signed copy of which Adams gave Lawson, links sensational literature and financial panic explicitly. In this text, a reform newspaper modeled after Hearst's *New York Journal* performs one audacious publicity stunt after another to feed the public's appetite for sensation and boost the paper's circulation. One of its reporters who is "perfectly daffy about news sensations" (117) causes a ruinous stock market panic by publishing rumors about the financial plans of several financial titans, kidnapping them, and then secreting them on an unmapped tropical island where they are given lectures about the injustice of the financial system they control.

89 Medbery, *Men and Mysteries of Wall Street*, 39.

90 "A Reply to Mr. Lawson."

91 Fales, *The Life of Lawson*, 22. Responding to the rumor that Lawson himself could never have achieved such a "miraculous . . . facility and force of expression" in his first literary attempt, Lawson's publishers explained that Lawson had distinguished himself as "a master of picturesque and forceful

English" when he was a promoter, long before he began *Frenzied Finance* ("Who Writes 'Frenzied Finance'?").

92 Barron, *More They Told Barron*, 87. Lawson inspired, provoked, and fascinated several prominent fiction writers. As I have noted, Lawson boasted that Upton Sinclair invited himself to Boston to show Lawson the manuscript of *The Jungle*, although no other record of any correspondence between the two writers exists; Sinclair discusses *Frenzied Finance* in *The Industrial Republic*, 159–66, and laments Lawson's ultimate ineffectiveness in *The Brass Check*, 57. Theodore Dreiser wrote Lawson a letter in July 1904, when *Frenzied Finance* first appeared, but I have been unable to discover its contents; Lawson's secretary acknowledged its receipt, responding only that Lawson was "too busy at the moment to take up anything new" (Clapp to Theodore Dreiser, 16 July 1904). Perhaps Dreiser, freelancing, wanted to do a story on Lawson. Dreiser read *Frenzied Finance* while researching *The Financier*, telling one interviewer that Lawson's book "had only nibbled at the barrel of cheese" ("Theodore Dreiser," in Pizer, *Theodore Dreiser*, 195). Dreiser mentions *Frenzied Finance* again in " 'Vanity, Vanity,' Saith the Preacher," 263. Lawson left his card for Mark Twain in June 1895, but Twain did not know who Lawson was at the time and apparently never saw him. Later, Twain came to despise Lawson when Lawson attacked Twain's financial savior, Henry H. Rogers, Standard Oil's chief financial officer, in *Frenzied Finance*. When the series came out, Twain offered to "take off my shirt and answer those articles, no matter what my publishers say" (Marcossan, *Adventures in Interviewing*, 246; see also Leary, *Mark Twain's Correspondence with Henry Huttleston Rogers*, 589–90). Jack London visited Lawson's Boston office, where he was struck by Lawson's collection of three thousand elephant figurines (Lockley, "A Westerner at Thomas Lawson's 'Dreamwold,' " 646).

93 "New Novels," 436; and "Mr. Lawson and the Personal Equation," 120.

94 "Friday the 13th," 453. Good reviews invite skepticism. In England, Lawson offered $5,000 to the papers that published the best reviews of his book. Critics in London, scandalized by Lawson's offer, characterized the bribe as "the most barefaced bid for public notice ever made" and declared that "never in the history of literature has [there] been such an open and unblushing attempt to purchase reviewers" ("Lawson's Literary Advertising Methods").

95 "Frenzied Fiction," 551. In 1916, the World Film Corp. produced a silent film melodrama based on the novel.

96 King, *The Light of Four Candles*, 248.

97 Lawson, "To My Readers," 718. It is unclear when Lawson actually drafted the novel; conflicting accounts can be found in E. J. Park, "How Lawson Writes"; and Barron, *More They Told Barron*, 87.

98   "With 'Everybody's' Publishers," 865; Lawson, "Fools and Their Money," 691.

99   Lawson himself blurred the line between fictional illustration and practical demonstration when he offered $5,000 to anyone who could demonstrate that Brownley's trick—in effect, selling massive amounts of stock without the means to purchase or deliver them—was impracticable. Responding to the challenge, a Philadelphia broker attempted to perform Brownley's gimmick and break the Philadelphia stock market. He tried this on the thirteenth of the month (a Thursday, alas) and failed. When he was unable to deliver the stocks he had sold, he fled town, but not, the *New York Times* wryly noted, to Boston, where he might have collected his $5,000 ("Broker Who Tried Lawson Plan Flees").

100 Hendler, *Public Sentiments*, 1.

101 Studies usefully complicating the once-conventional opposition between sentiment and the marketplace in nineteenth-century U.S. fiction include Fichtelberg, *Critical Fictions*; Hendler, *Public Sentiments*, 82–109; Merish, *Sentimental Materialism*; Zheng, *Moral Economy and American Realistic Novels*, 43–75; and Gillian Brown, *Domestic Individualism*, 39–60. On the mingling of sentimental and market values outside fiction, see Sandage, "The Gaze of Success"; and Fabian, "Unseemly Sentiments."

102 Adler and Adler, "The Market as Collective Behavior," 87. There are obvious differences between novelistic sympathy and market sympathy. Investors typically do not feel for each other or feel compassion toward each other; their sympathy is not something voluntarily extended but rather a structural fact of market sociality; and their sympathy is not toward individuals but rather with critical masses of anonymous investors. Nonetheless, there are compelling similarities, and I am suggesting that these similarities (and the differences as well) induced Lawson's readers to join his market insurgency. Both forms of sympathy describe a process of emotional identification and exchange sustained and intensified by imaginative projection. Sentimental novels typically work by inviting their readers imaginatively to identify with the emotions experienced by a witness to a victim's suffering. In the stock market, because market changes are influenced by the emotions of mass investors, individuals continually (and anxiously) imagine how other investors, most of whom are similarly vulnerable to market movements, feel. Indeed, unable to communicate directly with each other, most individuals can only imagine others' emotions. Even contrarians who bet against the mass of investors must sympathize in this sense: the market requires one to know, if not to experience, the feelings of others.

103 Jones, *Economic Crises*, 203–4.

104 Ibid., 205, 204.

105 Accounting for his turn from the "field of fact narrative" to that of "fiction story telling," Lawson explained that fiction, in addition to allowing his imagination free play, would allow him to create "human subjects," especially women characters ("To My Readers," 718). Although he did not elaborate on this claim, it seems clear enough from his novel that women characters suited his purpose because of their conventional capacity as sympathizers. Beulah's demise horrifies Lawson not because she is an innocent victim but rather because she becomes incapable of suffering and thus incapable of giving sympathy. *Friday, the Thirteenth* suggests that only in the market can the capacity for sympathy, once ruptured by the System, be restored. Lawson figures Beulah's capacity to sympathize as a "wire connecting heart and brain" that burns out when "the cruel 'System' [throws] on a voltage beyond the wire's capacity to transmit" (*Friday*, 156). This broken wire appears again late in the book in the form of the telegraph wire connecting Bob's office to the floor of the Stock Exchange (*Friday*, 191); Bob mentions this wire just as Jim, anguished by Bob's brutification, reawakens Bob's capacity for sympathy. The purifying panic at the end of the novel, unlike the merely destructive ones earlier, results directly from this revived capacity. We are led to believe that Bob's sentimental restoration somehow initiates the repair of Beulah's sympathetic faculty at the end—a repair all the more pathetic since it leads to her final trauma and death.

106 Walth, *Fire at Eden's Gate*, 19.

107 As Mary Templin shows, women's panic novels written during and after the crises of 1837 and 1857 are filled with such victims. See Templin, "Panic Fiction." In "Containing Sentiment," Templin argues that many of these novels link excessive emotionality, even compassion, with the excessive greed and excitement that contributed to the financial crisis; for this reason, authors overtly downplay sympathy for panic's victims, advocating emotionally restrained and pragmatic responses instead.

108 Tompkins, *Sensational Designs*, xi.

109 Lawson, "Why I Gave Up the Fight," 48r.

110 Lawson, "Fictitious Wealth," 832g.

111 Ibid. In later years, Lawson became more disposed to legislative remedies.

Chapter Three

1 Garland, *The Shadow World*, 138; subsequent citations appear parenthetically as TSW.

2 By confining the term "New Psychology" to the study of trance states and

hypnotism, I am following writers of popular books on psychic phenomena at the turn of the century. In *Telepathy and the Subliminal Self* (1897), for example, R. Osgood Mason notes that "now more than ever . . . the public [is] interested in matters relating to the 'New Psychology.' Scarcely a day passes that notice of some unusual psychical experience or startling phenomenon does not appear in popular literature" (iii).

3   Important discussions of the sublime that inform my analysis include Freeman, *The Feminine Sublime*; Tabbi, *Postmodern Sublime*; Nye, *American Technological Sublime*; de Bolla, *The Discourse of the Sublime*; Arsenberg, *The American Sublime*; Hertz, *The End of the Line*; Weiskel, *The Romantic Sublime*; Brooks, *The Melodramatic Imagination*; and Den Tandt, *The Urban Sublime in American Literary Naturalism*. Den Tandt discusses *The Pit*'s "sublime economics," 70–96.

4   Norris, "Inside an Organ," 9.

5   Norris, *The Pit*, 221; subsequent citations appear parenthetically as P.

6   Upon opening Nostradamus's text at the start of the play, Faust exclaims: "Was it a god who drew these signs which . . . unveil the powers of nature around me? All becomes clearer to me! I see in these pure lines creative nature lying open before my soul" (Goethe, *Goethe's Faust*, 9).

7   Norris pairs Wall Street speculation and literary art in "The True Reward of the Novelist," 1150; and "The Need of a Literary Conscience," 1158. We can discern the connection in his other essays as well: Jadwin typifies Norris's ideal novelist, a "mosaicist" who "has a design in his brain"; confronting the myriad signs of the wheat's movements, he "gets everything to fit, everything to harmonize" ("Fiction Is Selection," 1116; see also "The Novel with a 'Purpose,' " 1197–98). Jadwin doubles for the novelist not only in his totalizing manipulations but also in his speculative penetrations and excavations. In several essays, Norris remarks that the purpose of the novelist is to "find the value of x" (see "Novelists of the Future," 1153; and "Responsibilities of the Novelist," 1206). Howard Horwitz uses these equations to argue that the novel's final discomfort with speculation repudiates Norris's own novelistic ideal (*By the Law of Nature*, 146–67). In my reading, Jadwin's speculative failure is consistent with Norris's description of the writer's need to activate and then disengage himself from the mechanism latent in his work.

8   Norris, "The Mechanics of Fiction," 1163; subsequent citations appear parenthetically as "Mechanics."

9   John Philip Sousa, quoted in Roell, *The Piano in America*, 54. Roell notes that the first player piano sold in the United States was purchased by a speculator on the Chicago Board of Trade in 1897, the year of the famous Leiter corner on which Norris based the novel (*The Piano in America*, 40).

10 Fontenelle, A Plurality of Worlds, 15. I thank Michael Perelman for pointing me to Fontenelle as the source of Smith's trope. Smith used the image of the invisible hand to describe the providential agency ensuring that the economically self-serving behavior of individuals promoted the general welfare. I am using the phrase to describe what Norris and many of his contemporaries took to be the law of supply and demand governing the inexorably self-balancing operation of the wheat market—the tendency of high prices, for example, to induce farmers to plant more wheat, bringing prices down and disabling any attempt to corner the market. On Smith's varied deployments of the phrase, see Ahmad, "Adam Smith's Four Invisible Hands."

11 See Zimmerman, "The Mesmeric Sources of Frank Norris's The Pit." The mesmerist at the keyboard casting his adulterous influence on the heroine was a standard tableau in mesmeric romances, and the music's hypnotic effect on Laura conforms to a cliché of fin-de-siècle symbolist aesthetics, which was preoccupied with the hypnotic rapport between artist and audience. On the latter, see Silverman, Art Nouveau in Fin-de-Siècle France, 83–106, 234–42, 300–301; and Winters, Mesmerized, 309. For dated but still useful surveys of mesmerism and hypnotism's varied treatments by American writers in the nineteenth century, see Kerr, Mediums, and Spirit-Rappers, and Roaring Radicals; and Tatar, Spellbound, 189–269. Analyses of the political, racial, and economic work of such treatments include Castronovo, Necro Citizenship, 101–203; Schrager, "Mark Twain and Mary Baker Eddy"; Den Tandt, The Urban Sublime, 151–85; and Gillian Brown, Domestic Individualism, 63–132. Other discussions focusing on the importance of mesmerism and psychic research to the literary practices and aims of specific authors include Richards, "Lyric Telegraphy"; Coale, Mesmerism and Hawthorne; and Knoper, Acting Naturally, 119–40, 170–91.

12 See, for example, Hochman, The Art of Frank Norris, 108; and Horwitz, By the Law of Nature, 162.

13 As an apprentice journalist, Norris wrote about dual personality in "A Dual Existence" and "Romola between the Acts." Articles on double or multiple personality in the United States, redacted from clinical journals or from dozens of recently translated books on hypnotism, appeared regularly in mainstream magazines around the turn of the century. Laura's struggle to control her second self and her conception of a new, third self that "forgets" the other two echo the ongoing and well-publicized attempt by Morton Prince, the founder of the Journal of Abnormal Psychology, to suppress the reckless, melodramatic personality of his patient, Miss Beauchamp, as well as his attempts to find her "real" self and bring to birth, in similar revelatory fashion, a new, synthetic self that would not remember the others. On the

popular sensation of the Beauchamp case, see Marx, "Morton Prince and the Dissociation of a Personality." On the explosion of interest in multiple personality around this time, see Hale, "Introduction." On the prevailing symptomatology of hysteria and its association with a resistant femininity, see Smith-Rosenberg, "The Hysterical Woman."

14 Prince, "Some of the Revelations of Hypnotism," 52.

15 Myers, "The Subliminal Consciousness," 5; Breuer and Freud, "On the Psychical Mechanism of Hysterical Phenomena," 12. On the relation between hysteria and hypnotism in early clinical discourse, see Veith, *Hysteria*, 221–56; and Ellenberger, *The Discovery of the Unconscious*, 53–181.

16 On this confluence, see my introduction, n. 50.

17 Bernheim, *Automatisme et suggestion*, 49.

18 Sidis, *The Psychology of Suggestion*, 327; subsequent citations appear parenthetically as PS. On hypnotic suggestion and the origins of crowd psychology, see my introduction, n. 52.

19 See Fabian, "Speculation on Distress."

20 John Mills, "On Credit Cycles," 17.

21 Jones, *Economic Crises*, 207, 181.

22 Ibid., 206n.

23 Patrick, "The Psychology of Crazes," 292.

24 Le Bon, *The Crowd*, 35–36.

25 Writing about *The Pit* in *The Urban Sublime*, Den Tandt observes that "mesmeric paralysis overcomes men who face the chaos of the Board of Trade" (153) and refers in passing to "the mesmerizing energies of speculation" (90) and the "hysteria of the market" (84). Although he devotes a chapter to hypnotism, crowds, and the sublime, Den Tandt does not elaborate on these references to mesmerism in *The Pit*. On entrancement and psychic powers in other Norris works, see Newman, "Supernatural Naturalism"; and Crow, "The Real Vanamee and His Influence on Frank Norris's *The Octopus*." Spiritualism is mentioned in *The Pit*; Norris compares mediums' ability to see into the future and Jadwin's equally uncanny ability to predict the movements of wheat prices (P 114–15).

26 Crozier, *The Magnet*, 44.

27 On New Thought economics and success writing in the late nineteenth century, see Huber, *The American Idea of Success*, 124–76; Sklansky, *The Soul's Economy*, 137–70; Parker, *Mind Cure in New England*; Meyer, *The Positive Thinkers*; Leach, *The Land of Desire*, 225–60; and Satter, *Each Mind a Kingdom*, 150–80. Norris and his peers at the *Wave* regularly reviewed popular New Thought books such as Horace Fletcher's *Menticulture* (1895) and *Happiness as Found in Forethought Minus Fearthought* (1897).

28 Mulford, *Your Forces and How to Use Them*, 151.

29 Haddock, *Business Power*, 164–65. Several success writers saw mesmerism at work in the Chicago commodities pits. See, for example, Militz, *Prosperity through Knowledge and Power of Mind*, 15. At least two members of the Chicago Board of Trade belonged to the American Psychical Society, according to the society's membership list. One of them, Robert Lindblom, wrote finance fiction; F. J. Schulte, treasurer of the society's Chicago branch, was a publisher whose booklist in the 1890s included several finance novels.

30 On nineteenth-century attitudes toward spiritualist and psychic mediumship in the United States, see Braude, *Radical Spirits*; and Moore, *In Search of White Crows*.

31 Myers, *Human Personality and Its Survival of Bodily Death*, 127.

32 Norris was personally familiar with the psychic research that informs *The Pit*. He researched hypnotism and the New Psychology for pieces in the *Wave*, which, like many popular magazines in the 1890s, is filled with articles and reviews about spiritualistic and psychic phenomena, including "What Mesmerism Is" and "The Mesmerist Interviewed" (both 15 August 1896, 7). On Norris's friends and their devotion to psychic research and mysticism, see Zimmerman, "Frenzied Fictions," 252–55 n. 31.

33 Haddock, *The Personal Atmosphere*, 5.

34 Towne, *Practical Methods for Self-Development*, 42; Hudson, *The Law of Psychic Phenomena*, 25.

35 Mason, *Telepathy and the Subliminal Self*, 152.

36 Ibid., 143.

37 James, *The Bostonians*, 68.

38 Hart, *Hypnotism, Mesmerism, and the New Witchcraft*, 209–10.

39 Du Maurier, *Trilby*, 315.

40 On Charcot as an artist figure and disciplinarian of hysteria's anarchic significations, see Silverman, *Art Nouveau in Fin-de-Siècle France*, 91–106. For an overview of feminist and gender theorists' uses of hysteria's troubling of signification and narrative, see Showalter, *Hystories*, 54–58, 81–99; and Micale, *Approaching Hysteria*. On the effects of such troubling in late nineteenth-century literature, see Kahane, *Passions of the Voice*; Beizer, *Narratives of Hysteria in Nineteenth-Century France*; and Diamond, "Realism and Hysteria."

41 Jadwin's magnetic performance updates an old mesmeric manhood tale and reprises familiar tropes linking nature, the market, and sexual women. It also registers male writers' enduring anxieties about female influence. Jadwin, despite his mastery, is ultimately unmanned by his mesmerism. The market conjures forth his latent desire (something Laura is unable to do) and forces him to spill his seed in one final, fatal dissipation. His appetite

for control is only whetted by his plunges, and, in the end, he can contain neither himself nor the market's latent forces. *The Pit* is, after all, a story about seed, its embarrassing discharge and ruinous distribution. Jadwin's emasculation and the market's final hysteria, in this reading, are inseparable. The market, her latent power tapped by this alienist, unleashes her mad fury and suffocates him. For a different reading of *The Pit*'s troping of the market as feminine, one linked to the novel's political and ideological alignments, see Den Tandt, *The Urban Sublime*, 82–92.

42 Various sites and expressions of the economic sublime in the late nineteenth-century United States are examined in Den Tandt, *The Urban Sublime*; Bill Brown, *The Material Unconscious*, 46–56, 103–66; Freeman, *The Feminine Sublime*, 40–67; Nye, *American Technological Sublime*, 109–42; and Trachtenberg, *The Incorporation of America*, 41–42, 46–47.

43 For analyses of late nineteenth-century U.S. economic developments and their threat to proprietary capitalism's ideal of autonomous, boundaried selfhood, see Livingston, *Pragmatism and the Political Economy of Cultural Revolution*; Livingston, "The Strange Career of the 'Social Self' "; and Sklansky, *The Soul's Economy*. Livingston and Sklansky explicate the cultural, moral, and political promises, not merely the perceived dangers, of the reconstruction of subjectivity under the new corporate dispensation. For related analyses, see Horwitz, *By the Law of Nature*, 171–217; and Michaels, *The Gold Standard*, 183–213. For a Lacanian analysis that connects financial markets as signifying texts, financial traders' psychological investments, and traders' emulative subjectivity, see Knorr Cetina and Bruegger, "The Market as an Object of Attachment."

44 Binet, *On Double Consciousness*, 73.

45 Nordau, *Degeneration*, 26; Hirsch, "Epidemics of Hysteria," 549.

46 B. W. Richardson, "The Hypnotic Epidemic," 122; Bagehot, *Physics and Politics*, 92; William James, quoted in Jastrow, *Fact and Fable in Psychology*, 39.

47 Tarde, *The Laws of Imitation*, 77. The second French edition of this text was translated into English by the sociologist Elsie Clews Parson, the daughter of the prominent Wall Street banker and historian Henry Clews. Studies of representations of crowds in American literature include Esteve, *The Aesthetics and Politics of the Crowd in American Literature*; and Nicolaus Mills, *The Crowd in American Literature*.

48 Bagehot, *Physics and Politics*, 95.

49 Quoted in Barnett, *Business-Cycle Theory in the United States*, 22.

50 Jones, *Economic Crises*, 204.

51 See Oughourlian, *The Puppet of Desire*. Norris anticipates what Ruth Leys calls "the antimimetic turn within the mimetic paradigm" of American sociology

by exploring how market entrancement covertly reinstates the coherence of sovereign selfhood (Leys, "Mead's Voices," 286). Mark Seltzer, analyzing serial violence as a symptom of media-saturated "machine" culture, and drawing on the psychoanalytical theory of Mikkel Borch-Jacobsen and others, elaborates a related account of the connection between identification, identity, mimesis, and introjection in *Serial Killers*, 65–67, 70–72, 99 n. 7, 137–40, 145. On the deployment of Girard's notion of mimetic desire in Marxist monetary theory, see Grahl, "Money as Sovereignty."

52 On Laura's and Jadwin's distinct but equally doomed strategies for achieving a stable sense of self protected from internal and external flux, see Hochman, *The Art of Frank Norris*, 99–125. For Hochman, Laura's self-division represents the split between her identity before and after her marriage. Oughourlian's analysis also helps clarify *The Pit*'s insistent confounding of the Board of Trade and the theater. Laura experiences the pleasures and dangers of entrancement and suggestion in the theater. There, emulative desire fractures and suspends the actors' and the audience's self-identity, a breakdown reenacted in the panic scenes in the theater and the Board of Trade building. The presence of panics in both the theater and the marketplace highlights the connections between a runaway mimeticism and the loss of personal autonomy: panic, for Norris, presents the purest expression of theatrical emulation. However, if the theater in *The Pit* functions as the exemplary site where one gives one's self over to a dangerous mimeticism, it is the theatricality of this very self-surrender, the staging forth of one's second self, that protects the self from complete annihilation.

53 See Oughourlian, *The Puppet of Desire*, 169–70. For other accounts of the relation between hysteria, self-division, embodiment, and the market, see Gillian Brown, *Domestic Individualism*, 63–95; and Michaels, *The Gold Standard*, 3–28.

54 On this dynamic, see Oughourlian, *The Puppet of Desire*, 232.

Chapter Four

1 Quoted in "Predicting a Panic," 77, 78.

2 First-person accounts of the panic include White, *The Autobiography of William Allen White*, 195; Moody, *The Long Road Home*, 129–30; and King, *The Light of Four Candles*, 314–26. Useful secondary accounts include Strouse, "The Brilliant Bailout"; Sobel, *Panic on Wall Street*, 297–321; Kogan and Wendt, *Bet-A-Million!* 277–322; Filler, *Crusaders for American Liberalism*, 307–19; and Collman, *Our Mysterious Panics*, 223–69. Several of these accounts draw on congressional testimony given by the principal players in the panic, which

can be found in U.S. Congress, House Subcommittee of the Committee on Banking and Currency, *Money Trust Investigation*, 354–61, 430–57, 631–33, 683–84, 831–32, 1538–41; Senate Committee on the Judiciary, *Hearings before a Subcommittee of the Committee on the Judiciary Relating to the Absorption of the Tennessee, Coal, Iron, and Railroad Company*; and House, *Hearings before the Committee on Investigation of United States Steel Corporation*.

3 *Hearings before a Subcommittee of the Committee on the Judiciary Relating to the Absorption of the Tennessee, Coal, Iron, and Railroad Company*, 59.

4 This information comes from Brandeis, *Other People's Money*, 63; and Chernow, *The Death of the Banker*, 5.

5 Hovey, *J. Pierpont Morgan*, 5. Morgan's stunning capacity to tap the public's savings and put them to instant use—to ruin or rescue individual banks, to save a city, to avert a stock crash and mitigate a depression—offered such clear and, to many, ominous evidence of his financial dominance that it spurred the demand to establish a federal reserve system and contain banker titanism. As Ron Chernow notes, "Everybody saw that thrilling rescues by corpulent old tycoons were a tenuous prop for the banking system" (*The House of Morgan*, 128). For evidence of Morgan's astonishing power, see ibid., 147–56.

6 *Congressional Record—Senate*, 24 March 1908, 3796; *Congressional Record—Senate*, 17 March 1908, 3452.

7 *Congressional Record—Senate*, 24 March 1908, 3796.

8 *Congressional Record—Senate*, 17 March 1908, 3452.

9 Ibid., 3450.

10 The editor of the reformist monthly the *Arena* considered *The Magnet* to be "the most important politico-economic novel of the present year" (Flower, "The Battle of Privilege against Democratic Government," 485). Other reviews of *The Magnet* are excerpted in Crozier, *U.S. Money vs. Corporation Currency*, 392–401. See also Crozier, "The Recent Panic."

11 Crozier, *The Magnet*, 139.

12 According to Leon Harris, the phrase "How Wall Street manufactured the Panic of 1907" appeared on the book's cover (*Upton Sinclair*, 102). Sinclair discusses *The Moneychangers*' aims and sources in *The Brass Check*, 80–85; *The Autobiography of Upton Sinclair*, 144–46; and *Upton Sinclair Presents William Fox*, xii–xiii. *The Moneychangers* (1908) follows *The Metropolis* (1908) and precedes *The Machine* (1911), a drama published as one of E. Haldeman-Julius's Little Blue Books (No. 632), a series of five-cent socialist propaganda texts.

13 Sinclair, *The Brass Check*, 81. In a draft sketch of *The Metropolis-Moneychangers-Machine* trilogy included among Sinclair's manuscripts in the Lilly Library at Indiana University, Sinclair identified Waterman as Morgan; Ryder as

Charles T. Barney, president of the Knickerbocker Trust; Hegan as Thomas F. Ryan; and Wyman as E. H. Harriman. Sinclair does not identify his other characters, but Prentice clearly plays the role of Oakleigh Thorne, president of the Trust Company of America, and Price seems loosely based on the notorious John W. Gates, a Morgan nemesis. A number of these characters also appear in The Metropolis, and Hegan plays a central role in The Machine.

14 Sinclair, The Moneychangers, 187, 186; subsequent citations appear parenthetically as TM.

15 For a related representation of Morgan in fiction, see Frederick U. Adams's The Kidnapped Millionaires (1901). Examples of antibanker fiction in the late nineteenth century include T. S. Denison, An Iron Crown (1885); Ignatius Donnelly, Caesar's Column (1889); T. A. Bland, Esau, or the Banker's Victim (1892); William "Coin" Harvey, A Tale of Two Nations (1894); Minnie Lawson, Money to Lend on All Collateral (1895); and James B. Goode, The Modern Banker (1896). Rose provides a list, not always reliable, of additional postbellum antibanker novels in "A Bibliographical Survey of Economic and Political Writings," 387–88.

16 Studies of conspiracy's heuristic and cultural work include Wood, "Conspiracy and the Paranoid Style"; Hofstadter, "The Paranoid Style in American Politics"; Levine, Conspiracy and Romance; Graumann and Moscovici, Changing Conceptions of Conspiracy; Melley, Empire of Conspiracy; Knight, Conspiracy Nation; Barkun, A Culture of Conspiracy; West and Sanders, Transparency and Conspiracy; Marcus, Paranoia within Reason, 157–92; Ed White, "The Value of Conspiracy Theory"; and Bell, "Fear of Plot."

17 Haskell, "Capitalism and the Origins of the Humanitarian Sensibility, Part I," 358.

18 Seligman, "The Crisis of 1907 in the Light of History," xi, x.

19 Lefèvre was a respected financial journalist. Sinclair, Dreiser, and other fiction writers drew on his essays and anecdotes, often without attribution. Lefèvre, whom Frank Norris consulted when he was writing The Pit, also wrote several successful finance novels, including Sampson Rock of Wall Street (1907). His fictionalized autobiography, Reminiscences of a Stock Operator (1923), remains a popular investment book today.

20 "Notable Books and Authors," 504.

21 Barr, "A Deal on 'Change"; subsequent citations appear parenthetically as "Deal."

22 Ross, Sin and Society, 34; subsequent citations appear parenthetically as Sin. Ross also wrote on crowds and financial panics in "The Mob Mind." For a related account of the complexity of moral accounting under new economic

conditions, see J. M. Clark, "The Changing Basis of Economic Responsibility," 209–10, 222–23.

23 Wilson, "The Lawyer and the Community," 621.

24 Preoccupied with the uncertain difference between chaste and unchaste forms of seduction, the novel registers an anxiousness about the character of its own appeal to the reader. Like other melodramatic seduction novels, *The Moneychangers* must distinguish its own appeal to the reader from the seducer's appeal to his or her victim. Like other conspiracist novels, it must distinguish its virtuous enlistment of the reader from the conspiracy's vicious enlistment of its agents. The novel avoids seducing its readers by having us gaze on Lucy and her fate through Montague's conscientiously aloof eyes. Identifying with Montague, we see how Lucy refuses to comprehend the moral risks she assumes by continuing her romantic and business affair with Ryder. Most important, by inhabiting his vision, we stand behind Montague's chiding words and his active disavowal of her imprudence. The Lucy plot exists precisely so that we can refuse to be implicated in it—so that we can choose, instead, to join Montague and "the people" crying for reform. We disavow Lucy, that is, in order to become responsible citizens.

25 Like Lucy, the bankers find themselves subject to ruinous rumors—an epidemic of rumor punctures Ryder's financial reputation and prompts the fateful run on his bank. In 1911, congressmen investigating Morgan's role in the panic of 1907 pursued a similar connection, asking the president of one of the principal trust companies, "Your idea seems to be that the credit of a bank is a good deal like a woman's virtue—when you begin to talk about it, you are sure to do harm?" The banker responded, "I will talk about banks. I do not know anything about woman's virtue" (*Hearings before the Committee on Investigation of United States Steel Corporation*, 1693).

26 When he realizes that Lucy falls in too deep with Ryder, for example, Montague justifies terminating their relationship by observing to a friend, "I have told her about the mistake she's making, and she chooses to go her own way. So what more can I do?" (TM 71). Gazing on Lucy's seduction through Montague's castigating eyes may seem like a conventional literary means of highlighting the hazards of female independence and naturalizing male cultural authority. Indeed, Lucy comes to New York because her father and her husband have both recently died; her fall to Wall Street may thus seem to be the consequence of her freedom from patriarchal governance. Montague, authorized to dispose of her inherited property (her railroad stock) and witness to her early indiscretions and final self-abasement, might appear to occupy the role of such a governor. However, Montague himself resists such a role and such a reading since he insists that he is

powerless over her. He can advise her, but she must be accountable for her own fate.

27 Montague is modeled after Sinclair and also after Lincoln Steffens, who worked as a Wall Street reporter before gaining fame as a muckraker. Steffens, a friend of Sinclair, was unsuccessfully enlisted as the president of a corporation by Wall Street manipulators. James B. Dill, the corporation lawyer who advised Sinclair during the writing of The Moneychangers, also educated Steffens about Wall Street corruption.

28 In Martin Sklar's words, "Concentrated economic power meant the decline of the self-determining citizen in the market and in politics, and it meant the rise of massive political power capable of subordinating the individual to hierarchic organization and the government to special interest; it thus threatened democracy itself" (The Corporate Reconstruction of American Capitalism, 338). On the relation between dispersed, competitive markets and postbellum republicanism, see also Nancy Cohen, The Reconstruction of American Liberalism; and Ritter, Goldbugs and Greenbacks, 4–6.

29 Lippmann, Drift and Mastery, 47. On the challenges posed by new forms of property to the moral personality envisioned by the republican tradition, see Livingston, Pragmatism and the Political Economy of Cultural Revolution, 221–23, 273–77; and Sklansky, The Soul's Economy, 205–23.

30 Wilson, The New Freedom, 6.

31 The reformist monthly the Arena made the equation of exposure with accountability explicit; after a wave of exposés of business and municipal crime flooded the nation's magazines in 1906, it declared, "So long as the public was in ignorance of the criminality and corruption [in business and government] . . . , the people were not morally culpable; but now that it has been made plain, the whole nation will be morally responsible" ("In the Mirror of the Present," 627). Discussions of Progressivism's appeal to personal moral responsibility include Crunden, Ministers of Reform; Degler, Out of Our Past, 383, 402; Hofstadter, "Introduction," 3–6; and Mowry, The California Progressives, 89, 99.

32 Hofstadter, The Age of Reform, 202.

33 To understand the urgency of this project for Sinclair, we need to remember that supporters of the emergent corporate order (those who saw industrial combination as historically inevitable and, if properly regulated, socially beneficial and congenial to republicanism) also demanded that corporate practices, including stock dealings, be exposed to government scrutiny and public accountability. Even as the first banks collapsed in October 1907, a major advisory group, the National Civic Federation, argued that the full disclosure of corporate finances was necessary to boost public confidence in

the new corporate regime by preventing corporations from being "the hiding place of . . . irresponsible, dishonest, or corrupt" individuals (quoted in Sklar, *The Corporate Reconstruction of American Capitalism*, 189). *The Moneychangers*, countering this publicity campaign, highlights how there is nothing "safe, sane, moral, or respectable" about the leading financiers, nothing enlightened, paternal, or progressive about their public or private intentions (Flower, "The Money-Changers," 624). On corporate leaders' self-image as public stewards and trustees of stability, progress, and civilization, see chapter 1.

34 Quoted in Lippmann, *Drift and Mastery*, 82.

35 On audiences' preoccupation with melodrama's stage and cinematic machinery, see Singer, *Melodrama and Modernity*, 50.

36 Sinclair, "Synopsis of Metropolis-Moneychangers-Machine," 19; courtesy of Lilly Library, Indiana University, Bloomington, Ind. For an example of a Sinclair text overtly inviting attention to its own dramatic construction, see *The Pot Boiler* (1912), a melodrama about a playwright that features a play within a play as well as a stage design that emphasizes the difference between what Sinclair calls the "Real-play" and the "Play-play." In a postscript, Sinclair noted that there had been "many examples of the 'play within a play,' but up to that time there had never been a play which showed the *writing* of a play" (*The Pot Boiler*, 115). Sinclair confessed to his continuing use of dime-novel exaggeration and cliché in *The Autobiography of Upton Sinclair*, 51.

37 Review of *The Moneychangers*, *Nation*, 22 October 1908, 389.

38 Review of *The Moneychangers*, *Bookman*, October 1908, 112.

39 B. O. Flower, "The Money-Changers," 623.

40 *Congressional Record—Senate*, 17 March 1908, 3452.

41 Ibid.

42 Crozier, *The Magnet*, 139.

43 Crozier, *U.S. Money vs. Corporation Currency*, n.p. Crozier notes the date of the novel's composition in ibid., 392.

Chapter Five

1 Dreiser, "Change," 19; Dreiser, "Hey, Rub-a-Dub-Dub!" 17.

2 Thomas, *American Literary Realism and the Failed Promise of Contract*, 152, 153.

3 Dreiser, *The Financier* (New York: Harper, 1912), 693; subsequent citations of this edition of the novel appear parenthetically as TF. Dreiser published a significantly pared-down version of the novel in 1927; it is over two hundred pages and fifteen chapters shorter than the 1912 edition. On the differences

between the two editions, see Jett, "Vision and Revision"; and Hutchisson, "The Revision of Theodore Dreiser's *Financier*."

4 Quoted in Lingeman, *Theodore Dreiser*, 267. Although the novel's romance plot also details Cowperwood's unyielding drive for social mastery and pleasure, I have chosen to focus on the finance plot (that is, the financial and legal machinations of Cowperwood and his enemies) because it more clearly illuminates the sociological imperatives—the collusion and competition among interdependent, self-advancing individuals—and the forms of contagion and accounting that, in my reading, propel Dreiser's experiment with literary form. *The Financier* depicts an inescapably intersubjective conception of individuality, one that comprehends individuals only in relation to the social and financial matrices in which they perform their life activity and act out their desires. For related discussions of this social subjectivity and its aesthetic importance for *The Financier*, see Horwitz, *By the Law of Nature*, 192–217; and Lester Cohen, "Locating One's Self."

5 "Theodore Dreiser Now Turns to High Finance," 196.

6 Ibid., 197.

7 Ibid., 196, 197.

8 Gerber, *Theodore Dreiser*, 92. Dreiser provides a model for the nature special in *The Financier*'s famous account of the prolonged mortal combat between a lobster and a squid in a tank (TF 10–14). Dreiser adapted this aquatic scene from "A Lesson from the Aquarium," an article he published in 1906 that draws explicit parallels between the mercilessness and cunning of fish in an aquarium and the inexorably self-advancing activities and attitudes of captains of industry. In 1915, Stuart P. Sherman famously attacked Dreiser's imposition of a theory of animal behavior on human beings in "The Barbaric Naturalism of Mr. Dreiser." What Sherman saw as an artless insult to human nature, I see as the impetus for Dreiser's self-conscious and painstaking experimentation with genre. For an alternative view of the novel's craftsmanship, see Brennan, "*The Financier*."

9 Although the Cowperwood novels were later advertised as "The Trilogy of Desire," desire actually plays little role in *The Financier*, at least in its finance plot. To be sure, Cowperwood is compelled by an inborn desire for profit and power, but what moves him (and all the schemers) is less a personal characteristic or impersonal property than a transpersonal imperative that preexists him, acting itself out through him, binding him to its other agents. For *The Financier*'s first 275 pages, this imperative seems to be capital's, or money's, evolution. As the presence of so much detailed explication of Cowperwood's innovative schemes and accounting practices suggests, the opening tale of his financial rise does not focus on the title

character so much as on his mastery of increasingly abstract forms of profit-seeking. Money and the money form develop in the first third of The Financier, not Cowperwood, who never changes. The financier is simply a medium: he does not use money; rather, money uses him. He thrives because he is born with the requisite forcefulness of personality and accounting skills to serve as money's agent. Compelled by his own "chemic" nature, a will to profit always casting about for opportunities to express and actualize itself, he carries out money's seemingly inexorable expansion into new arenas, its drive to reproduce itself in increasingly efficient, abstract forms. Cowperwood represents money's avant-garde in both its imperialist and aesthetic senses, and he settles on municipal finance because this field, in the United States after the Civil War, is money's true frontier. In Cowperwood's hands, money reproduces itself by colonizing time, not trade, exploiting in ever more sophisticated ways the duration between when a loan is taken and when it must be paid back. Cowperwood's biography, until the financial panic, studies the career of money through the serialization and pyramiding of such durations. In short, The Financier, at least the first third of its narrative, offers a biography of money.

10 Biography fails as a generic model for The Financier not simply because this genre, plotting the life of an extraordinary individual, is insufficiently broad to illuminate the social psychology of a crisis and the web of interdependencies that in a panic turn cooperation into conflict; nor simply because the financier, requiring others with whom to open accounts, has no character or selfhood discrete from these social exchanges; but rather because biography—especially the financial kind in vogue around the turn of the century—privileges autonomous, self-determining subjects, not the career of an abstraction.

11 Quoted in Hutchisson, "The Creation (and Reduction) of The Financier," 249.

12 Quoted in Lingeman, Theodore Dreiser, 85.

13 Dreiser, "Equation Inevitable," 173.

14 Dreiser, "The Reformer," 210.

15 We cannot know for certain whether Dreiser intended this conventional visual form to advance his argument about accounting and its limits; it does, however, appear in all extant states of the text, as four inverted pyramids (one for each elliptical sentence) in the manuscript and typescript, and as a single large inverted pyramid in proof. The manuscript, typescript, and page proof can be found in the Theodore Dreiser Papers in the Rare Book and Manuscript Library at the University of Pennsylvania. I thank Nancy Shawcross, curator of the collection, for her help in tracking down these versions of the headline.

16 Dreiser, *The Titan*, 466.

17 Dreiser, "Ideals, Morals, and the Daily Newspaper," 152.

18 Ibid.; quoted in Lingeman, *Theodore Dreiser*, 277.

19 Dreiser, "Change," 21. Here we can clearly see Spencer's impact on Dreiser. For accounts of Spencer's influence on the novelist, see Dreiser, *A Book about Myself*, 457–58; and Zanine, *Mechanism and Mysticism*.

20 Dreiser, "Equation Inevitable," 173.

21 Dreiser, "Change," 21.

22 Dreiser, "Equation Inevitable," 166. For a similar meditation on "balance," see Dreiser, *The Titan*, 499–500.

23 Benjamin, "The Storyteller," 100.

24 Dreiser, *The Financier* (1927; repr., New York: Meridian, 1940), 227.

25 Ibid., 286.

26 Dreiser, "The Man on the Sidewalk," 167.

27 See Dreiser's exchanges with Mencken between August and October 1912 in Riggio, *Dreiser-Mencken Letters*, 1:96–103.

28 Gerber, "Dreiser's Debt to Jay Cooke." Dreiser wrote "Life Stories of Successful Men" and other biographical sketches for *Success* in 1898 and 1899, many following the conventional formulas of struggle-and-success tales. These articles can be found in Hakutani, *Selected Magazine Articles of Theodore Dreiser*, 111–201; and Hakutani, *Theodore Dreiser's Uncollected Magazine Articles*, 39–98. For a related study that views biography as a model, but a limited one, for explaining Cowperwood, his amoral activity, and the trajectory of his early career, see Hughson, *From Biography to History*, 122–59.

29 Notman, "Talks with Four Novelists," 164. Dreiser's generic innovation perplexed reviewers, many of whom identified the novel as a straightforward biography or history.

30 Cooper, "Theory of Endings," 115.

31 Riggio, *Dreiser-Mencken Letters*, 1:71.

32 Mencken, "Adventures among the New Novels," 751, 753.

33 Dreiser, "Hey, Rub-a-Dub-Dub!" 17.

34 Ibid., 10.

35 Lefèvre, "What Availeth It?" 836; subsequent citations appear parenthetically as "WAI." In *Theodore Dreiser, His World and His Novels*, 98, Richard Lehan lists this and other texts that Dreiser consulted.

36 In *The Titan*, Dreiser seems to poke deliberate fun at Lefèvre's essay. Commenting on Cowperwood's desire to build a museum that "might stand as a monument to his memory," Dreiser asks: "Until he could stand with [the nation's most famous magnates], until he could have a magnificent mansion, acknowledged as such by all, until he could have a world-famous

gallery, Berenice, millions—*what did it avail?*" (398; my emphasis). For an account of the relation between biography, death, and the "anticipation of retrospection" that organizes our reading of narrative, see Brooks, *Reading for the Plot*, 22–23.

37 Dreiser, "Equation Inevitable," 171, 173.

38 Dreiser, "Secrecy—Its Value," 142.

39 Ibid. For an analysis of the relation between the thematics of accounting's interminability and the Victorian novel's simultaneous compulsion toward and resistance to closure, as exemplified by Dickens's *Bleak House*, see Miller, *The Novel and the Police*, 58–106. Miller attributes this resistance to "the insoluble, abiding mysteriousness of human and literary experience" (97), a mysteriousness domesticated in his Foucauldian account by the disciplinary work of private novel reading. My argument is that *The Financier*, unlike *Bleak House*, overtly obviates the "shrewd administration of suspense" (88) that continually anticipates the prospect of totalizing retrospection, an "end of bafflement and the acquisition of various structures of coherence" (89). *The Financier* does not "reward" (91) the patience of the reader with the "payoff" (92) of closure.

40 "Traction Interests," 97.

41 This information dating the addition of the postscript comes from Pizer, *The Novels of Theodore Dreiser*, 161.

42 The first page of Dreiser's manuscript, cut from the published book, makes Cowperwood's predetermination overt: "He is fore-armed and set cap-a-pie for battle. Life has weighted the dice; marked the cards, given him odds in the game he is to play. He comes stamped with the tilka mark on his brow" (quoted in Hutchisson, "The Creation [and Reduction] of *The Financier*," 249).

43 Cooper, "Theory of Endings," 116.

44 "A Literary Show," 124.

45 Riggio, *Dreiser-Mencken Letters*, 1:99.

46 Quoted in Hutchisson, "The Creation (and Reduction) of *The Financier*," 249.

47 Riggio, *Dreiser-Mencken Letters*, 1:102. In November, Dreiser wrote Mencken that "the book should have been cut 170 pages instead of 77" (ibid., 1:103). Such apologies do not prove much about Dreiser's intentions in *The Financier*; they may simply be Dreiser's way of conveying his thanks for his friend's editorial labor and critical boost.

48 Mencken, "A Literary Behemoth," 755; "A Literary Show," 124.

49 Edgett, "Dreiser and His Titan," 235.

50 Critics frequently acknowledge the importance of the expository interruptions, observing, as Pizer does in *The Novels of Theodore Dreiser*, that "the great

bulk of detail is intrinsic both to character and to action" (177) and that it provides "that indefinable quality of fictional density, of a living canvas, which is one of the great achievements of the nineteenth-century novel" (178). However, no one, to my knowledge, has seen the inclusion of this material as reproducing or serving the philosophical argument of the novel. The compositional history of the novel lends support to my reading. As Pizer notes, Dreiser made a major structural revision of the manuscript in the summer of 1912. Dreiser decided "to dramatize rather than summarize" (164) Cowperwood's struggle against the city insiders after the panic and to move Butler's hiring of detectives closer to the start of the manuscript, to before the trial. For Pizer, the revision "enlivened a portion of the novel otherwise devoted to a tedious recounting of Cowperwood's postcollapse financial affairs" (164), but we might see the new link between the insiders' accounting, Cowperwood's desire to pay his debts and stay afloat, and the detectives' surveillance as an indication of Dreiser's decision to make the will to account (and its limits) the thematic crux of the novel. Further support for my claim includes the fact that Dreiser saved the speeches of the lawyers from cutting until the last moment, and he restored them in the 1927 edition—which suggests how integral the examination of criminal accountability's construction was to his formal and narrative aims.

51 Mencken, "A Literary Behemoth," 755; quoted in Hutchisson 255 n. 6; and Riggio, *Dreiser-Mencken Letters*, 1:99.

Epilogue

1 Clews, *Fifty Years in Wall Street*, 759.
2 Webster, *The Banker and the Bear*, 94.
3 Knorr Cetina and Bruegger, "The Market as an Object of Attachment," 149; subsequent citations appear parenthetically as "Market."

Works Cited

Ackerman, Kenneth D. *The Gold Ring: Jim Fisk, Jay Gould, and Black Friday, 1869.* New York: Dodd, Mead, 1988.

Adams, Frederick Upham. *The Kidnapped Millionaires.* Boston: Lothrop, 1901.

Adams, Henry. "The New York Gold Conspiracy." In Charles Francis Adams Jr. and Henry Adams, *Chapters of Erie,* 101–36. Ithaca, N.Y.: Great Seal Books, 1956.

Adler, Patricia A., and Peter Adler. "The Market as Collective Behavior." In Adler and Adler, *The Social Dynamics of Financial Markets,* 85–105.

——, eds. *The Social Dynamics of Financial Markets.* Greenwich, Conn.: JAI, 1984.

Ahmad, Syed. "Adam Smith's Four Invisible Hands." *History of Political Economy* 22, no. 1 (1990): 137–44.

Anthony, David J. "Banking on Emotion: Financial Panic and the Logic of Male Submission in the Jacksonian Gothic." *American Literature* 76 (December 2004): 719–47.

——. " 'Gone Distracted': 'Sleepy Hollow,' Gothic Masculinity, and the Panic of 1819." *Early American Literature* 40 (March 2005): 111–44.

Arsenberg, Mary, ed. *The American Sublime.* Albany: SUNY Press, 1986.

"The Artist Who Preaches." *American Magazine,* April 1907, 634–35.

Avrich, Paul. *The Haymarket Tragedy.* Princeton, N.J.: Princeton University Press, 1984.

Bagehot, Walter. *Physics and Politics.* 1872. Reprint, London: Paul, Trench, 1906.

Baker, Ray Stannard. *American Chronicle.* New York: Scribner's, 1945.

——. "Railroads on Trial." *McClure's,* March 1906, 535–49.

Barber, Bernard. "All Economies Are 'Embedded': The Career of a Concept, and Beyond," *Social Research* 62 (Summer 1995): 387–413.

Barkun, Michael. *A Culture of Conspiracy: Apocalyptic Visions in Contemporary America.* Berkeley: University of California Press, 2003.

Barnett, Paul. *Business-Cycle Theory in the United States, 1860–1900.* Chicago: University of Chicago Press, 1941.

Barr, Robert. "A Deal on 'Change: A Tale of Revenge." *McClure's,* October 1894, 436–42.

——. "The Revolt of the ——. A Page from the Domestic History of the Twentieth Century." *McClure's,* July 1894, 169–76.

Barrett, D. C. *The Greenbacks and Resumption of Specie Payments, 1862–1879.* 1931. Reprint, Gloucester, Mass.: Smith, 1965.

Barron, Clarence W. *More They Told Barron.* Edited by Arthur Pound and Samuel Taylor Moore. New York: Harper, 1931.

——. *The Record of the Boston News Bureau on Amalgamated.* Boston: Boston News Bureau, 1904.

Barrows, Susanna. *Distorting Mirrors: Visions of the Crowd in Late Nineteenth-Century France.* New Haven: Yale University Press, 1981.

Bazard, Philippe. "Homo Œconomicus Mesmerized: Jevons on Mind Reading." Unpublished essay, 1999.

Beizer, Janet. *Narratives of Hysteria in Nineteenth-Century France.* Ithaca, N.Y.: Cornell University Press, 1994.

Bell, Gregory R. "Fear of Plot: Conspiracy and the British Novel." Ph.D. diss., University of California, Berkeley, 2002.

Bellamy, Charles Joseph. *The Way Out: Suggestions for Social Reform.* New York: Putnam's, 1884.

Beltz, Lynda. "Preachers of Social Discontent: The Rhetoric of the Muckrakers." Ph.D. diss., Indiana University, 1968.

Benjamin, Walter. "The Storyteller." In *Illuminations,* edited by Hannah Arendt, translated by Harry Zohn, 83–109. New York: Schocken, 1968.

Bensel, Richard Franklin. *The Political Economy of American Industrialization, 1877–1900.* New York: Cambridge University Press, 2000.

——. *Yankee Leviathan: The Origins of Central State Authority in America, 1859–1877.* New York: Cambridge University Press, 1990.

Bernheim, Hippolyte. *Automatisme et suggestion.* Paris: Alcan, 1917.

Bernstein, Samuel. "The Impact of the Paris Commune in the United States." In *Revolution and Reaction: The Paris Commune 1871,* edited by John Hicks and Robert Tucker, 59–70. Amherst: University of Massachusetts Press, 1973.

Biggers, E. D. "The Frenzied Outcast." *Life,* 12 January 1905, 44.

Binet, Alfred. *On Double Consciousness.* 1890. In *Alterations of Personality and On Double Consciousness.* Vol. 5 of *Significant Contributions to the History of Psychology 1750–1920,* Series C, edited by Daniel N. Robinson. Washington, D.C.: University Publications of America, 1977.

Bird, S. Elizabeth, and Robert W. Dardenne. "News and Storytelling in American Culture: Reevaluating the Sensational Dimension." *Journal of American Culture* 13, no. 2 (1990): 33–37.

"Black Friday." *Literary World,* November 1904, 328–29.

"The Boston Claimant." *Life,* 9 March 1905, 277.

Brandeis, Louis D. *Other People's Money and How the Bankers Use It.* 1914. Reprint, edited by Melvin I. Urofsky. Boston: Bedford, 1995.

Brasch, Walter M. *Forerunners of Revolution: Muckrakers and the American Social Conscience.* Lanham, Md.: University Press of America, 1990.

Braude, Ann. *Radical Spirits: Spiritualism and Women's Rights in Nineteenth-Century America.* Boston: Beacon Press, 1989.

Brecher, Jeremy. *Strike!* Boston: South End, 1972.

Brennan, Stephen C. "*The Financier*: Dreiser's Marriage of Heaven and Hell." *Studies in American Fiction* 19 (Spring 1991): 55–69.

Breuer, Josef, and Sigmund Freud. "On the Psychical Mechanism of Hysterical Phenomena: Preliminary Communication." In *Studies on Hysteria*. Vol. 2 of *The Standard Edition of the Complete Psychological Works of Sigmund Freud*, translated and edited by James Strachey, 1–17. London: Hogarth, 1955.

"Broker Who Tried Lawson Plan Flees." *New York Times*, 14 June 1907, 2.

Brooks, Peter. *The Melodramatic Imagination: Balzac, Henry James, Melodrama, and the Mode of Excess*. New York: Columbia University Press, 1976.

——. *Reading for the Plot: Design and Intention in Narrative*. Cambridge, Mass.: Harvard University Press, 1992.

Brown, Bill. *The Material Unconscious: American Amusement, Stephen Crane, and the Economies of Play*. Cambridge, Mass.: Harvard University Press, 1996.

Brown, Gillian. *Domestic Individualism: Imagining Self in Nineteenth-Century America*. Berkeley: University of California Press, 1990.

Buhle, Mary Jo. *Women and American Socialism, 1870–1920*. Urbana: University of Illinois Press, 1981.

Burrows, Edwin, and Mike Wallace. *Gotham: A History of New York City to 1898*. New York: Oxford University Press, 1999.

Burton, Theodore E. *Financial Crises and Periods of Industrial and Commercial Depression*. New York: Appleton, 1902.

Casson, Herbert N. "The Trade-Unionist and the Monopolist." *Arena*, December 1902, 596–601.

Castronovo, Russ. *Necro Citizenship: Death, Eroticism, and the Public Sphere in the Nineteenth-Century United States*. Durham, N.C.: Duke University Press, 2001.

Chandler, Alfred D., Jr. *Henry Varnum Poor: Business Editor, Analyst and Reformer*. Cambridge, Mass.: Harvard University Press, 1956.

——. *The Visible Hand: The Managerial Revolution in American Business*. Cambridge, Mass.: Belknap Press, 1977.

Charvat, William. *The Profession of Authorship in America, 1800–1870*. Edited by Matthew J. Bruccoli. New York: Columbia University Press, 1992.

Chernow, Ron. *The Death of the Banker: The Decline and Fall of the Great Financial Dynasties and the Triumph of the Small Investor*. New York: Vintage, 1997.

——. *The House of Morgan: An American Banking Dynasty and the Rise of Modern Finance*. New York: Touchstone, 1990.

Chicago: Yesterday and Today. Chicago: Felix Mendelsohn, 1932.

Clapp, Charles C. Letter to Theodore Dreiser, 16 July 1904. Theodore Dreiser

Papers, Rare Book and Manuscript Library, University of Pennsylvania, Philadelphia, Pa.

Clark, Gordon. *Shylock: As Banker, Bondholder, Corruptionist, Conspirator.* Washington, D.C.: American Bimetallic League, 1894.

Clark, J. Maurice. "The Changing Basis of Economic Responsibility." *Journal of Political Economy* 24 (March 1916): 209–29.

Clews, Henry. *Fifty Years in Wall Street.* New York: Irving, 1908.

Clymer, Jeffory A. *America's Culture of Terrorism: Violence, Capitalism, and the Written Word.* Chapel Hill: University of North Carolina Press, 2003.

Coale, Samuel Chase. *Mesmerism and Hawthorne: Mediums of American Romance.* Tuscaloosa: University of Alabama Press, 1998.

Cochran, Thomas C., and William Miller, *A Social History of Industrial America.* Rev. ed. New York: Harper, 1961.

Cohen, Lester H. "Locating One's Self: The Problematics of Dreiser's Social World." *Modern Fiction Studies* 23 (Autumn 1977): 355–68.

Cohen, Nancy. *The Reconstruction of American Liberalism, 1865–1914.* Chapel Hill: University of North Carolina Press, 2002.

Cole, Arthur H. *The Historical Development of Economic and Business Literature.* Boston: Harvard Graduate School of Business Administration, 1957.

Collman, Charles Albert. *Our Mysterious Panics, 1830–1930.* New York: William Morrow, 1931.

"The Coming Woman." *Evening Star* [Washington, D.C.], 21 January 1869, 4.

Connery, Thomas B. "A Third Way to Tell a Story: American Literary Journalism at the Turn of the Century." In *Literary Journalism in the Twentieth Century,* edited by Norman Sims, 3–20. New York: Oxford University Press, 1990.

Cooley, Charles H. *Personal Competition.* New York: American Economic Association, 1899.

Cooper, Frederic T. "Theory of Endings and Some Recent Novels." In Salzman, *Theodore Dreiser: The Critical Reception,* 115–17.

———. "The Web of Life and Some Recent Books." *Bookman,* December 1904, 365–66.

"Copper Stock Speculation." *New York Times,* 1 January 1900, 10.

Crow, Charles L. "The Real Vanamee and His Influence on Frank Norris's *The Octopus.*" *Western American Literature* 9 (March 1987): 131–39.

Crozier, Alfred O. *The Magnet: A Romance of the Battles of Modern Giants.* New York: Funk, 1908.

———. "The Recent Panic and the Present Deadly Peril to American Prosperity." *Arena,* March 1908, 272–75.

———. *U.S. Money vs. Corporation Currency: "Aldrich Plan"; Wall Street Confessions! Great Bank Combine.* Cincinnati: Magnet, 1912.

Crunden, Robert M. *Ministers of Reform: The Progressives' Achievement in American Civilization, 1889–1920.* Urbana: University of Illinois Press, 1982.

Davis, David Brion, ed. *The Fear of Conspiracy: Images of Un-American Subversion from the Revolution to the Present.* Ithaca, N.Y.: Cornell University Press, 1971.

de Bolla, Peter. *The Discourse of the Sublime: Readings in History, Aesthetics and the Subject.* Oxford: Basil Blackwell, 1989.

Degler, Carl N. *Out of Our Past: The Forces That Shaped Modern America.* 3rd ed. New York: Harper Colophon, 1984.

Demaree, Albert Lowther. *The American Agricultural Press, 1819–1860.* New York: Columbia University Press, 1941.

Den Tandt, Christophe. *The Urban Sublime in American Literary Naturalism.* Urbana: University of Illinois Press, 1998.

Dewing, Arthur S. *Corporate Promotions and Reorganizations.* New York: Harper, 1969.

Diamond, Elin. "Realism and Hysteria: Toward a Feminist Mimesis." *Discourse* 13 (Fall–Winter 1990/1991): 59–92.

Dijkstra, Bram. *Evil Sisters: The Threat of Female Sexuality and the Cult of Manhood.* New York: Knopf, 1996.

Dill, James B. "Industrials as Investments for Small Capital." In *Corporations and Public Welfare,* 109–19. New York: McClure, Phillips, 1900.

"The Doctrine of the Destroyers and the Remedy of the Redeemers." *Appeal to Reason,* 21 December 1907, 1.

Donnelly, Ignatius. *Caesar's Column. A Story of the Twentieth Century.* 1890. Reprint, edited by Walter B. Rideout. Cambridge, Mass.: Belknap Press, 1960.

Donohoe, Denis. "The Truth about Frenzied Finance." *Public Opinion,* 5 January 1905, 9; 19 January 1905, 69–74; 26 January 1905, 109–12; 2 February 1905, 149–52; 11 February 1905, 189–95; 18 February 1905, 229–32; 25 February 1905, 271–74; 4 March 1905, 314–16; 11 March 1905, 367–69; 18 March 1905, 404–7; 25 March 1905, 442–46; 1 April 1905, 487–91, 505–7; 8 April 1905, 521–22, 545–46; 15 April 1905, 571–72.

Dorman, Jessica. " 'Deliver Me from This Muck-Rake': The Literary Impulse behind Progressive Era Muckraking." Ph.D. diss., Harvard University, 1996.

Dreiser, Theodore. *A Book about Myself.* New York: Boni and Liveright, 1922.

———. "Change." In Dreiser, *Hey Rub-A-Dub-Dub,* 19–23.

———. "Equation Inevitable." In Dreiser, *Hey Rub-A-Dub-Dub,* 156–81.

———. *The Financier.* New York: Harper, 1912.

———. *The Financier.* 1927. Reprint, New York: Meridian, 1940.

———. "Hey, Rub-A-Dub-Dub." In Dreiser, *Hey Rub-A-Dub-Dub,* 1–18.

———. *Hey Rub-A-Dub-Dub: A Book of the Mystery and Wonder and Terror of Life.* New York: Boni and Liveright, 1920.

———. "Ideals, Morals, and the Daily Newspaper." In Dreiser, *Hey Rub-A-Dub-Dub*, 152–56.

———. "A Lesson from the Aquarium." In Pizer, *Theodore Dreiser: A Selection of Uncollected Prose*, 159–62.

———. "The Man on the Sidewalk." In Pizer, *Theodore Dreiser: A Selection of Uncollected Prose*, 165–67.

———. "The Reformer." In Dreiser, *Hey Rub-A-Dub-Dub*, 206–11.

———. "Secrecy—Its Value." In Dreiser, *Hey Rub-A-Dub-Dub*, 142–51.

———. *The Titan*. 1914. Reprint, New York: Signet Classics, 1965.

———. *Twelve Men*. New York: Boni and Liveright, 1919.

———. " 'Vanity, Vanity,' Saith the Preacher." In Dreiser, *Twelve Men*, 263.

Du Maurier, George. *Trilby*. 1894. Reprint, London: Collins, 1953.

Dunne, Finley Peter. *Mr. Dooley Says*. New York: Scribner's, 1910.

Edgett, E. F. "Dreiser and His Titan." In Pizer, *Critical Essays on Theodore Dreiser*, 235–36.

"Editorial Announcement." *American Magazine*, October 1906, 569–75.

Edwards, Rebecca. *Angels in the Machinery: Gender in American Party Politics from the Civil War to the Progressive Era*. New York: Oxford University Press, 1997.

Ellenberger, Henri F. *The Discovery of the Unconscious: The History and Evolution of Dynamic Psychiatry*. New York: Basic Books, 1970.

Esteve, Mary. *The Aesthetics and Politics of the Crowd in American Literature*. New York: Cambridge University Press, 2003.

Ewen, Stuart. *PR! A Social History of Spin*. New York: Basic Books, 1996.

Fabian, Ann. *Card Sharps and Bucket Shops: Gambling in Nineteenth-Century America*. New York: Routledge, 1999.

———. "Speculation on Distress: The Popular Discourse of the Panics of 1837 and 1857." *Yale Journal of Criticism* 3 (Fall 1989): 127–42.

———. "Unseemly Sentiments: The Cultural Problem of Gambling." In *The Culture of Sentiment: Race, Gender, and Sentimentality in Nineteenth-Century America*, edited by Shirley Samuels, 143–56. New York: Oxford University Press, 1992.

"Fair Finance." *Appeal to Reason*, 18 April 1908, 1.

Fales, William E. S. *The Life of Lawson*. New York: Dixie, 1905.

Fayant, Frank. "The Real Lawson." *Success Magazine*, October 1907, 663–67, 701–3; November 1907, 719–22, 783–88; December 1907, 819–22, 868–69; January 1908, 23–25, 42; February 1908, 71–73, 105–7; March 1908, 145–46, 171.

———. "Sidelights on Lawson—His Creeds and Career." *New York Times* (magazine section), 23 August 1908, 3–4.

Felski, Rita. *The Gender of Modernity*. Cambridge, Mass.: Harvard University Press, 1995.

Fichtelberg, Joseph. *Critical Fictions: Sentiment and the American Market, 1780–1870*. Athens: University of Georgia Press, 2003.

Filler, Louis. *Appointment at Armageddon: Muckraking and Progressivism in the American Tradition*. Westport, Conn.: Greenwood, 1976.

———. *Crusaders for American Liberalism*. New York: Harcourt, Brace, 1939.

Flower, B. O. "The Battle of Privilege against Democratic Government." *Arena*, April 1908, 479–85.

———. "David Graham Phillips: A Twentieth Century Novelist of Democracy." *Arena*, March 1906, 252–58.

———. "The Money-changers." *Arena*, December 1908, 623–25.

Fontenelle, Bernard de. *A Plurality of Worlds*. Translated by John Glanvill. London: Nonesuch, 1929.

Forsyth, David P. *The Business Press in America, 1750–1865*. Philadelphia: Chilton, 1964.

Fowler, William Worthington. *Ten Years in Wall Street; or, Revelations of Inside Life and Experience on 'Change*. Hartford: Worthington, 1870.

———. *Twenty Years of Inside Life in Wall Street*. New York: Orange Judd, 1880.

Francke, Warren. "An Argument in Defense of Sensationalism: Probing the Popular and Historiographical Context." *Journalism History* 5 (Autumn 1878): 70–73.

———. "Sensationalism and the Development of 19th-Century Reporting: The Broom Sweeps Sensory Details." *Journalism History* 12 (Winter–Autumn 1985): 80–85.

Freeman, Barbara Claire. *The Feminine Sublime: Gender and Excess in Women's Fiction*. Berkeley: University of California Press, 1995.

"Frenzied Fiction." *Bookman*, February 1907, 551.

"Frenzied Poetry." *Public Opinion*, 18 February 1905, 263–64.

"Friday the 13th." *Outlook*, 6 April 1907, 453.

Gallagher, Catherine. "Undoing." In *Time and the Literary*, edited by Karen Newman, Jay Clayton, and Marianne Hirsch, 11–29. New York: Routledge, 2002.

Garland, Hamlin. *The Shadow World*. New York: Harper, 1908.

Gerber, Philip L. "Dreiser's Debt to Jay Cooke." *Library Chronicle of the University of Pennsylvania* 38 (1972): 67–77.

———. *Theodore Dreiser*. New York: Twayne, 1964.

"Get-Rich-Quick Lawson." *Outlook*, 5 September 1908, 9–10.

Givens, W. R. "Wall Street's Estimate of Mr. Lawson." *Independent*, 18 March 1905, 1110–14.

Glazener, Nancy. *Reading for Realism: The History of a U.S. Literary Institution, 1850–1910*. Durham, N.C.: Duke University Press, 1997.

Goethe, Johann Wolfgang von. *Goethe's Faust, Part I*. Translated by C. F. MacIntyre. New York: New Directions, 1957.

Goldman, Emma. *Living My Life*. 1931. Vol. 1. Reprint, New York: Dover, 1970.

Goode, James. *The Modern Banker*. Chicago: Kerr, 1896.

Goodwyn, Lawrence. *Democratic Promise: The Populist Moment in America*. New York: Oxford University Press, 1976.

Grahl, John. "Money as Sovereignty: The Economics of Michel Aglietta." *New Political Economy* 5 (July 2000): 291–316.

Grant, James. "Free Markets, Free Press." Museum of American Financial History. June–December 2000. <http://www.financialhistory.org/fmfp/fmfp_grant.htm>. August 2002.

Graumann, Carl F., and Serge Moscovici, eds. *Changing Conceptions of Conspiracy*. New York: Springer-Verlag, 1987.

Gullickson, Gay L. *Unruly Women of Paris: Images of the Commune*. Ithaca, N.Y.: Cornell University Press, 1996.

Haddock, Frank C. *Business Power*. Meriden, Conn.: Pelton, 1919.

———. *The Personal Atmosphere*. Meriden, Conn.: Pelton, 1918.

Hadley, Arthur T. "Jay Gould and Socialism." *Forum*, January 1893, 686–93.

Hakutani, Yoshinobu, ed. *Selected Magazine Articles of Theodore Dreiser: Life and Art in the American 1890s*. Vol. 1. Rutherford, N.J.: Fairleigh Dickinson University Press, 1985.

———, ed. *Theodore Dreiser's Uncollected Magazine Articles*. Newark: University of Delaware Press, 2003.

Hale, Nathan G. "Introduction." In Morton Prince, *Psychotherapy and Multiple Personality: Selected Essays*, edited by Nathan G. Hale, 1–18. Cambridge, Mass.: Harvard University Press, 1975.

Hapgood, Hutchins. *An Anarchist Woman*. New York: Duffield, 1909.

Hapgood, Norman. "The Epidemic of Exposure." *Collier's*, 25 March 1905, 23.

———. "How Much of a Liar Is Lawson?" *Collier's*, 22 April 1905, 22, 25, 27.

Harris, Charles T. *Memories of Manhattan in the Sixties and Seventies*. New York: Derrydale, 1928.

Harris, Leon. *Upton Sinclair: American Rebel*. New York: Crowell, 1975.

Hart, Ernest. *Hypnotism, Mesmerism, and the New Witchcraft*. 2nd ed. New York: Appleton, 1896.

Haskell, Thomas L. "Capitalism and the Origins of the Humanitarian Sensibility, Part 1." *American Historical Review* 90 (April 1985): 339–61.

———. "Capitalism and the Origins of the Humanitarian Sensibility, Part 2." *American Historical Review* 90 (June 1985): 547–66.

Haskell, Thomas L., and Richard F. Teichgraeber III, eds. *The Culture of the Market*. New York: Cambridge University Press, 1993.

Hellekson, Karen. *The Alternate History.* Kent, Ohio: Kent State University Press, 2001.

Hendler, Glenn. *Public Sentiments: Structures of Feeling in Nineteenth-Century American Literature.* Chapel Hill: University of North Carolina Press, 2001.

Henkin, David M. *City Reading: Written Words and Public Spaces in Antebellum New York.* New York: Columbia University Press, 1998.

Herron, George D. *From Revolution to Revolution: The Paris Commune and Its Lessons.* New York: Comrade Co-operative Company, 1903.

Hertz, Neil. *The End of the Line: Essays on Psychoanalysis and the Sublime.* New York: Columbia University Press, 1985.

Hicks, John D. *The Populist Revolt: A History of the Farmers' Alliance and the People's Party.* Lincoln, Neb.: Bison, 1961.

Hirsch, William. "Epidemics of Hysteria." *Popular Science Monthly,* August 1896, 544–49.

Hochman, Barbara. *The Art of Frank Norris, Storyteller.* Columbia: University of Missouri Press, 1988.

Hofstadter, Richard. *The Age of Reform: From Bryan to F.D.R.* New York: Vintage, 1955.

——. "Introduction." In *The Progressive Movement, 1900–1915,* edited by Richard Hofstadter, 1–15. Englewood Cliffs, N.J.: Prentice-Hall, 1963.

——. "The Paranoid Style in American Politics." In *The Paranoid Style in American Politics and Other Essays,* 3–40. New York: Knopf, 1965.

Holbrook, Stewart H. *The Age of the Moguls.* Garden City, N.Y.: Doubleday, 1954.

Horwitz, Howard. *By the Law of Nature: Form and Value in Nineteenth-Century America.* New York: Oxford University Press, 1991.

Hough, Emerson. *The Mississippi Bubble.* Indianapolis: Bowen-Merrill, 1902.

Hovey, Carl. *J. Pierpont Morgan.* New York: Sturgis and Walton, 1911.

Howe, Frederic C. *Confessions of a Monopolist.* 1906. Reprint, Upper Saddle River Junction, N.J.: Gregg, 1968.

Huber, Richard M. *The American Idea of Success.* New York: McGraw-Hill, 1971.

Hudson, Thomson Jay. *The Law of Psychic Phenomena.* 8th ed. Chicago: McClurg, 1895.

Hughson, Lois. *From Biography to History: The Historical Imagination and American Fiction, 1880–1940.* Charlottesville: University Press of Virginia, 1988.

Hutchisson, James M. "The Creation (and Reduction) of *The Financier.*" *Papers on Language and Literature* 27 (Spring 1991): 243–59.

——. "The Revision of Theodore Dreiser's *Financier,*" *Journal of Modern Literature* 20 (Winter 1996): 199–213.

Huyssen, Andreas. *After the Great Divide: Modernism, Mass Culture, Postmodernism.* Bloomington: Indiana University Press, 1986.

"Inferno of Packingtown Revealed." *Arena*, June 1906, 651–58.

"In the Mirror of the Present." *Arena*, June 1906, 623–27.

Irwin, Will. *The Making of a Reporter*. New York: Putnam's, 1942.

Isham, Frederic S. *Black Friday*. Indianapolis: Bobbs-Merrill, 1904.

James, Henry. *The Bostonians*. New York: Library of America, 1991.

Jameson, Fredric. "Progress or Utopia; or, Can We Imagine the Future?" *Science-Fiction Studies* 9 (July 1982): 147–56.

Jastrow, Joseph. *Fact and Fable in Psychology*. Boston: Houghton Mifflin, 1900.

Jett, Kevin W. "Vision and Revision: Another Look at the 1912 and 1927 Editions of Dreiser's *The Financier*." *Dreiser Studies* 29 (1998): 51–73.

Johnson, Helen Kendrick. *The Woman and the Republic: A Survey of the Woman-Suffrage Movement in the United States*. New York: Appleton, 1897.

Johnson, Joseph French. "The Crisis and Panic of 1907." *Political Science Quarterly* 23 (September 1908): 454–67.

Jones, Edward D. *Economic Crises*. London: Macmillan, 1900.

Josephson, Matthew. *The Money Lords: The Great Finance Capitalists, 1925–1950*. New York: Weybright, 1972.

———. *The Robber Barons: The Great American Capitalists, 1861–1901*. New York: Harcourt, Brace, 1934.

Kahane, Claire. *Passions of the Voice: Hysteria, Narrative, and the Figure of the Speaking Woman, 1850–1915*. Baltimore: Johns Hopkins University Press, 1995.

Kammen, Michael. *Mystic Chords of Memory: The Transformation of Tradition in American Culture*. New York: Knopf, 1991.

Kammer, Arjo. "Expectations." In *Business Cycles and Depressions: An Encyclopedia*, edited by David Glasner, 204–7. New York: Garland, 1997.

Katz, Philip M. *From Appomattox to Montmartre: Americans and the Paris Commune*. Cambridge, Mass.: Harvard University Press, 1998.

Keller, Morton. *Affairs of State: Public Life in Late Nineteenth Century America*. Cambridge, Mass.: Belknap Press, 1977.

Kemp, Richard W. "The Value of the Exposé." *Bookman*, November 1905, 162–64.

Kerr, Howard. *Mediums, and Spirit-Rappers, and Roaring Radicals: Spiritualism in American Literature, 1850–1900*. Urbana: University of Illinois Press, 1972.

King, C. F. *The Light of Four Candles*. Boston: King, 1908.

Kleppner, Paul. *Continuity and Change in Electoral Politics, 1893–1928*. New York: Greenwood, 1987.

Knight, Peter, ed. *Conspiracy Nation: The Politics of Paranoia in Postwar America*. New York: New York University Press, 2002.

Knoper, Randall. *Acting Naturally: Mark Twain in the Culture of Performance*. Berkeley: University of California Press, 1995.

Knorr Cetina, Karin, and Urs Bruegger. "The Market as an Object of Attachment: Exploring Postsocial Relations in Financial Markets." *Canadian Journal of Sociology* 25 (Spring 2000): 141–68.

Kogan, Herman, and Lloyd Wendt. *Bet-A-Million! The Story of John W. Gates.* Indianapolis: Bobbs-Merrill, 1948.

Kolko, Gabriel. *The Triumph of Conservatism: A Reinterpretation of American History, 1900–1916.* New York: Free Press, 1963.

Kurtz, Howard. *The Fortune Tellers: Inside Wall Street's Game of Money, Media, and Manipulation.* New York: Free Press, 2000.

Lamoreaux, Naomi R. *The Great Merger Movement in American Business, 1895–1914.* New York: Cambridge University Press, 1985.

Lawrence, George C. "How Truth Saved the Day." *Appleton's*, February 1908, 136–44.

Lawson, Thomas W. "Fictitious Wealth." In "What Caused the Panic." *Everybody's*, December 1907, 832f–g.

———. "Fools and Their Money: Some After-Claps of Frenzied Finance." *Everybody's*, May 1906, 690–95, 65–77 (advertising section).

———. *Frenzied Finance: The Crime of Amalgamated.* New York: Ridgway, 1905.

———. *Friday, the Thirteenth.* New York: Doubleday, 1907.

———. "Mr. Lawson's Advertised Stock Operations." *Everybody's*, January 1913, 98–104.

———. "The Muck-Raker." *Everybody's*, August 1906, 204–8.

———. "A Prediction Roll-Call." *Everybody's*, July 1906, 113–20, 65–74 (advertising section).

———. "The Remedy." *Everybody's*, October 1912, 472c–r; December 1912, 777–92.

———. "To My Readers." *Everybody's*, November 1906, 714–18.

———. "Why I Gave Up the Fight." *Everybody's*, February 1908, 287–88, 480–x.

"Lawson as a Prophet." *New York Times*, 17 December 1905, 1.

"The 'Lawson Panic,' with Lawson Left Out." *Literary Digest*, 17 December 1904, 832–33.

"Lawson's Frenzied Finance Answered." *Public Opinion*, 5 January 1905, 9.

"Lawson's Literary Advertising Methods." *New York Times Book Review*, 30 March 1902, 192.

"Lawson to Policy Holders." *New York Times*, 20 March 1905, 5.

Leach, William. *The Land of Desire: Merchants, Power, and the Rise of a New American Culture.* New York: Vintage, 1993.

Leary, Lewis, ed. *Mark Twain's Correspondence with Henry Huttleston Rogers.* Berkeley: University of California Press, 1969.

Le Bon, Gustav. *The Crowd: A Study of the Popular Mind.* New York: Viking, 1960.

Lefèvre, Edwin. "The American Newspaper, II: The Newspaper and Wall Street." *Bookman*, April 1904, 137–48.

———. "Panic Days in Wall Street." *Harper's*, 18 May 1901, 500–502.

———. "Pike's Peak or Bust." *McClure's*, June 1901, 153–63.

———. "What Availeth It?" *Everybody's*, June 1911, 836–48.

Lehan, Richard. *Theodore Dreiser, His World and His Novels*. Carbondale: Southern Illinois University Press, 1969.

Leonard, Thomas C. *The Power of the Press: The Birth of American Political Reporting*. New York: Oxford University Press, 1986.

Levine, Robert S. *Conspiracy and Romance: Studies in Brockdon Brown, Cooper, Hawthorne, and Melville*. New York: Cambridge University Press, 1989.

Levinson, Leonard Louis. *Wall Street: A Pictorial History*. New York: Ziff-Davis, 1961.

Leys, Ruth. "Mead's Voices: Imitation as Foundation, or, The Struggle against Mimesis." *Critical Inquiry* 19 (Winter 1993): 277–307.

Lingeman, Richard. *Theodore Dreiser: An American Journey*. New York: John Wiley, 1993.

Lippmann, Walter. *Drift and Mastery*. 1914. Reprint, Madison: University of Wisconsin Press, 1985.

"A Literary Show: A Great American Novel." In Salzman, *Theodore Dreiser: The Critical Reception*, 122–24.

"The Literature of Exposure." *Bookman*, September 1904, 16–17.

Livingston, James. *Origins of the Federal Reserve System: Money, Class, and Corporate Capitalism, 1890–1913*. Ithaca, N.Y.: Cornell University Press, 1986.

———. *Pragmatism and the Political Economy of Cultural Revolution, 1850–1940*. Chapel Hill: University of North Carolina Press, 1997.

———. *Pragmatism, Feminism, and Democracy: Rethinking the Politics of American History*. New York: Routledge, 2001.

———. "The Social Analysis of Economic History and Theory: Conjectures on Late Nineteenth-Century American Development." *Radical History Review* 92 (February 1987): 69–95.

———. "The Strange Career of the 'Social Self.'" *Radical History Review* 76 (Winter 2000): 53–79.

Lloyd, Henry Demarest. "The Political Economy of Seventy-three Million Dollars." *Atlantic Monthly*, July 1882, 69–81.

Lockley, Fred. "A Westerner at Thomas Lawson's 'Dreamwold.'" *Pacific Monthly Magazine*, December 1911, 644–55.

Lukács, Georg. "Narrate or Describe?" In Lukács, *Writer and Critic and Other Essays*, edited by Arthur D. Kahn, 110–49. London: Merlin, 1978.

Maas, Harro. "Mechanical Reasoning: William Stanley Jevons and the Making of Modern Economics." Diss., Universiteit van Amsterdam, 2001.

Mann, William D'Alton. *Fads and Fancies of Representative Americans at the Beginning of the Twentieth Century.* New York: Town, 1905.

Marchand, Roland. *Creating the Corporate Soul: The Rise of Public Relations and Corporate Imagery in American Big Business.* Berkeley: University of California Press, 1998.

Marcossan, Isaac F. *Adventures in Interviewing.* New York: Dodds, 1931.

Marcus, George E., ed. *Paranoia within Reason: A Casebook on Conspiracy as Explanation.* Chicago: University of Chicago Press, 1999.

Marsh, Margaret. *Anarchist Women, 1870–1920.* Philadelphia: Temple University Press, 1981.

Marx, Otto M. "Morton Prince and the Dissociation of a Personality." *Journal of the History of the Behavioral Sciences* 6 (April 1970): 120–30.

Mason, R. Osgood. *Telepathy and the Subliminal Self.* New York: Holt, 1897.

Masson, Tom. *Mary's Little Lamb.* New York: Life, 1905.

McCall, Dorothy Lawson. *The Copper King's Daughter.* Portland, Ore.: Binsford, 1972.

McClelland, J. S. *The Crowd and the Mob: From Plato to Canetti.* London: Unwin, 1989.

McLean, George N. *The Rise and Fall of Anarchy in America.* Chicago: Badoux, 1890.

Medbery, James. *Men and Mysteries of Wall Street.* Boston: Fields, Osgood, 1870.

Melley, Timothy. *Empire of Conspiracy.* Ithaca: Cornell University Press, 2000.

Mencken, H. L. "Adventures among the New Novels." In Riggio, *Dreiser-Mencken Letters*, 2:748–53.

——. "A Literary Behemoth." In Riggio, *Dreiser-Mencken Letters*, 2:754–59.

Merish, Lori. *Sentimental Materialism: Gender, Commodity Culture, and Nineteenth-Century American Literature.* Durham, N.C.: Duke University Press, 2000.

Meyer, Donald. *The Positive Thinkers.* New York: Doubleday, 1965.

Micale, Mark S. *Approaching Hysteria: Disease and Its Interpretations.* Princeton, N.J.: Princeton University Press, 1995.

Michaels, Walter Benn. *The Gold Standard and the Logic of Naturalism: American Literature at the Turn of the Century.* Berkeley: University of California Press, 1987.

Militz, Annie Ritz. *Prosperity through Knowledge and Power of Mind.* 4th ed. Los Angeles: Master Mind, 1916.

Miller, D. A. *The Novel and the Police.* Berkeley: University of California Press, 1988.

Mills, John. "On Credit Cycles and the Origin of Panics." *Transactions of the Manchester Statistical Society,* session 1867–68: 11–40.

Mills, Nicolaus. *The Crowd in American Literature.* Baton Rouge: Louisiana State University Press, 1986.

Miraldi, Robert. *Muckraking and Objectivity: Journalism's Colliding Traditions*. New York: Greenwood, 1990.

"Mr. Lawson and the Personal Equation." *Bookman*, March 1907, 120–23.

"The Moneychangers" (review). *Nation*, 22 October 1908, 389.

Moody, John. *The Art of Wall Street Investing*. New York: Moody, 1906.

———. *The Long Road Home: An Autobiography*. 1933. Reprint, New York: Arno, 1975.

Moore, R. Laurence. *In Search of White Crows: Spiritualism, Parapsychology, and American Culture*. New York: Oxford University Press, 1977.

Morison, Elting E., ed. *The Letters of Theodore Roosevelt*. Vol. 5. Cambridge, Mass.: Harvard University Press, 1952.

Morse, Sherman. "An Awakening in Wall Street." *American Magazine*, September 1906, 457–63.

Moscovici, Serge. *The Age of the Crowd: A Historical Treatise on Mass Psychology*. Translated by J. C. Whitehouse. Cambridge: Cambridge University Press, 1985.

Moses, Marlie. "Lydia Thompson and the 'British Blondes.' " In *Women in American Theatre*, rev. ed., edited by Helen Krich Chinoy and Linda Walsh Jenkins, 88–92. New York: Theatre Communications Group, 1987.

Mowry, George E. *The California Progressives*. Berkeley: University of California Press, 1951.

Mulford, Prentice. *Your Forces and How to Use Them*. Vol. 2. Wimbledon, Eng.: Anglo-American, 1908.

Myers, Frederic W. H. *Human Personality and Its Survival of Bodily Death*. Edited and abridged by Leopold Hamilton Myers. New York: Longmans, Green, 1907.

———. "The Subliminal Consciousness." *Proceedings of the Society for Psychical Research* 9 (1893–94): 3–25.

"Mysterious Instruments." *Nation*, 21 December 1905, 496–97.

Navin, T. R., and Marian V. Sears. "The Rise of a Market for Industrial Securities, 1887–1902." *Business History Review* 29 (June 1955): 105–38.

Neill, Humphrey B. *The Inside Story of the Stock Exchange*. New York: Forbes, 1950.

Newman, Robert D. "Supernatural Naturalism: Norris's Spiritualism in *The Octopus*." *Frank Norris Studies* 4 (Autumn 1987): 1–4.

"New Novels." *Athenaeum*, 13 April 1907, 436–37.

Newton, R. Heber. "Anarchism." *Arena*, January 1902, 1–12.

Nordau, Max. *Degeneration*. Translated from the 2nd German edition. New York: Appleton, 1895.

Norris, Frank. "A Dual Existence." *Wave*, 27 February 1897, 8.

———. "Fiction Is Selection." In Norris, *Frank Norris: Novels and Essays*, 1115–18.

———. *Frank Norris: Novels and Essays*. New York: Library of America, 1986.

———. "Inside an Organ." *Wave*, 2 January 1897, 9.

——. "The Mechanics of Fiction." In Norris, *Frank Norris: Novels and Essays*, 1161–64.

——. "The Need of a Literary Conscience." In Norris, *Frank Norris: Novels and Essays*, 1157–60.

——. "Novelists of the Future." In Norris, *Frank Norris: Novels and Essays*, 1152–56.

——. "The Novel with a 'Purpose.' " In Norris, *Frank Norris: Novels and Essays*, 1196–1200.

——. *The Pit: A Story of Chicago*. New York: Penguin, 1994.

——. "The Responsibilities of the Novelist." In Norris, *Frank Norris: Novels and Essays*, 1206–10.

——. "Romola between the Acts." *Wave*, 24 October 1896, 7.

——. "The True Reward of the Novelist." In Norris, *Frank Norris: Novels and Essays*, 1147–51.

"Notable Books and Authors." *McClure's*, September 1901, 504.

Notman, Otis. "Talks with Four Novelists: Mr. Dreiser." In Pizer, *Theodore Dreiser: A Selection of Uncollected Prose*, 163–64.

Noyes, Alexander D. "A Year after the Panic of 1907." *Quarterly Journal of Economics* 23 (February 1909): 185–212.

Nye, David E. *American Technological Sublime*. Cambridge, Mass.: MIT Press, 1994.

Nye, Robert. *The Origins of Crowd Psychology: Gustave Le Bon and the Crisis of Mass Democracy in the Third Republic*. London: Sage, 1975.

Oberholtzer, E. P. *Jay Cooke: Financier of the Civil War*. Vol. 2. Philadelphia: Jacobs, 1907.

Osborn, E. B. "Frenzied Finance and Its Author." *Outlook*, 3 March 1906, 307–8.

Oughourlian, Jean-Michel. *The Puppet of Desire: The Psychology of Hysteria, Possession, and Hypnosis*. Stanford, Calif.: Stanford University Press, 1991.

Painter, Nell Irvin. *Standing at Armageddon: The United States, 1877–1919*. New York: Norton, 1987.

Palmer, Bruce. *"Man over Money": The Southern Populist Critique of American Capitalism*. Chapel Hill: University of North Carolina Press, 1980.

Park, Edwin J. "How Lawson Writes." *New Englander Magazine*, March 1909, 21–25.

Park, Robert E. "The Public and the Crowd." 1904. In Park, *The Public and the Crowd and Other Essays*, edited by Henry Elsner Jr., 5–81. Chicago: University of Chicago Press, 1972.

Parker, Gail Thain. *Mind Cure in New England: From the Civil War to World War I*. Hanover, N.H.: University Press of New England, 1973.

Parrini, Carl P., and Martin J. Sklar. "New Thinking about the Market, 1896–

1904: Some American Economists on Investment and the Theory of Surplus
Capital." *Journal of Economic History* 43 (September 1983): 559–78.

Parsons, Wayne. *The Power of the Financial Press: Journalism and Economic Opinion in
Britain and America.* Aldershot: Elgar, 1989.

Patrick, G. T. W. "The Psychology of Crazes." *Popular Science Monthly*, July 1900,
285–94.

Payne, Will. "In the Panic." *Century Illustrated Monthly*, July 1900, 427–36.

———. *Mr. Salt.* 1903. Reprint, Boston: Houghton, Mifflin, 1904.

Perkins, George W. "The Modern Corporation." In *The Currency Problem and the
Present Financial Situation*, 155–70. New York: Columbia University Press,
1908.

Pizer, Donald. *The Novels of Theodore Dreiser: A Critical Study.* Minneapolis:
University of Minnesota Press, 1976.

———, ed. *Critical Essays on Theodore Dreiser.* Boston: Hall, 1981.

———, ed. *Theodore Dreiser: A Selection of Uncollected Prose.* Detroit: Wayne State
University Press, 1977.

Preda, Alex. "Financial Knowledge, Documents, and the Structures of Financial
Activities." *Journal of Contemporary Ethnography* 31 (April 2002): 209–42.

"Predicting a Panic." *Literary Digest*, 20 January 1906, 77–78.

Prince, Morton. "Some of the Revelations of Hypnotism: Post-hypnotic
Suggestion, Automatic Writing, and Double Personality." In *Psychotherapy
and Multiple Personality: Selected Essays*, edited by Nathan G. Hale, 37–60.
Cambridge, Mass.: Harvard University Press, 1975.

Reaves, Shiela. "How Radical Were the Muckrakers? Socialist Press Views, 1902–
1906." *Journalism Quarterly* 61 (Winter 1984): 763–70.

Red Ruin; or, The Romance of Anarchy in America: Its Origin, Rise, and Crimes. New
York: Fox, 1888.

Reeve, Sidney A. *The Cost of Competition.* New York: McClure, 1906.

Regier, C. C. *The Era of the Muckrakers.* Gloucester, Mass.: Peter Smith, 1957.

Reising, Russell. *Loose Ends: Closure and Crisis in the American Social Text.* Durham,
N.C.: Duke University Press, 1996.

"A Reply to Mr. Lawson." *New York Times*, 6 January 1905, 8.

"Rest for the Weary." *New York Times*, 15 December 1905, 8.

Rezneck, Samuel. *Business Depressions and Financial Panics.* New York: Greenwood,
1968.

Richards, Eliza. "Lyric Telegraphy: Women Poets, Spiritualist Poetics, and the
'Phantom Voice' of Poe." *Yale Journal of Criticism* 12, no. 2 (1999): 269–94.

Richardson, B. W. "The Hypnotic Epidemic." *Asclepiad*, November 1890,
118–35.

Richardson, Heather Cox. *The Death of Reconstruction: Race, Labor, and Politics in the*

Post–Civil War North, 1865–1901. Cambridge, Mass.: Harvard University Press, 2001.

Rideout, Walter. "Introduction." In Donnelly, *Caesar's Column,* vii–xxxii.

Riggio, Thomas P., ed. *Dreiser-Mencken Letters: The Correspondence of Theodore Dreiser and H. L. Mencken, 1907–45.* 2 vols. Philadelphia: University of Pennsylvania Press, 1987.

Ritter, Gretchen. *Goldbugs and Greenbacks: The Antimonopoly Tradition and the Politics of Finance in America.* New York: Cambridge University Press, 1997.

Roell, Craig H. *The Piano in America, 1890–1940.* Chapel Hill: University of North Carolina Press, 1989.

Roosevelt, Theodore. Speech, 14 April 1906. In *The Progressive Movement, 1900–1915,* edited by Richard Hofstadter, 18–19. Englewood Cliffs, N.J.: Prentice-Hall, 1963.

Rose, Lisle Abbott. "A Bibliographical Survey of Economic and Political Writings, 1865–1900." *American Literature* 15 (January 1944): 381–410.

Ross, Edward Alsworth. "The Mob Mind." *Popular Science Monthly,* July 1897, 390–98.

———. *Sin and Society: An Analysis of Latter-Day Iniquity.* 1907. Reprint, Gloucester, Mass.: Peter Smith, 1965.

Russell, Charles Edward. *Bare Hands and Stone Walls.* New York: Scribner's, 1933.

Salzman, Jack, ed. *Theodore Dreiser: The Critical Reception.* New York: David Lewis, 1972.

Sandage, Scott A. "The Gaze of Success: Failed Men and the Sentimental Marketplace." In *Sentimental Men: Masculinity and the Politics of Affect in American Culture,* edited by Mary Chapman and Glenn Hendler, 181–201. Berkeley: University of California Press, 1999.

Satter, Beryl. *Each Mind a Kingdom: American Women, Sexual Purity, and the New Thought Movement, 1875–1920.* Berkeley: University of California Press, 1999.

Schabas, Margaret. "Victorian Economics and the Science of Mind." In *Victorian Science in Context,* edited by Bernard Lightman, 72–93. Chicago: University of Chicago Press, 1997.

Schiller, Dan. *Objectivity and the News: The Public and the Rise of Commercial Journalism.* Philadelphia: University of Pennsylvania Press, 1981.

Schrager, Cynthia D. "Mark Twain and Mary Baker Eddy: Gendering the Transpersonal Subject." *American Literature* 70 (March 1998): 29–62.

Schudson, Michael. *Discovering the News: A Social History of American Newspapers.* New York: Basic Books, 1978.

Sedgwick, Ellery. "The Man with the Muck Rake." *American Magazine,* May 1906, 111–12.

Selden, G. C. *Psychology of the Stock Market.* New York: Ticker, 1912.

Seligman, Edwin R. A. "The Crisis of 1907 in the Light of History." In *The Currency Problem and the Present Financial Situation*, ix–xxvii. New York: Columbia University Press, 1908.

Seltzer, Mark. *Serial Killers: Death and Life in America's Wound Culture*. New York: Routledge, 1998.

Sherman, Stuart P. "The Barbaric Naturalism of Mr. Dreiser." In *The Stature of Theodore Dreiser*, edited by Alfred Kazin and Charles Shapiro, 71–80. Bloomington: Indiana University Press, 1955.

Shiller, Robert J. *Irrational Exuberance*. Princeton, N.J.: Princeton University Press, 2000.

Showalter, Elaine. *Hystories: Hysterical Epidemics and Modern Culture*. New York: Columbia University Press, 1997.

Sidis, Boris. *The Psychology of Suggestion*. New York: Appleton, 1898.

Silverman, Debora L. *Art Nouveau in Fin-de-Siècle France: Politics, Psychology, and Style*. Berkeley: University of California Press, 1989.

Sinclair, Upton. *The Autobiography of Upton Sinclair*. New York: Harcourt, Brace, 1962.

——. *The Brass Check: A Study of American Journalism*. Pasadena, Calif.: Sinclair, 1919.

——. *The Industrial Republic: A Study of the America Ten Years Hence*. New York: Doubleday, 1907.

——. *The Machine*. Girard, Kans.: Haldeman-Julius, 1911.

——. *The Metropolis*. New York: Moffat, 1908.

——. *The Moneychangers*. 1908. Reprint, Amherst, N.Y.: Prometheus, 2001.

——. *The Pot Boiler: A Comedy in Four Acts*. Girard, Kans.: Haldeman-Julius, 1913.

——. "Synopsis of Metropolis-Moneychangers-Machine." Manuscripts Department, Lilly Library, Indiana University, Bloomington, Ind.

——. *Upton Sinclair Presents William Fox*. Los Angeles: Sinclair, 1933.

Singer, Ben. *Melodrama and Modernity: Early Sensational Cinema and Its Contexts*. New York: Columbia University Press, 2001.

Sklansky, Jeffrey. *The Soul's Economy: Market Society and Selfhood in American Thought, 1820–1920*. Chapel Hill: University of North Carolina Press, 2002.

Sklar, Martin J. *The Corporate Reconstruction of American Capitalism, 1890–1916: The Market, the Law, and Politics*. New York: Cambridge University Press, 1988.

Smith, Carl. *Urban Disorder and the Shape of Belief: The Great Chicago Fire, the Haymarket Bomb, and the Model Town of Pullman*. Chicago: University of Chicago Press, 1995.

Smith, Matthew Hale. *Bulls and Bears of New York*. 1873. Reprint, New York: Books for Libraries, 1972.

Smith-Rosenberg, Carroll. "The Hysterical Woman: Sex Roles and Role Conflict in 19th-Century America." In *Disorderly Conduct: Visions of Gender in Victorian America*, 197–216. New York: Oxford University Press, 1985.

Snow, David A., and Robert Parker, "The Mass Media and the Stock Market." In Adler and Adler, *The Social Dynamics of Financial Markets*, 153–72.

Sobel, Robert. *The Big Board: A History of the New York Stock Market*. New York: Free Press, 1965.

———. *Panic on Wall Street: A History of America's Financial Disasters*. New York: Collier, 1968.

Sonnichson, C. L. *Colonel Greene and the Copper Skyrocket*. Tucson: University of Arizona Press, 1974.

Steeples, Douglas, and David O. Whitten. *Democracy in Desperation: The Depression of 1893*. Westport, Conn.: Greenwood, 1998.

"Stock Market Stirred by Lawson Manoeuvres." *New York Times*, 8 December 1904, 16.

"Storm Dies Out, Lawson Subsides." *New York Times*, 10 December 1904, 5.

Strouse, Jean. "The Brilliant Bailout." *New Yorker*, 23 November 1998, 62–77.

Studenski, Paul. *Financial History of the United States*. 2nd ed. New York: McGraw-Hill, 1963.

Sullivan, Mark. *Our Times: The United States, 1900–1925*. Vol. 3. New York: Scribner's, 1930.

Tabbi, Joseph. *Postmodern Sublime: Technology and American Writing from Mailer to Cyberpunk*. Ithaca, N.Y.: Cornell University Press, 1995.

The Tale of Coppers. New York: Business Development Company of America, 1906.

Tarbell, Ida M. *All in the Day's Work*. New York: Macmillan, 1939.

Tarde, Gabriel. *The Laws of Imitation*. Translated from the 2nd French edition by Elsie Clews Parson. 1903. Reprint, Gloucester, Mass.: P. Smith, 1962.

Tatar, Maria M. *Spellbound: Studies in Mesmerism and Literature*. Princeton, N.J.: Princeton University Press, 1978.

Tax, Meredith. *The Rising of the Women: Feminist Solidarity and Class Conflict, 1880–1917*. New York: Monthly Review Press, 1980.

Taylor, Walter F. *The Economic Novel in America*. Chapel Hill: University of North Carolina Press, 1942.

Templin, Mary. "Containing Sentiment: Antebellum Women's Panic Fiction." Paper delivered at the American Studies Association annual meeting, Houston, 2002.

———. "Panic Fiction: Women's Responses to Antebellum Economic Crisis." *Legacy* 21, no. 1 (2004): 1–16.

"A Test of Friendship." *Everybody's*, January 1907, 144, 85–86.

Thayer, John Adams. *Astir: A Publisher's Life Story*. Boston: Small, 1910.

"Theodore Dreiser." In Pizer, *Theodore Dreiser: A Selection of Uncollected Prose*, 192–95.

"Theodore Dreiser Now Turns to High Finance." In Pizer, *Theodore Dreiser: A Selection of Uncollected Prose*, 196–99.

Thomas, Brook. *American Literary Realism and the Failed Promise of Contract*. Berkeley: University of California Press, 1997.

Thornton, Brian. "Muckraking Journalists and Their Readers: Perceptions of Professionalism." *Journalism History* 21 (Spring 1995): 29–41.

Tichi, Cecelia. *Exposés and Excess: Muckraking in America, 1900/2000*. Philadelphia: University of Pennsylvania Press, 2004.

Tompkins, Jane. *Sensational Designs: The Cultural Work of American Fiction, 1790–1860*. New York: Oxford University Press, 1985.

Towne, Elizabeth. *Practical Methods for Self-Development*. Holyoke, Mass.: Towne, 1904.

Trachtenberg, Alan. *The Incorporation of America: Culture and Society in the Gilded Age*. New York: Hill and Wang, 1982.

"Traction Interests." In Salzman, *Theodore Dreiser: The Critical Reception*, 97–98.

Tracy, Frank Basil. "Menacing Socialism in the Western States." *Forum*, May 1893, 332–42.

U.S. Congress. House. Subcommittee of the Committee on Banking and Currency. *Money Trust Investigation: Investigation of Financial and Monetary Conditions in the United States Under House Resolutions Nos. 429 and 504 before a Subcommittee of the Committee on Banking and Currency*. 62nd Cong., 3rd sess., 1913. Washington: Government Printing Office, 1913.

——. House. *Hearings before the Committee on Investigation of United States Steel Corporation*. 62nd Cong., 1st sess., 1911. Washington: Government Printing Office, 1911.

——. Senate. Committee on the Judiciary. *Hearings before a Subcommittee of the Committee on the Judiciary Relating to the Absorption of the Tennessee, Coal, Iron, and Railroad Company by the United States Steel Corporation*. 60th Cong., 2nd sess., 1909. Washington: Government Printing Office, 1909.

Untermyer, Samuel. "Is There a Money Trust? An Address Delivered before the Finance Forum in the City of New York, December 27th, 1911." New York, 1911.

Vandervelde, Emile. *Collectivism and Industrial Evolution*. Translated by R. P. Farley. London: Independent Labour Party, 1907.

van Ginneken, Jaap. *Crowds, Psychology, and Politics, 1871–1899*. Cambridge: Cambridge University Press, 1992.

Veblen, Thorstein. *The Theory of Business Enterprise*. 1904. Reprint, New Brunswick, N.J.: Transaction, 2002.

Veith, Ilza. *Hysteria: The History of a Disease*. Chicago: University of Chicago Press, 1965.

Wallace, Mike. *Mickey Mouse History and Other Essays on American Memory*. Philadelphia: Temple University Press, 1996.

"The Wall-Street Panic." *Revolution*, 7 October 1869: 216.

Walth, Brent. *Fire at Eden's Gate: Tom McCall and the Oregon Story*. Portland: Oregon Historical Society Press, 1994.

Watson, Charles N., Jr. *The Novels of Jack London: A Reappraisal*. Madison: University of Wisconsin Press, 1983.

Weaver, James B. *A Call to Action: An Interpretation of the Great Uprising, Its Source and Causes*. 1892. Reprint, New York: Arno, 1974.

Webb, Richard. *Me and Lawson*. New York: Dillingham, 1905.

Webster, Henry K. *The Banker and the Bear: The Story of a Corner in Lard*. New York: Macmillan, 1900.

Wegner, Phillip E. *Imaginary Communities: Utopia, the Nation, and the Spatial Histories of Modernity*. Berkeley: University of California Press, 2002.

Weinberg, Arthur, and Lila Weinberg. *The Muckrakers*. New York: Simon and Schuster, 1961.

Weiskel, Thomas. *The Romantic Sublime: Studies in the Structure and Psychology of Transcendence*. Baltimore: Johns Hopkins University Press, 1976.

West, Harry G., and Todd Sanders. *Transparency and Conspiracy: Ethnographies of Suspicion in the New World Order*. Durham, N.C.: Duke University Press, 2003.

Wharton, Edith. *The House of Mirth*. New York: Oxford University Press, 1994.

White, Ed. "The Value of Conspiracy Theory." *American Literary History* 14 (March 2002): 1–31.

White, Hayden. "The Historical Text as Literary Artifact." In *The Writing of History: Literary Form and Historical Understanding*, edited by Robert H. Canary and Henry Kozicki, 41–62. Madison: University of Wisconsin Press, 1978.

White, Horace. "Commercial Crises." In *Cyclopaedia of Political Science, Political Economy and of the Political History of the United States*, edited by John J. Lalor, 1:523–30. Chicago: Cary, 1883.

White, William Allen. *The Autobiography of William Allen White*. 2nd edition, revised and abridged. Edited by Sally Foreman Griffith. Lawrence: University Press of Kansas, 1990.

"Who Writes 'Frenzied Finance'?" *Everybody's*, April 1905, 578.

Wicker, Elmus. *Banking Panics of the Gilded Age*. New York: Cambridge University Press, 2000.

Wiebe, Robert W. *Businessmen and Reform: A Study of the Progressive Movement*. Cambridge, Mass.: Harvard University Press, 1962.

Wilson, Woodrow. "The Lawyer and the Community." *North American Review*, November 1910, 604–22.

——. *The New Freedom: A Call for the Emancipation of the Generous Energies of a People.* New York: Doubleday, Page, 1913.

Winters, Alison. *Mesmerized: Powers of Mind in Victorian Britain.* Chicago: University of Chicago Press, 1998.

"With 'Everybody's' Publishers." *Everybody's*, December 1906, 865.

"Women of Montmartre." *Harper's Weekly*, 8 July 1871, 620.

Wood, Gordon S. "Conspiracy and the Paranoid Style: Causality and Deceit in the Eighteenth Century." *William and Mary Quarterly* 39 (July 1982): 401–41.

Wood, Henry. *The Political Economy of Natural Law.* Boston: Lee and Shepard, 1894.

Zanine, Louis J. *Mechanism and Mysticism: The Influence of Science on the Thought and Work of Theodore Dreiser.* Philadelphia: University of Pennsylvania Press, 1993.

Zelizer, Viviana A. "Beyond the Polemics on the Market: Establishing a Theoretical and Empirical Agenda." *Sociological Forum* 3 (Fall 1988): 614–34.

Zheng, Da. *Moral Economy and American Realistic Novels.* New York: Peter Lang, 1996.

Zimmerman, David A. "Frenzied Fictions: The Writing of Panic in the American Marketplace, 1873–1913." Ph.D. diss, University of California, Berkeley, 2000.

——. "The Mesmeric Sources of Frank Norris's *The Pit*." *Frank Norris Studies* 26 (Autumn 1998): 1–4.

Index

158, 163–64, 182–85; panic of 1907 as, 156–57, 185–89
Mencken, H. L., 214, 216, 221, 222
Mesmeric romance, 125, 135, 139, 144
Mesmerism, 31, 132, 133, 135–36, 137. *See also* Hypnotism; Suggestion
Miller, William, 16
Mimetic desire, 142–47
Money Trust Investigation, 16–17, 154
Morgan, John Pierpont, 16, 17, 152, 154–57, 186, 187, 188, 189
Most, Johann, 70
Muckraking, 98–101, 180; and reform fiction, 102–4. *See also* Lawson, Thomas W.: *Frenzied Finance*
Myers, Frederic W. H., 138

Narrative and markets, 11, 13, 31, 131–32, 141, 223–28. *See also* Narrative form
Narrative form, 2, 4, 7, 9, 12, 33, 74, 227; and conspiratorial plotting, 7, 185–90; and capitalist history, 23–24, 74–78; limits of, 36, 193–94, 214–17, 219, 221–22
Naturalism, 9, 35, 138, 191–92, 193–97, 211, 215
New Psychology, 124–25, 134, 138, 139, 144
New Thought, 136–37, 138
New York Gold Exchange, 46
New York Stock Exchange, 4, 17, 94, 109, 111
Norris, Frank, 8–9, 161, 227; *The Pit*, 31–32, 124–49; "Inside an Organ," 126–28; "The Mechanics of Fiction," 131, 141; familiarity with New Psychology, 138

Oughourlian, Jean-Michel, 144, 145

Painter, Nell Irvin, 40
Panic novels, 1–13, 17, 20–22, 223, 227–28; *Friday, the Thirteenth* (Lawson), 10, 82, 105, 108–21; *The Magnet* (Crozier), 10, 17, 135–36, 156–57, 161, 189; *The Mississippi Bubble* (Hough), 10, 232 (n. 40); *The Moneychangers* (Sinclair), 17, 20, 34–35, 151, 157–60, 166–78, 179–88, 190, 192; *Mr. Salt* (Payne), 19, 23, 70–71; *Black Friday* (Isham), 22–23, 40–45, 48–56, 60–66, 70–80; *The Modern Banker* (Goode), 22, 65; *The Kidnapped Millionaires* (Adams), 29, 247 (n. 88); *The Pit* (Norris), 31–32, 124–49; *The Financier* (Dreiser), 35–36, 191–222; *The Banker and the Bear* (Webster), 223–24
Panics, 1–2, 11–12, 14; equated with cultural collapse, 3, 20, 42–43, 52–53, 63, 78; and sympathy, 5, 112–21; as endemic feature of capitalism, 13, 19, 45, 63, 77, 164; conspiracy as cause of, 17–18, 34, 46–48, 65, 83, 86, 155–58, 161, 164, 179, 185, 188; antimonopolist representation of, 17–18, 65, 179; as cause of class conflict, 18–19, 20, 44, 60, 63, 75, 78–80; socialist representation of, 18–20; market reading as cause of, 24, 26–29, 81–82, 89–93, 106–8, 122, 225; as form of hysteria, 30–31, 124–25, 132, 133, 140, 144; and hypnotism, 31, 124–25, 132, 133–35; moral responsibility for, 32, 33, 151, 158–61, 164, 166–70, 177–78, 182; importance of for Dreiser's naturalism, 35–36, 191–93, 197, 198–200, 211, 214–15; and breakdown of patriarchal authority,

prise, 44–45, 48–49, 65–66, 70–71; psychological ramifications of, 124–25, 137–39, 140–42, 144–46; and narrative imagination, 223–26. *See also* Black Friday

Speculators, 18, 65–66, 69, 135–36; equated with anarchists, 52, 71, 73, 78, 240 (n. 61), 241

Spencer, Herbert, 192, 196, 206

Standard Oil Company, 81, 83, 86, 93

Stanton, Elizabeth Cady, 56, 57, 78

Steffens, Lincoln, 83, 98, 260 (n. 27)

Stock advertising, 81, 84–90, 96–97, 122

Stockholders, 102; moral accountability of, 159, 166, 180, 190

Stock market, 4, 5, 83, 109–21 passim, 192; emergence as linchpin of U.S. economy, 10–11, 15, 16, 17; writing's effect in, 24–29, 81–82, 96–97, 106–8, 111, 225; psychology of, 26–27, 29–31, 113–14, 124, 133–35, 143–44; stock manipulation as means of reforming, 27, 82, 88–89, 93–95, 121–22; Lawson's manipulation of, 84–93; and sympathy, 112–21, 126, 134–35, 143–44; as exemplary naturalist arena, 196–97. *See also* New York Stock Exchange; Stockholders: moral accountability of; Wall Street; Wall Street in fiction

Sublime, 31–32, 125, 126–28, 136, 141–42, 147–48, 185

Subliminal self. *See* Second self

Suggestion, 5, 29–30, 125, 134, 137, 143

Sympathy, 30, 82, 103, 112–21, 183; market emulation as form of, 5,

107, 113–14, 120–21, 126, 134, 143–44

Tarbell, Ida, 83, 98, 99, 247 (n. 86)

Tarde, Gabriel, 134, 143

Tarkington, Booth, 109

Thomas, Brook, 192

Thompson, Lydia, 52–53

Tompkins, Jane, 121

Untermyer, Samuel, 17

Veblen, Thorstein, 29

Wallace, Mike, 22

Wall Street, 10–11, 16–17, 28, 83, 94, 96, 107, 121, 136, 223; populist vision of, 17–18, 64–65, 67, 156–57, 179; moral risk of acting in, 158–60, 164, 166, 167–80 passim, 184, 192. *See also* Black Friday; New York Stock Exchange; Stock market: manipulation as means of reforming; Wall Street in fiction

Wall Street in fiction, 10, 17–18, 75, 76, 135–36, 156–57, 161–64. *See also* Isham, Frederic S.: *Black Friday*; Lawson, Thomas W.: *Friday, the Thirteenth*; Sinclair, Upton: *The Moneychangers*

Walth, Brent, 118

Webster, Henry K.: *The Banker and the Bear*, 223–24

White, Hayden, 70

Wilson, Woodrow, 21, 166, 181

Woodhull, Victoria, 56–57, 73

Yerkes, Charles T., 191, 216–17